D0940327

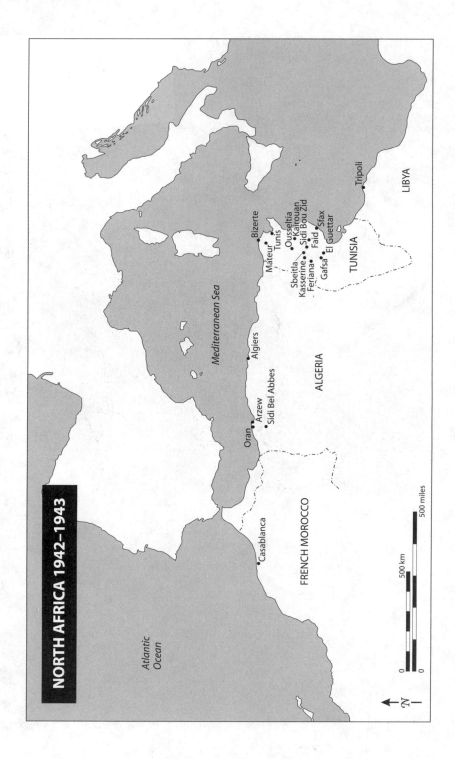

NORTH AFRICA 1942–1943

Atlantic
Ocean

Mediterranean Sea

FRENCH MOROCCO

Casablanca

Oran
Arzew
Sidi Bel Abbes

Algiers

ALGERIA

Bizerte
Mateur
Tunis
Ousseltia
Kairouan
Sidi Bou Zid
Faid
Sfax
El Guettar
Gafsa
Feriana
Kasserine
Sbeitla

TUNISIA

Tripoli

LIBYA

500 km
500 miles
0
0

N

ERNIE PYLE

HERE IS YOUR WAR

STORY OF G. I. JOE

Introduction to the Bison Books Edition by Orr Kelly

Drawings by Carol Johnson

UNIVERSITY OF NEBRASKA PRESS · LINCOLN AND LONDON

Introduction and map © 2004 by the Board of Regents of the University of
Nebraska
Manufactured in the United States of America

⊗

First Nebraska paperback printing: 2004

Library of Congress Cataloging-in-Publication Data
Pyle, Ernie, 1900–1945.
Here is your war: story of G.I. Joe / Ernie Pyle; introduction by Orr Kelly; drawings
by Carol Johnson.
p.   cm.
Originally published: New York: H. Holt, 1943. With a new introd.
ISBN 0-8032-8777-1 (pbk.: alk. paper)
1. Pyle, Ernie, 1900–1945.   2. World War, 1939–1945—Personal narratives,
American.   3. World War, 1939–1945—Campaigns—Tunisia.   4. War correspondents—United States—Biography.   I. Kelly, Orr.   II. Title.
D811.5.P92   2004
940.54'2311—dc22
2003023752

ORR KELLY

Introduction

Ernie Pyle has long been famous as the reporter who gave the American public a foxhole–eye view of World War II. His columns—larded with the names and hometowns of soldiers who were more often privates and corporals than colonels and generals—were all told in short sentences and short paragraphs with plenty of quotes.

But wait a minute. Couldn't the same be said of every wire service reporter who ever hurried out to cover a story, copy paper and thick-leaded pencil in hand, hard-wired to produce punchy copy filled with names (first, middle initial, and last, always spelled correctly)?

Here Is Your War, based on columns written some sixty years ago, covers the war's first ground combat, in North Africa, between American and German troops. What separates Ernie Pyle from the countless other reporters who covered the war? One obvious difference was that Pyle was a columnist. His columns, distributed by the United Features syndicate, appeared in newspapers all across the United States. So, unlike newspaper and wire service reporters whose copy might appear every day for a week and then not again for a month, Ernie Pyle's words were seen six days a week, usually in a familiar place in the newspaper. In that pre-television era Americans got almost all of their news from their daily newspapers.

As a columnist Pyle was free from the rigid printing strictures that shackled newspaper and wire service reporters. In those days metal type was cast, one line at a time, on Linotype machines and then fitted into a page by compositors. The story had to be written with the most important news appearing at the beginning and the less important coming after, so the compositor was free to simply throw away the concluding paragraphs to fit the story in the available space. Pyle, on the other hand, was expected to deliver a column of a certain length each day. But neither he nor his syndicate could control what was done with the column by individual editors, some of whom, to his dismay, hacked away with a too-heavy pencil.

In addition to the built-in advantages he had as a syndicated columnist,

Pyle also had something else going for him: he was very, very good at what he did. While many wire service reporters followed the same formula used by Pyle—short sentences and paragraphs, lots of names, lots of quotes—their copy was often choppy and disjointed. Pyle's sentences and paragraphs, on the other hand, are short, but they have a kind of cadence to them that carries the reader smoothly along.

Ironically, Pyle himself seems not to have realized how good and effective his style was. He envied both Ernest Hemingway and A. J. Liebling, the latter of whom covered the war for *The New Yorker*. Pyle even devoted one column to praising Liebling. The column did not appear, however. Lee G. Miller, Pyle's friend and editor back in the states, spiked the column because Liebling, who also served as *The New Yorker's* media critic, had recently let go some harsh words about Roy W. Howard, chairman of the Scripps Howard newspaper chain and Pyle's boss. In his book, *The Story of Ernie Pyle* (Viking 1950), Miller adds: "As for Ernie's modest judgment of his own pen in comparison with Liebling's, one book reviewer presently mentioned Liebling as '*The New Yorker's* own Ernie Pyle.' "

Pyle and Liebling both got their first taste of war—with the exception of their coverage of the Blitz in London—when American troops landed in North Africa in November 1942. The troops met scattered resistance—some of it intense and bloody—from French colonial forces for about three days before a cease-fire was arranged and the Americans moved off to Tunisia to confront the Werhmacht for the first time.

In Algeria, as the correspondents waited to join the troops moving east toward Tunisia, Pyle got what was probably his biggest scoop of the war. It did not take long for Pyle and the other reporters to see that the American military leaders had retained in positions of authority many of the French officials who had administered the French colony of Algeria, the same officials who had opposed the Allied landings for three bloody days. Many of these French officers were brutally antisemitic and just as bad as the Nazis who had conquered France two years before.

The official excuse given for retaining these French police and other civil administrators was that they were needed to keep order among the native population. (Today such a move could be compared to retaining Saddam Hussein's government, even Saddam himself, after the U.S. invasion of Iraq.) In press conferences held at American headquarters, reporters angrily questioned military leaders about this policy of favoring the "bad guys" while ignoring the French officers who had risked everything to help make the landings a success. Loudly as they protested, the reporters were prevented by the censors from letting people back home know what was happening—until Ernie Pyle filed a couple of columns.

In columns dated January 4 and 5, 1943 (included here as chapter 4), Pyle reported that American casualties at Oran had been substantially higher than admitted in official reports. He went on to lay bare the American policy of favoring the German-installed French administration: "We have left in office most of the small-fry officials put there by the Germans before we came," he wrote. "We permitted fascist societies to continue to exist. Actual sniping had been stopped, but there was still sabotage. The loyal French saw our tactics and wondered what manner of people we were. They were used to force, and expected us to use it against the common enemy, which included the French Nazis. Our enemies saw it, laughed, and called us soft."

The columns caused a sensation back home. How they slipped past the censors remains a mystery. The likeliest explanation is that the censors, familiar with the "soft news" character of Pyle's dispatches, simply passed them through without carefully reading their contents. Ironically, when Pyle later went to cover the conflict in the Pacific he complained of overzealous censors who blacked out the names of those he interviewed—in essence the very heart of his kind of column.

Pyle was very good at "hard news" too, despite his reputation for telling human-interest stories of individual servicemen. His columns lagged behind the news of the war, but they often gave a better feel for what was happening on the battlefield than the official news releases and the hurried dispatches of newspaper and wire service reporters.

On Valentine's Day, 1943, German tank columns surged out of the Faid Gap in a mountain chain that runs north and south through Tunisia. The tanks overwhelmed American forces near a dusty little town called Sidi Bou Zid. The Americans counterattacked but were even more soundly beaten. They retreated far back through the Kasserine Pass before finally stopping the German assault led by Field Marshal Erwin Rommel.

In columns dated March 1, 2, and 3, 1943 (chapter 10), Pyle set out to "describe what a tank battle looks like." These columns appeared two weeks after the beginning of the initial battle at Sidi Bou Zid, so readers were already familiar with what had happened there. Pyle's words come as close as words can to describe the confusion and the violence of tank warfare. Here the reader will find no names of individual soldiers, no lists of units involved, no precise description of how the opposing forces are arrayed. Yet in a first-rate example of war reporting Pyle somehow captures the "feel" of the whole violent day.

Pyle began the day with a briefing by the American general in charge, some ten miles behind the line of battle. He then sat on the ground drinking tea and eating British crackers with jam, hoping to find a way to get closer to the action. Finally a young lieutenant procured an army jeep and offered to take him forward. They moved to the spot the general had recommended for a view of the battle but decided it wasn't close enough; they then went bouncing forward through the stubble of wheat fields and the ruts made by tank tracks.

Pyle and the young officer, together in their little jeep, stayed out of the thick of the fighting, although they learned later that there had been fighting both behind and in front of them. The two managed to escape safely, which was more than most of the soldiers in the American tanks did.

Pyle's willingness to ride an unarmored jeep into the fringes of a vast, sprawling tank battle is in curious contrast to his attitude about flying combat missions. Before the war Pyle had been the aviation editor for the *Washington Daily News* and was a friend of Gen. Jimmy Doolittle and other officers who had risen to command of the Army Air Forces. Yet when offered the chance to fly with bomber crews out of Biskra, in southern Tunisia, Pyle declined the offer:

> I knew the day of that invitation would come, and I had dreaded it. Not to go branded a man as a coward. To go might make him a slight hero or a dead duck. Actually I never knew what I'd say until the moment came. When it did come, I said, "No, I don't see any sense in my going. Other correspondents have already gone, so I couldn't be the first anyhow. I'd be in the way, and if I got killed my death would have contributed nothing. I'm running chances just being here without sticking my neck out and asking for it. No, I think I won't go. I'm too old to be a hero." (p. 83)

At the time, in the late winter of 1942–43, Pyle was forty-two years old, at least twice as old as most of the soldiers he had interviewed and befriended and with whom he lived. He was already becoming something of a hero to many soldiers and to readers back home.

Before the war Pyle had been a newspaperman in Washington DC, and then he and his wife Jerry took off on a driving tour of the country. Along the way Ernie wrote folksy, human-interest columns about the people they met. When he went to England in 1942 he was syndicated in some forty papers and was unsure of his future. He even considered joining the army.

Through his columns from North Africa he suddenly became a household name. The number of papers carrying his work quickly doubled, and then soared to nearly seven hundred. He was employed by Scripps Howard at $175 a week—a handsome salary for a newspaperman in those days—and the revenue from his syndicated columns added hundreds more to his income. He reluctantly acknowledged to an interviewer that his income had gone from $13,000 in 1942 to about $25,000 in 1943. Here is one measure of how well Pyle was doing financially: Shortly after the war the American

Newspaper Guild set a goal of $100 a week—$5,200 a year—as the pay for a journeyman reporter or desk editor. It was a goal that, considering inflation, has never been reached.

And then came the book offers. One publisher offered $2,500 for the right to convert Pyle's North Africa columns into a book, and then quickly doubled the offer. In response to a wire from Lee Miller, who was handling Pyle's business affairs, he cabled: "Christ, Miller, if something doesn't happen to stop all this nonsense, we're going to get rich. Everything about the book deal sounds okay to me. I'm not nuts about the proposed title, but so far haven't been able to think of anything better." The proposed title was *With the Yanks in Africa*, but before publication it was changed to *Here Is Your War: Story of G. I. Joe*.

Pyle was sitting on top of the world. He was not only wealthy, he had a kind of a superstar status never achieved by another newspaper columnist before or since. He was interviewed by other reporters and featured on the cover of *Time* magazine. He was invited to the White House to meet President Franklin D. Roosevelt and Mrs. Roosevelt. And yet those who might have been tempted to envy his popularity would probably have been unwilling to change places had they known what else came with the fame. There was, of course, the danger and discomfort of war that Pyle shared with the soldiers about whom he wrote. There was the anguish, shared by millions of others, of long separations from loved ones. Separation was especially painful for Pyle, who was constantly worried about the health of his wife, Jerry (who suffered from mental illness and abused both alcohol and narcotics).

In letters, often delayed by weeks, they tried to keep in touch with each other. Finally, after the fall of Paris in the autumn of 1944, Pyle came home and joined Jerry in Albuquerque. A short time later the woman who cared for her found her covered with blood and jabbing a small scissors into her neck. Fortunately, the wounds were not fatal. Jerry was subjected to a series of electrical shock treatments and was still in an institution when Pyle, reluctantly but under intense pressure from the Navy to come cover "their war," flew to Hawaii and the war in the Pacific.

As he headed toward this new war zone, so different from the familiar European theater, he wrote in a column, "Anybody who has been in war and wants to go back is a plain damn fool in my book. I'm going simply because there's a war on and I'm part of it and I've known all the time I was going back. I'm going simply because I've got to, and I hate it."

He made a promise to himself, and to Jerry, that he wouldn't go ashore in any more amphibious landings. But he didn't think he was breaking that promise when he went ashore on the tiny island of Ie Shima after the initial landing and after much of the island had been more or less secured. On the morning of April 18, 1945, Pyle and several Marines were in a jeep traveling over a road he had used the previous day. Several other vehicles preceded them up the road. Suddenly a Japanese machine gunner, hidden on a coral ridge, opened fire. Pyle and the others in the jeep dove into a ditch, but one bullet caught Pyle in the temple and killed him. Jerry was well enough to go to Washington to accept a posthumous Medal of Merit from the War, Navy, and State Departments, but her health declined and she died on November 23, 1945.

Pyle's career as a columnist covering the war had lasted two months short of three years. And then, like one of the stories he told in his column, it came to an end. But Pyle's words remain to help future generations understand what World War II was like for the Americans whose wartime lives he chronicled.

To My Father

CONTENTS

HERE IS YOUR

WAR

1. CONVOY TO AFRICA

A TRIP by troop transport in convoy is a remarkable experience. I came to Africa that way.

Convoys are of three types: slow ones, made up of freighters carrying only supplies; medium-fast troop convoys, which run with heavy naval escort; and small convoys of swift ocean liners, carrying vast numbers of troops and depending for safety mainly on their speed. Our convoy from England to Africa was the second type. We were fairly fast; we carried an enormous number of troops; and we had a heavy escort, although no matter how much escort there is, it never seems enough. The ships in our convoy were both British and American, but the escort was entirely Royal Navy.

At noon one late October day, I got the word we were to leave London that night. There were scores of last-minute things to do: I'd sent my laundry off that morning and there was no hope of getting it back, so I had to rush out and buy extra socks and underwear. The army was to pick up my bedroll at 2:00 P.M. to take it somewhere for its mysterious convoy labelings.

Everything else I had to pack in a canvas bag and my army musette bag. Four friends came and had a last dinner with me. At leaving I put on my army uniform for the first time, and said good-bye to civilian clothes for God knew how long. My old brown suit, my dirty hat, my letters—all the little personal things went into a trunk to remain in London, and I would probably never see it again. I felt self-conscious and ridiculous and old in army uniform.

It was nighttime. I took a taxi to the designated meeting place; other correspondents were there when I arrived. Our British papers were taken away for safekeeping by the army and we were told to take off our correspondents' arm bands, for they might identify us to lurking spies, if any, as a convoy party. Then an army car picked us

1

up and drove clear across London through the blackout; I lost all track of where we were. Finally we stopped at a little-used suburban station and were informed we'd have two hours to wait before the troop train came. We paced the station platform, trying to keep warm. It was very dark and it seemed the train would never come. When it finally did, we piled into two compartments and I fell asleep immediately.

We sat up all night on the train, sleeping a little, as I had at first, but not much because it was too cold. We hadn't known what port we were going to, but on the way somebody told us the embarkation point. We were all surprised, and some of the boys had never even heard of the place.

Just after daylight our train pulled up alongside a huge ship. We checked in at an army desk in the pier shed, gathered our baggage, and climbed aboard, feeling grubby and cold but very curious. Our party was assigned to two cabins, four men in each. The staterooms were nice, better than any of us had expected, and much the same as in peacetime, except for an extra bunk built in over each bed. Many officers were in cabins far more crowded than ours.

We all expected to sail shortly after getting aboard, but we had forgotten that the ship had to be loaded first. Actually we didn't sail for forty-eight hours. All during that time one long troop train after another, day and night, pulled alongside and unloaded its human cargo. Time dragged on. We stood at the rails and watched the troops marching aboard. They came through the rain, heavily laden— in steel helmets, in overcoats, carrying rifles and huge packs on their backs. It was a thrilling sight, and a sad sight too, in a way, to see them marching in endless numbers up the steep gangway to be swallowed into the great ship.

They came on silently, most of them. Now and then one would catch sight of somebody he knew at the rail, and there would be a shout. For men who were going off to war, they carried odd things aboard. Some had books in their hands, some carried violin or banjo cases. One soldier led a big black dog. And one, I found later, carried two little puppies under his shirt. Like the Spartan boy in the story, he was almost scratched to death, but he had paid $32 for the pups and he treasured them.

The British (ours was a British ship) are finicky about allowing dogs on troop transports. The officers ordered all dogs turned in. They said they'd be sent ashore, and promised that good homes would be found for them. Somehow the dogs disappeared and were never located by the officers. But the morning we filed off the boat in North Africa and began the long march to our quarters, a black dog and two little puppies from England marched with us up the strange African road.

After two days of loading American soldiers aboard our troopship, and of hoisting aboard thousands of bedrolls and barracks bags, we sailed at last. It was a miserable English day, cold, with a driving rain; too miserable to be out on deck to watch the pier slide away. Most of us just lay in our bunks, indifferent even to the traditional last glance at land. Now it was all up to God— and the British Navy.

Our ship carried thousands of officers and men and a number of army nurses. I felt a little kinship with our vessel, for I'd seen her tied up in Panama two years before. I never dreamed then that someday I'd be sailing to Africa on her.

The officers and nurses were assigned to the regular cabins used by passengers in peacetime. The soldiers were quartered below decks, in the holds. The ship had once been a refrigerator ship, but all the large produce-carrying compartments had been cleared out, and there the men were packed in. Each compartment was filled with long wooden tables, with benches at each side. The men ate at those tables, and at night slept in white canvas hammocks slung from hooks just above.

It seemed terribly crowded, and some of the men complained bitterly of the food, and didn't eat for days. Yet many of the boys said it was swell compared to the way they had come over from home to Britain. Sometimes I ate below with the troops, and I'll have to say that their food was as good as ours in the officers' mess, and I thought that was excellent. On any troop transport, some crowding is unavoidable. It's bad, but I don't know how else enough men could be shipped anywhere fast enough.

The worst trouble aboard was a lack of hot water. The water for washing dishes was only tepid, and there was no soap. As a result the dishes got greasy, and some troops got a mild dysentery from it. In our cabins we had water only twice a day—7:00 to 9:00 in the morning and 5:30 to 6:30 in the evening. It was unheated, so we shaved in cold water. The troops took lukewarm salt-water showers, by army orders, every three days.

The enlisted men were allowed to go anywhere on deck they wished, except for a small portion of one deck set aside for officers. Theoretically the officers weren't permitted on the enlisted men's deck, but that regulation soon broke down. We correspondents could go anywhere we pleased, being gifted and chosen characters.

Instructions for "battle stations" in case of attack were issued. All officers were to stay in their cabins, all soldiers must remain below. Troops in the two bottom decks, down by the water line, were to move up to the next two decks above. Only we correspondents were to be allowed on deck during an attack. Being useless as well as gifted, we were honored with the divine right of getting ourselves shot if that was what we wanted.

American gunners manned all the ship's guns, but they never had to fire a serious shot. On our first morning out, all the ships in the convoy tested their guns, and for a while it was a vivid and noisy display of shooting all over the place.

We correspondents knew where we were going. Some of the officers knew too, and the rest could guess. But an amazing number of soldiers had no idea where they were bound. Some of them thought we were going to Russia over the Murmansk route, others thought our destination was Norway, and still others thought it was Iceland. A few sincerely believed we were returning to America. It wasn't until the fifth day out, when advice booklets were distributed on how to conduct ourselves in North Africa, that everybody knew where we were bound.

The first couple of days at sea our ship seemed to mill around without purpose. Then we stopped completely, and lay at anchor for a day. But finally we made our rendezvous with other ships and at dusk —five days after leaving London—we steamed slowly into a prearranged formation, like floating pieces of a puzzle drifting together to form a picture. By dark we were rolling, and the first weak ones were getting sick.

The sea was fairly rough for a couple of days, and there was considerable seasickness. Especially below, among the troops. But they handled themselves well, and the holds didn't get into the frightful condition they do on some voyages.

After a while the sea calmed, and it was in the main a happy voyage. The soldiers were routed out at 6:30 A.M., and at 10:00 A.M. every day they had to stand muster and have boat drill for an hour. Outside of that they had little to do, and passed the time just standing around on deck, or lying down below reading, or playing cards. There wasn't any saluting on board during the whole trip. Lots of the soldiers started growing beards.

It's a terrific task to organize a shipful of troops. It was not until our convoy had been at sea nearly a week that everything got settled down and running smoothly. An Air Force colonel was appointed commanding officer of troops on board. An orderly room was set up, aides were picked, deck officers appointed, and ship's regulations mimeographed and distributed. The troops were warned about smoking or using flashlights on deck at night, and against throwing cigarettes or orange peels overboard. A submarine commander can spot a convoy, hours after it has passed, by such floating debris.

The warning didn't seem to make much impression at first. Soldiers threw stuff overboard, and one night a nurse came on deck with a brilliant flashlight guiding her. An officer near me screamed at her. He yelled so loudly and so viciously that I thought at first he was doing it in fun.

"Put out that light, you blankety blank-blank! Haven't you got any sense at all?"

Then suddenly I realized he meant every word of it, and her one little light might have killed us all.

The ship, of course, was entirely blacked out. All entrances to the deck were shielded with two sets of heavy black curtains. All ports were painted black and ordered kept closed, but some people did open them in the daytime. In the holds below, the ports were opened for short periods each day, to air out the ship. If a torpedo hit when many of the ports were open, however, enough water might rush in to sink her immediately if she listed.

Everybody had a life preserver, and had to carry it constantly. These were of a new type, rather like two small pillows tied together. They went on over the head, were pulled down over the shoulders and chest, and then tied there. We merely slung them over our shoulders for carrying. They were immediately nicknamed "sandbags."

After the second day we were ordered to wear our web pistol belt, with water canteen attached. Even going to the dining room, we had to take our life preserver and our water canteen.

There were nine members of our special little group. We were officially assigned together, and we stuck together throughout the trip. We were: Bill Lang, of *Time* and *Life*; Red Mueller, of *Newsweek*; Joe Liebling, of the *New Yorker*; Gault Macgowan, of the New York *Sun*; Ollie Stewart, of the Baltimore *Afro-American*; Sergeant Bob Neville, correspondent for the Army papers *Yank* and *Stars and Stripes*; two army censors, Lieutenants Henry Meyer and Cortland Gillett; and myself.

Sergeant Neville, being an enlisted man, wasn't permitted to share cabin space with us, but had to go to general quarters in the hold and sleep in a hammock. We did manage to get him up to better quarters after a couple of days. Neville was probably the most experienced and traveled of all of us—he spoke three languages, was foreign news editor of *Time* for three years, had worked for the *Herald Tribune* and *PM*, was in Spain for that war, in Poland for that one, in Cairo for the first Wavell push, and in India and China and Australia. But he turned down a commission and went into the ranks, and consequently he had to sleep on floors, stand for hours in mess line, and stay off certain decks.

Ollie Stewart was a Negro, the only American Negro correspondent then accredited to the European theater. He was well-educated, conducted himself well, and had traveled quite a bit in foreign countries. We all grew to like him very much on the trip. He lived in one of the two cabins with us, ate with us, played handball on deck with the officers, everybody was friendly to him, and there was no "problem."

We correspondents already knew a lot of the officers and men aboard, so we roamed the ship continuously and had many friends. Bill Lang and I shared a cabin with the two lieutenants. We'd get out the regulations about correspondents, which said that we must be treated with "courtesy and consideration" by the army. We'd read those rules aloud to Lieutenants Meyer and Gillett, and then order them to light our cigarettes, and shine our shoes. Humor runs pretty thin on a long convoy trip.

Our troopship had a large hospital, and it was filled most of the time. The long train rides in unheated cars across England seemed to have given everybody a cold, and it was a poor man indeed who couldn't sport a deathlike cough aboard ship. We even had two pneumonia cases, both of whom pulled through. I myself came down with one of the Ten Best Colds of 1942 the day after we got aboard, and spent the next five days in bed, feigning seasickness. But the ship was lousy with army doctors, so I had lozenges, injections and consultations, all without charge.

The ship had never carried American troops before, and the British waiters were somewhat shocked by the appetites and the dining-room manners of the younger officers. Second lieutenants, muscular and still growing, would order a complete second dinner after finishing the first. And betweentimes they'd get up and serve themselves with bread, carry off their own plates, play loud tunes on their glasses with their forks, make rude jokes about the food, and generally conduct themselves in a manner unbecoming to the dignity of a British cruise-ship waiter. Also, smoking was prohibited in the dining room. The poor waiters had a terrible time enforcing it, but finally succeeded. I must say, in behalf of the British, that they finally broke down and entered into the spirit of the thing. Eventually, I think, they enjoyed the wild West camaraderie as much as the Americans did.

Those of us in the cabins were awakened at seven each morning by the cabin steward, bearing cups of hot tea. Meals were in two sittings, an hour apart. The headwaiter wore a tuxedo at dinner-time and, as I have said, the food was excellent. We had fried eggs and real bacon for breakfast every morning—the first real eggs I'd tasted in four months. There was also tea in the afternoon, and sandwiches at night.

Once under way, two canteens were opened for the troops. One sold cigarettes, chocolates, and so forth; the other, called a "wet canteen," sold hot tea. There was a constant long queue at each one. Soldiers often had to stand in line for three hours.

There was a bar in the evening for soft drinks, but no liquor was sold. Some officers brought whiskey aboard, but it was all gone after a day or two, and from then on it was probably the driest ocean voyage ever made. As someone observed, "We catch it both ways. We can't smoke in the dining room because it's a British ship, and we can't buy liquor because it's an American trooper."

Of all the spots on earth where rumors run wild, I think a convoy trooper must lead, hands down. Scores of rumors a day floated about the ship. We got so we believed them all, or didn't believe any.

It was rumored we would rendezvous with a big convoy from America; that an aircraft carrier had joined us; that we'd hit Gibraltar in six hours, twenty-four hours, two days; that the ship behind us was the West Point, the Mount Vernon, the Monterey; that we were eighty miles off Portugal, and two hundred miles off Bermuda. None of these turned out to be true.

The rumormongering got so rife that one officer made up a rumor to the effect that we were going to Casablanca, and timed it to see just how long it would take to encircle the ship. It came back to him, as cold fact right from the bridge, in just half an hour.

The trip had no sooner started than rehearsals for an enlisted men's variety show began. I believe you could take any thousand soldiers in our army, and out of them create a good orchestra. From our troops they dug up an accordionist, saxophonist, trumpeter, violinist, two banjo players, a dancer, a tenor, a cowboy singer and several pianists —all professionals. They rehearsed every afternoon. The big night

came a couple of evenings before we got to Gibraltar. They put on two shows that night, for the enlisted men only. It was a burlesque, and I mean burlesque. Word got around, and the officers and nurses wanted to see it. So the night we were approaching Gibraltar they put it on again. They cleaned it up some, by the colonel's request, but it still sparkled.

The show went over terrifically. There was genuine talent in it, and serious music, as well as the whiz-bang stuff. But the hero of the evening was a hairy corporal—Joe Comita of Brooklyn—who did a strip-tease burlesque of Gypsy Rose Lee. His movements were pure genius. Gypsy herself couldn't have been more sensuous. Joe twirled and stripped, twirled and stripped. And then when he was down to his long heavy GI underwear he swung to the front of the stage, lifted his veil, and kissed a front-row colonel on top of his bald head!

The whole show was marvelously good, but there was something more to it than just that. There was the knowledge, deep in everybody's mind, that this was our night of danger. The radio had just brought word that Germany's entire U-boat pack was concentrated in the approaches to Gibraltar. More than fifty submarines were said to be waiting for us. I doubt there was a soul on board who expected the night to pass without an attack.

It was a perfect night for romance or for death. The air was warm and the moon laid a brilliant sheen across the water. By its very gentleness, the night seemed in collusion with the evil that lay beneath the waters. And in that environment the boys went buoyantly through their performances. We sat with life preservers on and water canteens at our belts. We laughed and cheered against a background of semiconscious listening for other sounds.

As the show ended a major whom I did not know turned to me and said, "That's wonderful, those boys doing that when they're being taken to war like galley slaves down there in the hold. When you think of people at home squawking their heads off because they can have only twenty gallons of gasoline, it makes my blood boil."

Our ship had two funnels, or smokestacks. The forward one was a dummy—empty inside. About three feet from its top a steel platform had been built. It was reached by a steel ladder. The army kept a lieutenant and three enlisted men up there all the time, on lookout with binoculars.

It was a grandstand seat and I went up almost every afternoon. Lieutenant Winfield Channing, who had charge of an antiaircraft battery, usually had the afternoon watch up there, and we'd chat for hours about his job before the war, and of our chances for the future, and of what we'd do when it was over. The sun was bright, the funnel sides cut off the wind, there were deck chairs, and it was really like a few square feet of Miami Beach. We called our little post "The Funnel Club." From our perch we could get a perfect view of the convoy's zigzagging maneuvers. Once we saw three rainbows at once, one of them making a horseshoe right over the ship. Occasionally on the horizon we could dimly sight a sailing sloop or a fishing vessel.

My special hangout down below was in a section where I ran onto a bunch of soldiers from New Mexico, where my home is now. One of them was Sergeant Cheedle Caviness, a nephew of Senator Hatch. Cheedle had grown a blond mustache and goatee, and looked like a duke.

There was no trouble at all among the troops during the voyage but we did have a couple of small "incidents" in the officers' section of the ship. One officer, monkeying with his revolver in his cabin, "didn't know it was loaded" and shot a nice hole through the wardrobe, thoughtfully missing his cabinmates. Another officer was arrested for taking pictures of the convoy.

The troop commander issued orders that no movies were to be shown during the trip and that electric razors were not to be used. He was afraid the enemy could pick up our position from the current, but we found out later this precaution had been unnecessary.

We got radio news broadcasts twice a day from BBC. It was rumored they would be discontinued after we were a couple of days at sea, but they weren't. They were piped over the ship by loud-speakers so that the troops could hear the news.

Chaplains aboard ship said that church attendance among the troops went up noticeably after we sailed, and continued to rise as we approached submarine waters.

The nurses and doctors aboard were mainly from Roosevelt Hospital in New York. There were two other detachments of nurses on other ships in the convoy, we learned later. The nurses teamed up with the officers and together they played cards, walked the decks, sat in the lounge. That moonlight was pretty enchanting, and I wouldn't be surprised if some romances got started.

As time wore on, acquaintanceships grew broader and broader, just as they do on a peacetime cruise. The days were purposeless and without duties, yet they seemed to speed by. For many of us the trip was a grand rest. Toward the end some of us even hated to have it over—we felt the sad sense of parting from new friends and of returning to old toils, and we were reluctant. But war doesn't humor such whims.

I had often wondered in just what sort of formation a big convoy moved, and whether a person could see the whole thing all the time or not, and how the escort vessels acted.

Well, ours was a medium-big convoy. The day we left, we counted a certain maximum number of ships. We were never able to count the same number again until we got almost to port. Not because they were out of eye range, but because they were lined up in rows and we couldn't see those behind other ships. Usually our convoy was wider than it was long, which surprised me.

The convoy seemed to use three or four different geometric patterns. Every little while the entire formation changed from one pattern to another, like a football team shifting after a huddle. It was fascinating to watch some ships speed up, others drop back, and the new pattern take shape. In addition, the entire convoy, moving in unison, zigzagged constantly. The turns were sudden, and so sharp that the ships would heel over. These zigzags were made at frequent intervals—very frequent when we were in suspicious waters.

British corvettes and warships were ahead and on all sides of us. They didn't do much dashing about but seemed to keep their positions just as steadily as we kept ours. In the daytime we ran half a mile or so apart, and at night the entire convoy tightened up. Then we could distinguish two or three dark shapes close around us. I do not know whether it was true, but they said we had additional escorts out of sight over the horizon.

So far as we know, the convoy had only one "incident" during the entire trip. Our ship was on the outside. The corvette on out beyond us and the transport running aft of us both signaled that a torpedo had passed just behind us and just ahead of the other transport.

The corvettes dashed around and dropped depth charges, and that was all there was to it. Nobody on our ship saw the torpedo, and nobody at all saw the submarine.

As we progressed southward, the weather became downright heavenly—softly warm and so calm that there was no roll whatever in the ship. Often the voyage seemed like a peacetime tropical cruise, instead of a packed trooper going dangerously to war. Many soldiers slept on deck those last few nights, and for the last three we were all ordered to sleep in our clothes. It would be wrong to deny that people were tense those days, but it also would be wrong to say that fear was shown by anybody.

Dawn and dusk were the crucial times, and the last two mornings I managed to get awake and on deck just before daylight. I never saw any submarines, but I saw two of the most thrilling sunrises I've ever known.

As we drew closer and closer to journey's end, we acquired a feeling something akin to family love for our team of ships. We had come so far together, had so perfectly consummated our endless shifting of formation, our eternal zigzagging. We somehow became like an enormous oceanic machine, engaged in a giant rhythmic rotation, our ability to go on and on forever ensured by the perfection of our own discipline.

Hour after hour I stood at the rail looking out over that armada of marching ships—they did really seem to march across the ocean —and an almost choking sense of its beauty and power enveloped me.

At last we came to the Strait of Gibraltar—to lights on both sides of us—and then on into the calmness of the Mediterranean. We still sailed a long time, still in danger waters, but a pleasant relief took hold of us.

We started to pack. We were issued our desert gear of dust masks, water purifiers, and so on. We tipped our stewards, returned borrowed books, traded our money for the new American issue, and took down outfit numbers, for looking up new army friends.

Finally we reached our port. Slowly and intricately, like twine from a hidden ball, the ships poured us out onto the docks in long brown lines. We lined up and marched away. Some of us marched three miles, some of us twenty miles. We marched at first gaily and finally with great weariness, but always with a feeling that at last we were beginning the final series of marches that would lead us home again —home, the one really profound goal that obsesses every one of the Americans marching on foreign shores.

2. THE AMERICANS HAVE

LANDED

ARMY photographers are soldiers who fight with cameras instead of guns. They are in the Signal Corps, and their purpose is twofold— to get newsreels for showing in the theaters back home and to make a permanent pictorial record of the war. There are many of these men, in both the army and the navy, scattered in our forces throughout the world and already they have done some historic work. Many of them will die behind their cameras before it is all over.

I had been in Africa a few days when I ran into Private Ned Modica and Sergeant Norman Harrington, both army cameramen. Ned was thirty-five, and had coal-black hair, slightly graying. Even in battle dress he looked and spoke like an officer. As a youth he went to the New York School of Fine Arts, then on to two years' study in Paris. Before the war Ned had his own studio on fashionable Madison Avenue.

Ned's teammate had been a civic leader back home in Easton, Maryland—an odd thing for a boy of sixteen just out of high school. At seventeen he became the youngest Rotarian in America. At nineteen he opened a studio of his own. Norman didn't even bother to wear his stripes. His only interest was in doing for the army what he had been doing as a civilian—superb photography. Ned claimed that Norman was the best newsreel man in the army.

On the morning of November eighth Sergeant Harrington and Private Modica stood in the darkness on the hurricane deck of a troopship lying off the coast of Algeria. They were spellbound by the scenes their cameras were recording—the fantastic searching of tracer bullets along the shore, the fiery splash of colored flares in the sky, the laying of smoke screens by our armored speedboats.

13

Then, just at dawn, their ship moved in close to shore. As it dropped anchor, a French mortar shell came looping over. It missed the two cameramen by three feet. A moment later a second shell blew up the spot where they had been sleeping the night before.

Adventure starts almost too soon in some cases.

The two cameramen looked at each other in wonder, but their tension was broken by a voice on the ship's loud-speaker calling their numbers. The job for which they had trained and waited was at hand. Grabbing their kits they jumped into their steel-sided assault boat. As soon as they reached shallow water they tumbled out of the barge and landed waist-deep in the Mediterranean. Holding their cameras high over their heads, they waded ashore. After dumping their bags and extra film, they waded back, and began grinding away at the hordes of soldiers landing. By that act they became the first army newsreel men to go into action on this side of the ocean.

The water was cold, but they didn't feel it.

"Honestly, we were hardly aware of anything around us," Ned Modica said. "We were so consumed with what we were doing that we didn't know anything that was happening outside the radius of our lenses."

They worked for fifteen minutes waist-deep in the water and then ran up and down the beach getting shots of the troops dashing ashore. They filmed their first blood when they found some navy medical men tending a wounded French soldier lying on the beach. The soldier still wore his red fez, and the color must stand out in the technicolor film; so must the bare African mountains, the curve of the beach, and the great waiting convoy in the background, and the white bandages.

At the end of that first day of the Battle of Oran the two photographers sprawled on the floor of a country schoolhouse near the little Algerian town of Arzeu. Other soldiers lay all around them. Both cameramen were dead-tired. They had been on the go all day without stopping, running up and back, ditching extra equipment, and returning later to get it.

Their clothes were still wet, and they were cold. They had come ashore without blankets or overcoats. Instead of one musette bag, they carried three over their shoulders, and the bags weren't filled with food or ammunition. They were filled with extra film for their cameras, and of cameras they had aplenty. Ned carried two movie color cameras and one still camera. Norman lugged a huge newsreel job and a still camera. Their personal effects consisted of two toothbrushes.

In their first twelve hours on African soil, Norman and Ned filmed wounded Americans and wounded Frenchmen, photographed the actual capture of a seaplane base, and got pictures of their first wartime corpse. That was the body of a sniper who had shot at them and missed.

They slept little that first night. Bullets pinged on the walls and thumped into the yard. The soldiers in the schoolroom were nervous all night. In the darkness they could hear the click of cartridge clips in pistols. Just before dawn one touchy doughboy heaved a hand grenade out the window at an imagined shadow. One of the bunch sat up all night telling endless anecdotes about his fraternity days in college.

At dawn the next morning the two photographers luckily found a jeep and drove forward to where the fighting for Saint-Cloud was going on. Eventually they left the jeep and worked their way up to the front line. In the infantry a man learned to walk in ditches for protection. He learned to walk a little, then to lie down and wait for a mortar shell to burst. His head jerked down involuntarily when he heard the zing of a passing bullet. These two boys learned that in a hurry.

Ned Modica found an American machine-gun crew, and ground away at them with his camera. It was good action stuff. Then they went on into Oran and filmed the dramatic welcome given the American troops by the French and Arab people. Finally they boxed up their film and scouted around till they found an accommodating RAF pilot to fly it to London.

During their second night on African soil the two photographers "slept" in another country schoolhouse—that time on desks. They actually managed to get about three hours' sleep out of their first sixty ashore. At dawn the third day a colonel rushed up and asked Harrington if he wanted to ride along on a reconnoitering trip that Captain Paul Gale was making in a jeep. Harrington grabbed his cameras and jumped in.

The driver, a nice looking youngster whose name the cameraman didn't catch, set off down the road at a good clip. They went ahead several miles, passing troops on the way, and finally came to a small town. There they parked the jeep. While Captain Gale went about his business, Harrington got out his equipment and took pictures of the local people and the shell-marked walls. Everybody was cordial. Things seemed normal.

They were about ready to leave when some American troops came marching in. Only then did they realize they had unwittingly spent a pleasant hour in a town that hadn't yet been captured.

They started back in their jeep to a command post several miles to the rear. Captain Gale was sitting beside the driver. Sergeant Harrington was in the back seat. The top was down, and the windshield folded flat and covered—for a windshield can create a glare that makes a perfect target for snipers. It's funny the things a man learns in war.

For instance, the soldiers were issued sunglasses before coming ashore, but they had to abandon them because the glasses caught the sun and made nice targets.

The three drove on along the highway, among vineyards, under a warm African sun. Everything was quiet. The Algerian phase of the war seemed about over.

Suddenly the driver, for no apparent reason, fell over his steering wheel, and the jeep swerved. Blood splashed down over his uniform. He never uttered a sound. Unheard and unseen, a sniper's bullet had taken him just over the right eye. He died instantly.

Harrington reached over the body and grabbed the wheel. Captain Gale got his foot around the dead driver's leg and shoved the throttle to the floor. Two more shots zipped past but missed. The jeep roared on down the road and out of danger, with one man steering and another man at the throttle.

In the meantime, Ned Modica had gone by foot up to the front line of the attack upon Saint-Cloud. The French there put up a terrific resistance, and in fact stopped us cold for a while. The fight was spectacular, and Ned became momentarily oblivious to the danger about him, lost in the craftsman's enthusiasm of getting his pictures.

As Ned stood rigid, snapping his pictures, he felt someone leaning against him. Making conversation, he said, "It's getting pretty hot, isn't it?" There was no reply, for just at that moment all the soldiers jumped up and began to retreat.

The move was on orders from the commander, who was altering the battle tactics, but Ned didn't know that at the time.

He said to a chap leaning against him, "Let's get the hell out of here," and whirled about to start running. And as he turned the soldier fell heavily to the ground—dead.

Modica never knew who had died while leaning against him.

The next day the two cameramen bivouacked in tiny shelter tents pitched in an olive grove, miles out in the country, and waited for the next move. That's where I found them.

"Here in Africa is the first place I ever picked an orange off a tree," said Modica.

"After our film is edited and censored it should still be enough for a thirty-minute newsreel, most of it in technicolor," said Harrington. "It should be beautiful."

"When we get to Italy we can get us some wonderful things to eat," said Modica. "At least we can ask for them. I can speak Italian."

"You'll get to Italy and lots of other places," said Harrington. "We're going to be the beach-busters of every landing and be in on every kill. You'll see."

"When it's all over I'm going to get discharged in Paris and have my wife take a sabbatical leave," said Modica. "We'll do these countries as tourists."

"You'll be in China by the time it's all over," said Harrington.

"Well, I've always wanted to see China, so we might as well get discharged there," said Modica.

"If we live that long," said Harrington.

When Ralph Gower was a little fellow in Arkansas, a deaf man lived across the street from his home. The man could read lips, and Ralph learned the trick from him. He did it mainly to show off before the other kids.

A quarter of a century later, Sergeant Ralph Gower was sitting on the edge of a folding cot in a tent way out in a field in Africa. It was a hospital tent, and wounded soldiers in red bathrobes lolled around in it. Ralph Gower could talk to them and understand what they were saying solely because he learned lip reading as a stunt when he was a child. For he was newly deaf from the explosion of an enemy shell.

When I went to see him he had been deaf only a few days, but his lip reading was already perfect. It had all come back to him across those twenty-five years. We talked for half an hour and he never made a single mistake.

Sergeant Gower escaped without serious wounds other than the loss of his hearing. There was a fifty-fifty chance of his recovering his hearing, but even if he didn't he had two strikes on deafness to begin with.

Ralph Gower was thirty-seven and, although he was born in Arkansas, his home town was Sacramento, California. Before the war he worked as a draftsman and machine-screw operator. In his early twenties he served a hitch in the army and as soon as England and Germany started fighting he joined up again. He was a machine-gun sergeant.

Gower came to Africa aboard one of a group of combat boats that got into trouble trying to take an Algerian harbor. Those who lived to tell the tale were miraculously lucky.

"Do you want to hear what it felt like?" Ralph asked.

I sat down on the edge of the next cot. "Sure I do. What did it feel like?"

"It felt just like going into hell and back out again," he said.

The boys around the tent all laughed loudly. That startled me, for I couldn't see anything to laugh at. But gradually I caught on. Sergeant Gower's dead-pan Arkansas wit was keeping the whole tentful howling day and night. He never said anything obviously clever. He just said things with an odd twist to them and never cracked a smile. His expression never changed.

Six dozen wounded soldiers gathered on near-by cots to listen as Ralph told me the whole story. He told it very gravely, but he was frequently interrupted by shattering laughter from his convalescing audience. It was friendly and admiring laughter.

"We were all down in one of the compartments of the boat," he said. "That French ship came right up against us, and one of their shells came through the side. The damn' thing exploded right in my face."

Some of the wounded soldiers in the tent had been through the same lethal nightmare he was describing, but they laughed at that remark just as if Bob Hope had pulled a fast one.

"I never heard a sound," Ralph went on. "It just went 'shisht-ppfftt.' That's all I ever heard. Then I passed out.

"When I came to everything was quiet. I thought the battle was over. The ship was full of ammonia and smoke. I couldn't hardly breathe. I like to choked to death. My heart was shooting pains out in all directions. [Laughter] I couldn't get enough air in my lungs. I couldn't even get enough smoke, for that was all I was getting anyhow. [More laughter]

"I finally started climbing a ladder. When I stuck my head out on deck I couldn't hear anything, but the air was full of tracer bullets. Then I realized there were dead men lying on the deck. I passed out. That fresh air was too much for me. [Laughter]

"When I came to again I was lying over by the rail with a stack of dead men. We had a hell of a time. Them dead men wouldn't move much. [Laughter] I thought I was never gonna get out from under there."

Thus the story went. It was getting late, and we shook hands.

"Are you married?" I asked.

"Am I married?" he said. "No, I'm single. I mean to say I'm sensible."

The wounded boys all roared.

Probably the hardest fighting in the whole original North African occupation took place in Oran. Many of the soldiers whom I had known in England went through it, and they told me all about it. Without exception, they admitted they were scared stiff.

Don't get the wrong idea from that. They kept going forward. But it was their first time under fire and, being human, they were frightened. As one private said, "There was no constipation in our outfit those first few days."

I asked an officer how the men manifested fright. He said, largely by just looking pitifully at each other and edging close together to have company in misery.

Once the first phase was over, a new jubilance came over the troops. There was among them a confidence and enthusiasm that hadn't existed when they were in England, even though their morale was high there. Then they were impatient to get started and get it over, but once they had started they were eager to sweep on through.

That first night of landing, when they came ashore in big steel motorized invasion barges, many funny things happened. One famous officer intended to drive right ashore in a jeep, but they let the folding end of the barge down too soon and the jeep drove off into eight feet of water. Other barges rammed ashore so hard the men jumped off without even getting their feet wet.

It was moonlight, and the beach was deathly quiet. There was one small outfit that didn't hear a shot till long after daylight the next morning, but the moonlight and shadows and surprising peacefulness gave them the creeps, and all night, as they worked their way inland over the hills, nobody spoke above a whisper.

Each outfit was provided with the password beforehand. In the shadows, soldiers couldn't tell who was who, and everyone was afraid of getting shot by his own men, so all night the hillsides around Oran hissed with the constantly whispered password directed at every approaching shadow.

A friend of mine, Lieutenant Colonel Ken Campbell, captured eight French soldiers with a pack of cigarettes. It was all accidental. He stumbled onto an Arab sleeping on the beach and the man told him there were soldiers in the building up the hill. Campbell sneaked up, revolver in hand, and opened the door. The soldiers were all asleep. With quick decision, he stuck the gun back in its holster, then woke the soldiers. They were very startled and confused. Campbell, who spoke perfect French, chatted with the men, passed around the cigarettes, told them they were captured, and after a bit marched them away.

Private Chuck Conick from Pittsburgh, telling me how the soldiers felt during that first advance, said everybody was scared but didn't talk about it in the rest periods between advances. They mainly wondered what the papers at home were saying about the battle. Time after time he heard the boys say, "If my folks could only see me now!"

Boys from New Mexico and Arizona were amazed at how much the North African scenery resembled their own desert Southwest. In the moonlight that first night the rolling, treeless hills looked just like home country to them.

All through the advance the troops were followed in almost comic-opera fashion by hordes of Arab children, who crowded around the guns until they were actually in the way. The Arab men were very calm and quiet and there was a fine dignity about even the most ragged of them. But our boys couldn't resist the sad and emaciated little faces of the children, and that was when they started giving away their rations.

It was hot in the daytime, so hot that the advancing soldiers kept stripping and abandoning their clothes until some were down to undershirts, but at night it turned sharply chilly and they wished they hadn't.

French resistance ran the whole scale from eager co-operation to bitter fighting to the death. In most sectors the French seemed to fire only when fired on. Later we learned that many French troops had only three bullets for each rifle, but in other places the 75-mm. guns did devastating work.

The more experienced of our troops said they didn't mind the machine-gun and rifle fire so much, but the awful noise and uncanny accuracy of the 75's made their hearts stand still.

The boys who went through it will have memories forever. Many of them said that chiefly they remembered little things of beauty like the hills shadowed in moonlight and the eerie peacefulness of the beach when they landed.

On the whole, the American forces were welcome in North Africa. Oran gave a terrific demonstration for them. The first thing into the city after the original few days of fighting was a tank. It pulled up and stopped in the city square. A throng gathered around, and the people didn't know whether the tank was French, British, American, or what. They were still bewildered by the suddenness of it all. Finally an officer stuck his head out of the turret and somebody yelled and asked his nationality. The officer couldn't understand French, and said something in English. The crowd recognized his American accent, and then the cheering started. Women kissed him, and the crowd almost carried him away. He went around for hours with lipstick all over his face.

Soldiers who were with the first party reported that the town was almost deliriously happy over the Americans' arrival. They analyzed the feeling about as follows: Forty per cent of the demonstration was based on the Frenchman's love for show, for cheering anything that passes; twenty per cent was due to the farseeing knowledge that it eventually meant the liberation of France; and another forty per cent was based on personal and bodily gratitude at the prospect of getting something to eat again.

The Germans had shipped vast quantities of African foodstuffs across the Mediterranean to France and on to Germany. The people of Oran were in a pitiful condition. They were starving. The American occupation naturally stopped the flow to Germany. Further, our army donated huge food stocks to the city, and the people gradually began to eat once more. A starving man is likely to feel better than well-disposed toward almost anyone who comes offering him something to eat.

Americans, notoriously, are often foolishly generous. The troops in the first wave came ashore with only canned field rations carried on their backs, yet our soldiers gave much of that food to the pitiful-looking Arab children. The result was that pretty soon the soldiers themselves hadn't much left to eat, and for days they lived on oranges.

In England, oranges were practically unknown, so we gorged ourselves on them. Some troops ate so many they got diarrhea and broke out in a rash. I bought tiny tangerines, very juicy, to carry around in my pockets. They cost a franc each, about one and a third cents.

We were all equipped with foreign-issue American money. The smallest denomination, a dollar bill, looked just like our regular money except for a yellow stamp. The stamp was in case any of the currency fell into the hands of the enemy. The earmark would render it useless to them. This money of ours was accepted everywhere, but we got our change in francs. The exchange was seventy-five francs to a dollar. Prices promptly began to rise, but still they were low according to our standards. Good wine cost only forty-four francs a bottle, and wine was about the only thing left to buy. The stores had pitifully small stocks, and the restaurants listed horse meat on their menus.

Oran is a big city. It reminded me very much of Lisbon. There are modern office buildings and beautiful apartment buildings of six and eight stories. The Renault automobile showroom was full of brand-new cars when we arrived. In a few days the army had bought every car, and in a few more days the Red Cross had taken over the showrooms, turned it into a club for troops, and the soldiers were standing around the piano singing "The White Cliffs of Dover."

Some of our soldiers spoke French, but not many. Every French dictionary in Oran was sold in a few days, but the boys had no inhibitions in the matter of language and get along on pidgin French and loud shouting.

As soon as the Americans came the stores began pasting shatter tape on the windows, for they knew that German bombing probably would follow. It was interesting to see the difference between French and British temperaments displayed in the way windows were taped. In England the taping was in very conventional patterns, but here it was a work of art. Designs often were so intricate that they resembled the fantasies of a snowflake under a microscope. One store worked its name into a design; another made the tape into a framework for a dozen pictures hanging in the window.

German planes did fly over several times in those early days. There was considerable shooting from the ground too, but no damage was done by bombs or shells. Oran was not even blacked out. It was dimmed out, but the result was really not very dim. When planes actually came over, however, all the lights were turned out. Also, the army ringed the city with smoke pots. When those were set off, they created what seemed to be a heavy fog, very effective for hiding the city.

*   *   *

Oran, we found, was not a bad place at all. But most of the Americans there would have traded the whole layout for the worst town in the United States, and thrown in a hundred dollars to boot. That's the way Americans are, including me. Most of us had never heard of Oran till the war started, yet it is a bigger city than El Paso. It has palm-lined streets, broad sidewalks, outdoor cafés, a beautiful harbor, restaurants with soft colored lighting, and apartments with elevators. On the other hand, it also has Arabs dressed in ragged sheets, garbage in the gutters, dogs that are shockingly gaunt, and more horse carts than automobiles.

Most of the Americans talked about how dirty Oran was. Which just goes to show they hadn't been around. Oran was cleaner than some of the poorer Latin cities in our own hemisphere. And at that season it didn't even smell very bad.

World travelers had told me that Oran had an Oriental atmosphere, but I couldn't detect it. It seemed much more like a Latin city than an Oriental one. And it could be compared in many ways with El Paso, discounting the harbor. The climate is roughly the same. Both cities are in semiarid country. Both are dusty in the spring and very hot in summer. Both are surrounded by fertile, irrigated land that produces fruit and vegetables and grain.

The population of Oran is actually mostly French, Spanish and Jewish. The Arabs are a minority. They run all the way from hideous beggars up to solemn men in long white robes and bright turbans, sitting in the most expensive cafés and sipping tall drinks. But there are many more Europeans than Arabs.

At first, our troops were rather lost in Oran, officers and men alike. There weren't the usual entertainments to be had at home and in England. Nothing much was left to drink but wine, and most Americans hadn't learned to drink wine with relish. The movies were few and pretty poor. There were no dances. There was a professional "line," but the parents of nice girls in Oran were very fussy and wouldn't let the girls out.

Everybody felt an odd sense of irritation at not being able to talk to the local people. The soldiers tried hard with French but it wasn't much fun. Officers stationed here at desk jobs were itching to move onward. Troops camped far out in the country—which the vast majority were—really felt better satisfied than those in town.

Lieutenant Nat Kenney, of Baltimore, had an old broken-down motorcycle that he rode about the country. One day he took off for

Arzeu, about twenty miles from his camp. He passed a monstrous-looking lizard lying on the pavement, so he stopped and went back.

The lizard was about a foot long, plus six inches of tail. The thing kept changing color. Its eyes could move separately, and in any direction. It was an evil-looking customer indeed. Nat poked it gingerly with his shoe, but it didn't attack him. Then he poked it with his gloved hand, and still it didn't try to bite. Then he stuck his hand in front of its nose, and the lizard crawled up on the glove, just as if it had been waiting for Nat all the time.

So Nat held still and the lizard continued its crawl—up his arm, over his shoulder, up the back of his neck and clear to the top of his head. There it curled up, resting on the top of his cap and looking forward snakelike over his brow. Nat, crowned with this dragon, got back on his motorcycle and rode into Arzeu.

He parked the motorcycle and walked down the street. He kept running into soldiers he knew. They would start to salute, and right in the middle of the salute their mouths would fly open and they would gurgle out, "Lieutenant, for God's sake don't!"

Nat had dinner with the lizard still poised comfortably on top of his head, spent a pleasant hour walking around the town and startling his friends, then got back on the motorcycle and rode back almost to Oran. Finally he stopped at a field hospital where he knew some of the doctors. He left his friend there for them to experiment with.

Altogether the lizard spent about three hours and rode about thirty miles on top of Nat's head. The army began to think of transferring Lieutenant Kenney to Iceland for fear he would go riding to town next with a camel on his handle bars.

The American soldier will not be denied fraternization with his fellow man. Regardless of barriers, somehow our soldiers got along and made themselves understood, even though they couldn't speak a word of French or Arabic. I saw a soldier sitting at a café table with two French girls and their father, apparently spending the whole evening just smiling and making gestures. And I also saw Americans walking arm in arm with Frenchmen of the Foreign Legion. What they talked about or tried to talk about, I have no idea. A really comic sight was one of our boys standing on the street with an English-French dictionary in his hand, talking to a girl and looking up each word as he spoke it.

One night, far out in the country, I passed a small roadside fire with two American soldiers and two turbaned and bewhiskered Arabs squatted closely over it like old pals—a really touching sight.

Our soldiers were filthy rich, for there was little to buy. They loaded up on perfume and lipsticks, which were plentiful. They sent perfume to their girls in America and lipsticks to their girls in England, the old Lotharios.

The native crafts are largely silverwork, rugs, and leather. Some of the Algerian rugs resembled our Navajo Indian ones. They were beautiful and the prices were about the same. One officer I know thought he'd have an Arabian horseman's regalia made, to wear to costume balls after the war. But he found it would cost about $100, that he'd have to get a special dispensation to obtain the materials, and that it would take anywhere from several weeks to six months to make.

There weren't many American sailors in Oran at first, but the navy, as usual, took excellent care of those who were. One day I bumped into Lieutenant William Spence, a good friend of mine, who invited me down to look at the navy's hospital, of which he was in charge.

Lieutenant Spence was at Bellevue, in New York, before the war. He came ashore here, the morning of the American landings, with eight men, and they spent the next few days tending wounded sailors and soldiers on the beach. Then they went to Oran and started looking for a place to set up their hospital. They found a French Red Cross building standing empty and promptly moved in. In a day or two the navy was all set in what probably was the nicest hospital in North Africa.

I always like to hang around with navy men, they take such good care of me. At the time I still had a cough from the convoy trip, so they fixed me up a bottle of cough medicine and even made a blood count, to get a line on whether I was going to live or not.

It turned out that the pharmacist's mate who poured the medicine was an old Hoosier boy—in fact, he used to live only twenty miles from where I was raised. His name was Ben Smith of 620 South Fifth Street, Terre Haute, Indiana.

One of the army hospital commandants who came ashore the first morning of the occupation had a tale to tell. It seems the Medical Corps took over a barracks that the French had vacated in haste, and turned it into a hospital. The Americans found the place full of ammunition, and the officer got the creeps for fear the French would come back that night and try to retake it.

His problem was solved when he spied two tommy-gunners walking along the street. He rushed out and asked them if they would guard the ammunition all night. They said, "Sure," and the doctor went on about his business.

It was a couple of days before the fighting was all over, and the two guards never entered his mind again until about a week later, when he happened to see them. They hadn't reported back to their own outfit, they were still hanging around, faithfully guarding the ammunition.

And why did they do that? The answer is simple. Hospital food was always better than could be had anywhere else. These guys hadn't spent their months in the army for nothing.

Our troops found the African climate a welcome change, most of the time, from the wet bitterness of England. From December till late March there were few mosquitoes, and there wasn't much danger of malaria. The hospitals reported only an occasional case. On the average, the nights even as early as November were quite chilly. It began to be cold as soon as the sun got low, around four o'clock. By dark it was usually cold enough for an overcoat. We slept under all the blankets we could get.

In the morning the sun wasn't well up until after eight o'clock. Usually the sky was a clear blue before noon, and it seemed to be a larger sky than ours back home. Maybe that was because we were out where we could see more sky than ordinarily. Some days high white clouds covered the sky. Other days the sky was entirely cloudless, and then the sun was as warm as it is at home in late June.

In fine weather the troops went around stripped to the waist, and practically everybody got a sun tan.

Once a week or so we had a bad spell that was thoroughly miserable. For two days it would pour rain, and a cold and bitter wind blew at such times. It was exactly like a bad winter day in England.

Our troops lived mostly in the fields. Many company commanders used to march their men up and down just to keep them warm. I felt sure that half of them would be sick, but there was no such reaction at all. The doctors said that the constant living outdoors, even in bad weather, was healthier than living inside. Also, our troops were getting tougher.

Most of the men abandoned their heavy underwear, but they wouldn't wear their summer uniforms until spring. During a cold spell the men filled their mattress covers with straw, put down one blanket to lie on, and had five spread over them. There was just room in each tent for two men, and the two usually slept together so they could pile both men's blankets across them.

They lived pretty primitively in their scattered camps. They were on American rations by then and the food was really wonderful. But there was very little water. At some camps a man ordinarily got a gallon a day for drinking, shaving and washing his clothes. But at many camps it was as little as a quart.

There was no room for small niceties and homey touches as in the bigger tents in England. There were no lights either, but two boys did rig up an Eskimo lamp. They bought some liquid paraffin in a near-by town, poured it into an empty can, then cut a few inches off one man's waist belt which was too big for him, and shoved this through the top of the can for a wick. It really made a serviceable light.

Military police patrolled the streets in the cities. Usually it was quiet as the grave by 10:30 P.M. The local people were terrified of air raids and wouldn't venture out at night. Their fear was so intense that I think Germany must have done an extra propaganda job in scaring them before we arrived.

For some reason communications were faint, I might even say mystic. I couldn't find out how my copy was transmitted. The censors themselves didn't know. I wrote my stuff and sent it away with about the same assurance of delivery as if I had put it in a bottle and tossed it into the Mediterranean. One morning I was positive I saw a small Arab boy feeding my latest dispatch to his goat.

We Americans actually knew less about what was happening throughout North Africa than you did at home. We got the daily communiqués in the local French papers, but there weren't many details, and anyway most of us couldn't read French well enough to get the fine points.

Some of us listened to the 9:00 P.M. news from BBC in London, and a few camps had short-wave radios and got hourly news from America. It seemed ironic that what was happening two hundred miles from us had to be flashed to America and then back again before we could hear it. But that's the way things are in this crazy world.

3. NOT TOO DARK AFRICA

OF ALL the American troops who were about to bust their traces to get into battle, I suppose the Rangers were the worst. That was because they had been trained like race horses, and if they couldn't race every day they got to pawing the ground.

As you know, the Rangers are American commandos. For months their training had been a violent, double-barreled curriculum of body toughening and scientific elimination of the enemy. All summer and fall in the cold waters of Scotland, troops of Rangers had practiced until they were as indestructible as Popeye and as deadly as executioners. Then they had had a shot of the real business. A few had gone on the Dieppe raid, and all of them had come to Africa.

They had one specific and highly dangerous job to do. And they did it so expertly that they suffered almost no casualties and spared all the Frenchmen's lives.

After the first assault those Rangers had had nothing to do. They were encamped, running through mock landings, swimming in the Mediterranean on the coldest days, doing military police duty in a near-by town. And they were gradually going nuts waiting to get into action again.

Since the specialty of the Rangers is landing on enemy beaches and storming gun positions, I asked one of them, "Do you suppose you'll just have to sit here until we invade another continent?"

"My God, I hope not! It might be too long a wait," was the wistful reply.

I made friends with one Ranger officer, Captain Manning Jacob. He called Morristown, New Jersey, home, but before the war he was an oil operator in South Texas.

Captain Jacob took me on a cross-country walk, following a detachment of Rangers. I had to run to keep up. Finally I couldn't go on any longer, and had to sit down and pant. I thought to myself, I'm ashamed of being so soft and feeble, but after all I'm past forty and I shouldn't be expected to keep up with guys like Jacob.

And then it turned out that this lethal athlete called Captain Jacob was forty years old himself. Maybe he got more vitamins than I did.

At any rate, the Rangers were good, and I was afraid if somebody didn't think up a new shore for them to storm pretty quick, they might resort to storming Africa all over again.

The Army's Special Services Branch, whose job was to provide relaxation and entertainment for the soldiers, had a tough time at first. There were lots of reasons why it was so tough. They hadn't any money and there wasn't much to buy even if they had had money. Lots of their athletic equipment never showed up, and they didn't know where it was. There were no stage or movie facilities at the camps, and they ran onto all kinds of snags in dickering with the local business people for theaters, restaurants, and auditoriums.

But they made some progress. They picked up a local troupe of singers and dancers with the very un-French name of Robert Taylor Shows, who traveled from camp to camp. They also hired a local circus, with wild animals and trapeze performers, to visit camps. Since the Special Services Branch had no money, the soldiers had to pay admission, but they had plenty of money.

They say that a soldier's three first needs are: (1) good mail service; (2) movies, radios, and phonographs; (3) cigarettes and candy. Cigarettes were issued free, six packs a week, but the other items were very short. Every radio in Oran had been bought up by the army. Music stores were cleaned out. All the camps wanted more musical instruments; they even advertised in the newspapers for secondhand ones.

Many camps rigged up their own forms of entertainment. Some had bands, and gave big dances which delighted the local people since dancing had been banned during more than two years of German rule.

Boxing was popular in the camps, and tournaments were arranged. Boxing gloves were one of the things that did show up in sizable amounts. But it was simple athletic games in which lots of men could participate that the Special Services Branch concentrated on in lieu of better things. Three such games—kick baseball, speedball, and touch football—were inaugurated. In addition, I saw lots of handball and even badminton being played at the more remote camps.

In town the Red Cross as usual did a good job of setting up clubs and restaurants for troops on leave. The army itself supervised the opening of two night clubs for officers, and also negotiated for clubs for enlisted men, noncoms, and Negro troops.

But with the shortage of sports equipment in the camps, and the towns so far away and no regular transportation, and with the different customs and different language, in a country stripped of almost everything a person would want to buy, life was considerably different from what it had been in England. Some of the harder heads said, "Well, this is war and we're at the front. The time for coddling troops is over."

But then it happened that only a very tiny percentage of our troops in Africa were at the front. The rest were far behind the lines, doing the drab, hard work of supplying the army or waiting impatiently to get into action. And as the war grew fiercer and troops came back from the front to rest, they would have to have something to do. So if that was the spot we had picked to do our fighting in, I was in favor of doing as much as possible to brighten dull and cheerless hours.

Being with the troops in Africa was, in many ways, like attending a national political convention—especially around one of the headquarters set up in the various coastal cities.

In Oran, for instance, the censor's office served as the press box, and that was where correspondents met and exchanged dope and listened to the radio news. Everybody ate at two big messes set up by the army. If we wanted to see somebody and couldn't find him, we waited till mealtime and we were bound to see him then.

As at a convention, we ran our legs off from one building to another, looking up various officers and having confabs. Everybody handed out an earful of dope, rumor, and fact. Most of it we couldn't use, and most of it wasn't true anyway.

Convention-like, people wandered in and out of my room all day and night. Some of them I knew, and some I didn't. Rooms were scarce, and I usually had one friend and two strangers sleeping on my floor. I shook hands with scores of people whose faces I knew, but I couldn't remember their names or at what camp in Ireland or England I had met them. And, surprisingly, I was always running onto some genuine acquaintance.

One fine day Private Crosby Lewis walked into my room. He was a brilliant young American who had joined the Canadian Army and had been sent to England two years before. After we got in the fight he transferred to our forces. The last time I had seen him was at a cocktail party in London when he announced his engagement.

Another time, I bumped into Lieutenant Colonel Louis Plain of the Marine Corps, one of my friends at Londonderry. He was a big Clevelander; hard as nails. Here in Africa, he got the Marine situation well in hand and then lost his voice, so he was reduced to making motions.

On my first day in Oran a beaming fellow in British uniform came up and started pumping my hand. It was Guy Ramsey, of the London *News-Chronicle*, whom I had last seen when we were following Wendell Willkie in England. Ramsey was the greatest reciter of limericks in England, all of them unprintable.

Away out in the country one night I was introduced in the darkness to Major William H. Pennington. We chatted a few moments, and it turned out we had been in school together at Indiana University twenty years ago.

I ran into another fellow I hadn't seen for ten years, Grainger Sutton, once a linotype operator on the Washington *Daily News*, and he was sporting a major's leaf.

So it went. Friends I had known in England, good friends from America, people I hadn't seen for two decades. And the next day they disappeared again.

In wartime people leave without saying good-bye—a fellow would be gone for three or four days before we realized his absence. It was no use to inquire. We just accepted it, and months later we were likely to be pumping his hand in some other foreign country. Or maybe we would never see him again. There was no telling.

Personal luggage in wartime is a paradox. A man must have it, and in order to have it he must carry it with him, and he can't carry it with him because there's too much of it. He has to carry his own bed and tent, some extra rations, his clothes, and a lot of purely military stuff such as gas mask, dust mask, tin hat, canteen, mess kit, and so on.

No man can carry all that on his back; I personally couldn't have carried all my stuff if there had been two of me. Consequently, it had to go on trucks. And inevitably it got lost. The result of this overweight of baggage was that people simply abandoned part of it, even if they didn't lose it. They were less comfortable, but they just couldn't lug it all. In almost every billet or barracks we found bedding or clothes or barracks bags that the guys ahead of us had left.

In the room I had in Oran I picked up a nice cap which fitted me better than my own, and I also took the blankets I found on the floor and left mine in their place, because they were nicer than mine. There was also a brand-new mess kit I was big enough to leave for the next fellow.

My own special bomber crew arrived shortly after I landed in Africa. I had met them first in England. It was the one known as the House of Jackson—the one where everybody in the crew called every-

body else "Jackson." We had a reunion out under the wing of their
Flying Fortress. The crew and the plane both looked a little shop-
worn. Neither had had a bath in a long time.

The ground crew hadn't arrived yet, so the boys were doing all their
own mechanical work. They lived in their little shelter tents out on
the field, under the wing of the bomber. Sometimes they ate C rations
out of tin cans, and sometimes they went to headquarters to eat in
the mess hall.

"What do you do about washing your shirts and such?" I asked
them, and they all laughed uproariously.

"We don't," they said.

But at that, they didn't have much on me; I had worn the same
shirt for two weeks.

They had already flown on several missions over Tunisia. Some of
their comrades had had trouble, but the House of Jackson continued
to supply itself with round-trip tickets. "We don't want to be heroes,"
they said. "We just want to get back every time."

But, of course, the chooser doesn't always get to make his own
choice. The battle camps of the world are filled with heroes who'd
have preferred not to be heroes.

The House of Jackson's service stripes made a long line then. There
were ten little bombs in a row painted on the nose of their plane,

signifying ten missions under fire. And beneath the little bombs there were three little swastikas, representing three German planes destroyed. "Those three were confirmed," said the skipper. "But we actually got seven more."

Two members of the crew had been decorated since we had parted in England. Their Fortress didn't have a name then, but in Africa the nose bore a painting of a vicious-looking devil dancing in a fire and brandishing a pitchfork, and above it the words "Devils from Hell."

My boys thought they were pretty tough, and I guess they were. They had been hit only once. Shortly before, they had dug a piece of flak half as big as a man's fist out of a wing close to the fuselage, although they hadn't even been aware of it when it hit them. Another day they flew five hundred miles with only three motors. They weren't hit that time—the fourth motor just went out, and later they installed a spare—outdoors, right on the field.

The boys said it was just as cold at high altitudes over Africa as it had been over England. When they went to bomb Bizerte or Tunis, they knew there was fighting going on down there on the ground, but they never had been able to see it. One day, as they headed east for Bizerte, they met a large formation of Junker 88s coming west to attack an Allied convoy. The Americans and the Germans passed about ten miles apart and just ignored each other.

"What a war!" said Captain Jackson. "We met each other on the way to bomb each other."

The ten men of the House of Jackson were enjoying themselves. They had no kicks at all. They had become used to being dirty now, and they were glad to be in Africa.

There was always a little bunch of Arabs squatting around their plane, selling them oranges and other native things. The boys traded cigarettes for eggs, which they cooked over their campfire. A day before they were to change bases they "sold" their Fortress to an Arab for twenty thousand eggs.

"Won't he be surprised when he brings those eggs and finds us gone!" said one of the boys.

Probably not half as surprised as they would have been if he really had brought twenty thousand eggs.

They went into the city only once the whole time I was there. Two of them went to my room, took a bath, then got a bottle of vino. They ran into some American nurses and bought them Algerian black wooden carved dolls as souvenirs. Then they went to a new night club, danced and had what seemed like a hell of a time, but actually wasn't much.

I was away that day, but they left a note on my pillow, thanking me for the baths, and signed it "Two Clean Fellows."

They had already lost some of their good friends, and one of my other airmen friends had gone too. He got it on the very first American mission. It was all like the old early days of the night Air Mail, when one by one my good friends left and didn't come back.

I could see each one of these Jackson youngsters going through the same mental phase—always believing it could happen to the other fellow, but never to him. A man has to feel that way, or he'd go crazy.

I survived a tour of one hundred and fifty miles in a jeep. After that distance in a jeep it takes twenty-four hours to stop vibrating. At the hospitals they told me they even had soldiers down in bed after riding all day in a jeep. So I felt pretty tough and proud of myself.

We made a grand tour of American camps. I went along with a couple of security officers, whose job it was to set up and supervise security detachments in each camp. By security is meant keeping silent about military secrets, and watching for snakes in the grass such as Axis sympathizers and agents.

The security officers had a terrible job because they said Americans simply weren't security-minded—we wouldn't keep our mouths shut and we insisted on trusting everybody. They said the French practiced better security in peacetime than we did in wartime.

We stopped at the first airport and I ran into some of my fighter-pilot friends that I'd last seen in Northern Ireland. One of them had an arm in a cast. I immediately visualized a good thriller story, but it turned out he had merely fallen off the wing of his plane and broken his arm, the unromantic cur.

Next we stopped at an antiaircraft gun set in a hole in the ground, and talked to Sergeant John Muir of Chicago. He said that if the Spitfires flying about two thousand feet overhead were enemy planes they would be dead ducks.

At a château out in the country, we had lunch with a couple of generals. I tried to lunch with some general at least once a week to keep up my social standing and my dignity.

Afterward we visited a big tent hospital, just being set up. There I ran onto Lieutenant Dick Alter and Nurse Katie Bastadiho, both of New York, who came down on the same boat with us. They were all crazy about living out under canvas. Katie said she had been washing her feet in her steel helmet, and it turned out her feet were bigger than her head.

We made quick stops at a supply depot full of railroad rails and at an engineer company that was building some roads. Finally we wound up at Sidi-bel-Abbes, home of the famed Foreign Legion. Somehow or other we got acquainted with a Major Fuzeau of the Foreign Legion and sat with him for an hour at a sidewalk café, though the major spoke no English and we no French, at least hardly any.

We spent the first fifteen minutes asking the major such primary questions as how old he was, if he was married, how long he had been in the Legion, and what his native city was. That exhausted our vocabulary, so we spent the last forty-five minutes complimenting each other on our hospitality, extending hands across the sea, touching our hearts, and recalling wonderful Franco-American incidents of the last war.

I knew we were doing that because the major kept saying, "Quatorze-dix-huit," which I happened to know meant "fourteen-eighteen," and those of course were the war years. We just assumed from his gestures that he was telling us brotherly-love incidents. The major actually was about the most hospitable person I've ever met. We planned to return another day, and he was to show us all over the town.

On the way back we put in at a place where American tank crews were teaching Frenchmen to run our tanks. They were camped on a sloping hillside, on ground covered with sagebrush exactly like hillsides in the American West. The tank boys worked from daylight to dark when they were on the move. They worked all night too, for the ground crews hadn't arrived and they had to do their own repairing.

They were really roughing it. It was cold out there at night, and they sat around bonfires before going to bed in their little tents. They were the first troops into Oran, but they had never been back to the city. For some reason they weren't allowed to go there on leave. Even their officers thought it was ironic that they captured the city and then couldn't go into it.

It was long after dark when we left the tank boys. Fortunately there was no blackout and we could drive with headlights on. Even so we almost spilled ourselves a couple of times shying around Arabs who loomed up suddenly with immense bundles of sticks on their backs.

We lurched back to Oran at fifty miles an hour, deeply wind-burned and feeling exactly like men who had seen practically all there was to see. Yet we hadn't seen the tiniest fraction of what we actually had around there then.

The roads in North Africa were surprisingly good. They were macadamized, with banked curves just like ours. Driving around the country, we often remarked that it was hard to realize we were not somewhere in the United States.

The long coastal plain stretching across North Africa, between mountains and sea, was, as I've said before, very much like parts of our own Southwest. It was bare of trees, but it was not exactly desert. In fact, it was very fertile and almost wholly under cultivation.

The soil resembled red clay, and was a regular gumbo after rain. The Arabs raised some oats, and I saw some uncommonly long straw-stacks, but most of the land was in vineyards and olive groves. Across the slightly rolling land, a person could see for long distances—fifty miles or more. The fields were quite large, and at that season most of them were freshly plowed.

Many American soldiers had their first experience of picking olives right from the trees and eating them—or, I should say, biting them, for they tried it only once. There followed the most violent spitting, spluttering and facemaking you ever saw. It seems an olive has to be ripened in brine before it's edible. They're black and beautiful on the trees, but they have a bitter, puckering taste that's beyond description.

We were all impressed by the neatness and cleanliness of the farming country, even though I can't say the same for the cities. The fields were immaculate. There was no refuse or squandered growth or stuff lying around, as on so many American farms.

The Arabs did all their farming with horses, which appeared to be in good shape. But we seldom saw one of those beautiful Arab steeds that we read about in "sheik" books. Out in the country there were many herds of goats and sheep, usually tended by small children. We saw cute little shepherdesses, not more than eight years old, in hoods and nightgownlike dresses, who smiled and made the V-for-Victory sign as we passed.

The Arabs seemed a strange people, hard to know. They were poor, and they looked as tight-lipped and unfriendly as the Indians in some of the South American countries, yet they were friendly and happy when we got close to them. As we drove through the country, Arab farmers by the hundreds waved at us along the road, and the children invariably shouted their few American words—"good-bye" or "okay" —as we passed, and either saluted like soldiers or gave the V sign with their fingers. In half a day's driving there I got more V signs than I saw the whole time I was in England.

Once in a while there were clusters of cactus, and frequently fields were fenced with hedgelike rows of what is known in Mexico as maguey, the plant from which pulque and tequila are made. Apparently the Arabs don't keep themselves as well oiled on their native drinks as do the people in some countries. I saw some drunken Arabs, but they were very rare. The good ones never drink anything alcoholic. It's against their religion.

I still haven't got the religion question straight. Some Arab women wore white sheets and hoods that covered the face, except for one eye peering out. The soldiers called them "One-eyed Flossies." But they were in the minority. Most of the women showed their faces. As far as I could figure out, the ones who covered their faces were the severely religious, just as at home only a few of the Jewish people are what they call orthodox. The rest were good people, but they didn't observe the ancient customs and restrictions.

Just at sunset one day we passed a team and a wagon carrying a whole Arab family. The man was down on his knees and elbows at the edge of the pavement, facing east toward Mecca, but the women

and children were sitting in the wagon. One of our party remarked, "I guess he's making a deal for the whole family."

That was the only Arab I saw praying.

In the northern part of Africa, we never saw a camel. Apparently those beasts weren't needed in that fertile region. The Sahara proper didn't begin until nearly three hundred miles south, and we were told we would have to go there to see camels in action.

There were few native-owned passenger cars on the roads, but quite a lot of heavy trucks. That was because of gasoline shortage. The trucks burned alcohol, but even that was scarce, for the Germans turned most of the grape-crop alcohol into their own motors.

As far as I could discover, there was no such thing as interior heating of homes in winter. The region used to get coal from France, but that was cut off when France fell. We brought our own coal with us.

Our convoy unloading ports in North Africa were pleasant places to be in—when the Germans were too busy to drop bombs on them, which fortunately was most of the time. There on the open docks the sun beamed down warmly, and the air was clear and fresh. Vast quantities of bombs and trucks and guns and food came pouring out of the busy hatches.

Thousands and thousands of American troops unloaded those ships as they came in. At one port where I visited, enough American soldiers to make a good-sized city were working as stevedores. About a fourth of them were colored troops. In addition, there were thousands of Arab stevedores. The Americans were working a three-shift day, right around the clock.

The amount of material pouring out of those ships was impressive. As I stood and looked around I felt that further shipments could be stopped right then, that it was enough. Yet on soberer thought I realized that it was only a drop in the bucket. The British and Germans in the Middle East had often captured many times that much stuff from each other without stopping the fight. The flood then coming in must continue indefinitely and grow to an absolute cascade before it would be enough.

Convoys were coming through with remarkable safety, even the slow ones. And ships were turned around quickly, although they weren't approaching any world's records. With escort ships scarce as they were, I had supposed that one convoy a fortnight would be a good average. Actually there were many times that.

There was never a time when there were not ships unloading. There was never a time when new convoys were not about due to take their places. Day by day the whole of North Africa grew nearer the saturation point with American soldiers, machines of war, and supplies. Before long they would be ready to spill out in a smothering flow over the enemy.

At one port the commanding officer was given a table of expectancy —he was to have the port ready to unload a certain number of tons per day within a certain time after the occupation. Within a week he had exactly tripled his goal.

To do that he had to clear scuttled ships out of the harbor, clear battle debris off the docks, repair damaged utilities, organize thousands of men at the docks.

The whole thing was magnificently planned ahead of time, just as was the whole occupation. For example, they knew just how many ships would be in the harbor. They even assumed that those ships would be sunk or scuttled, and they came prepared to raise them, with soldier-divers trained in England.

Another example of detailed planning: Photographic planes took pictures of the docks. By careful study of the pictures the army could tell the exact amount of coal piled on the docks and then figure the total needed to run the utilities and railroads. They brought exactly the amount necessary beyond what was on the docks. It amounted to one whole shipload.

At first all the thousands of stevedoring troops were quartered in tents right on the docks. Later, they were billeted in empty buildings around the town and in a tent camp out in the country. The men worked in brown coveralls and all kinds of headgear.

The Arabs' working shift was ironically called "the vacation." Their normal working day consisted of two "vacations" of three hours and twenty minutes each, but in time they worked three hours overtime. They got the going scale of fifty francs a day, which was about sixty-seven cents.

In many harbors on the night of the occupation the French scuttled their ships with a degree of co-operation. That is, on many ships they only opened the seacocks and let the ships ease over on their sides, leaving them in condition to be raised easily.

In other cases, their ships lay on the bottom badly damaged. Long after our arrival there were still masts and funnels sticking above the surface of harbors. Some of the hulks were completely under water. They impeded navigation, but the harbors were usable with careful maneuvering.

Under our arrangements with the local government, French pilots took all ships in and out. Once they accidentally ran a number of ships over sunken hulks and tore out their bottoms. Diving crews worked for two weeks patching a hulk sunk close to the channel, and finally had it ready to start pumping air. They expected it to be afloat the next day. That morning a ship leaving the harbor with a French pilot somehow happened to hit the submerged hulk, and it tore off all the patches. So the repairers had to start all over again. It took two more weeks to raise the ship.

There were many wars besides the big one up at the front.

The American soldier is an incurable wishful-thinker. At that time the average soldier in North Africa, despite the slow going in Tunisia and the long distances we still had to go, thought the war would be over by April of 1943.

The censors told me that the soldiers' letters home were full of such belief, and I know that in the camps they were willing to bet good money on it whenever they could find a taker. If I tried to point out that such a quick victory was against all logic, and that even a year from then would be pretty optimistic, they looked at me as if I was nuts.

Our soldiers were all over being seriously homesick but they did constantly think about home. Even a general said one day, "What I wouldn't give for twenty-four hours in New York. I'd just like to see how it looks and hear what people are saying."

And as I traveled about the camps the question I most frequently heard was, "What are the folks at home thinking about?"—never "What are the papers saying?"

Unfortunately I didn't know any more about it than they did. All I knew was what I read in the French newspapers, such as an item about America building thirty-two thousand "chars" in the past year. I assumed that a "char" was a chair or a charwoman, but my French dictionary swore it meant chariot. So all I could tell the boys at the camps was that there was apparently some mighty funny business going on in America. Thirty-two thousand chariots, indeed!

No, we didn't know what you were thinking at home, but I hope you weren't letting yourselves believe we would all be headed for New York by spring. My powers of prediction are pretty feeble, but I thought that our part of North Africa might not be very exciting for some little time. After the initial occupation there necessarily would follow a period of getting established and building up immense stocks of men and supplies. We were in the middle of that period then.

Only a very small portion of our troops in North Africa were in action. The remainder of the combat troops were just waiting, and a huge organization of supply troops was busy day and night back of the lines.

We were, it seemed to me, in another period of waiting to strike, as Mr. Churchill said, when it suited us best and Hitler least. I had no idea when or where that would be.

On the map El Agheila looks like an afternoon's drive from Algeria, but actually it's as far as from New York to Kansas City. I hoped the people back home wouldn't get impatient if nothing much seemed to happen for a while.

Suddenly we had a flood of mail both from England and from America. Mail sacks were piled on the docks by the thousand, making mounds as big as strawstacks. The Army Post Office, working with remarkable speed, sorted and delivered all of it in three days.

Some people got as many as seventy-five letters all at once. One fellow I know got two letters—one a notification that a friend had subscribed to the Reader's Digest for him, which he already knew, and the other a mimeographed letter which his wife had sent him, about some church festival. He had received no personal letter from her in weeks. The recipient used very unchurchly language when he told about it.

Another man I knew, a colonel from San Francisco, hadn't heard from his wife in three months or from his friends in longer than that.

The deluge of mail brought him just one letter. It was from a vice-president of the Goodrich Tire Company, warning him that it was his patriotic duty to conserve his tires.

But this I think was the best one: Captain Raymond Ferguson of Los Angeles had a Christmas box from his aunt. It was the first one she had sent in many years, and he was quite touched when he saw it came from her. Ferguson opened the box with eager fingers. Then his face fell. The gift was a large stack of blank V-mail forms, for him to write home on. And Captain Ferguson, being head of the army's postal service in that section, already had millions of V-forms.

Lieutenant Herbert Desgorges, a friend of mine from Gallup, New Mexico, got twenty letters from his wife. Another friend, Lieutenant Bill Wilson of Des Moines, got thirty personal letters in one day.

They told a story about one soldier who hadn't heard from his wife in three months, and finally was so disgusted he wrote her and told her to go to hell, saying he was going to get a divorce. Then in one huge batch came fifty letters, covering the whole three months. So he had to cable her and take back the divorce threats.

As for me, I was the recipient of only two letters—one from a girl in Pittsburgh wanting me to say hello to her soldier sweetie and one from a man in Iowa telling me that eggs were plentiful and only thirty-eight cents a dozen. I could only suppose that my fifty family letters were at the bottom of somebody's ocean.

American movies, prohibited during the German occupation, were being shown again. There were some modern theaters in the bigger cities, but no new films had arrived as yet.

They were dragging out some unbelievable antiques. One theater showed a film starring Sessue Hayakawa, who has been gone so long you have to be middle-aged to remember him at all. Another star was the dog Rin Tin Tin, dead lo! these many years.

Captain Stan Pickens, Charlotte Coca-Cola king, went to town and bought an Algerian violin in a wooden case, to while away his spare hours at camp. He paid twenty-two dollars for it and was lucky to find one at any price, as the music stores were nearly bare . . . Lieutenant Colonel Gurney Taylor took to visiting me in town in order to use my bath. Once he had two baths in less than a week. It made him so damned clean he was conspicuous . . . Private Chuck Conick of Pittsburgh got a whole flock of Pittsburgh *Presses* one day. Unfortunately these papers were four months old . . . I had the novel experience of driving an army truck fifty miles along African roads at nighttime, to help out a fellow who was getting a little tired. It was the first time I'd driven since leaving America six months before, and it felt wonderful. Traffic in Africa, incidentally, was right-handed, the same as at home. After all those months in left-handed England I felt, during the first few days, that I was on the wrong side of the road . . . We heard a rumor that the ship which brought us from England was sunk on the way back. I hated to think of that faithful ship being on the bottom of the ocean . . . A large batch of officer promotions came through, catching many officers without the insignia of their new rank. They had to continue wearing their old ones, as no American insignia were available. I heard of one ambitious and farsighted second lieutenant who came loaded with all possible insignia up to three stars . . . The army newspaper *Stars and Stripes* began printing an African edition. Lieutenant Colonel Egbert White and Lieutenant Harry Harchar flew down to Algiers from London, and with Sergeant Bob Neville set up shop and were printing in less than a week. The paper started as a weekly but promised to become a daily.

4. POLITICAL PICTURE

DECEMBER, 1942

MEN who brought our convoys from America, some of whom I met shortly after I arrived, told me the people at home had a false impression of things in Africa.

Merchant Marine officers, after they had been in Oran a couple of days, were astonished by the difference between what they thought the situation was and what it actually was. They said people at home thought the North African campaign was a walk-away and would be over quickly; that our losses had been practically nil; that the French loved us to death, and that all German influence had been cleaned out.

If you thought that, it was because we newspapermen here failed at getting the finer points over to you.

The mixup of French emotions that showed itself during the fighting was fantastic. One French motor launch went about Oran Harbor firing a machine gun at wounded Americans, while other Frenchmen in rowboats were facing the bullets trying to rescue the Americans.

I knew of one landing party sent ashore with the special mission of capturing four merchant ships. They took them all without firing a shot. The captain of one ship greeted the party with "What was the matter? We expected you last night," and the skipper of another met the party at the gangway with a bottle of gin. There was much fraternization. In one town where fighting was heavy, the bodies of five men were found in a burned truck. Three were Americans and two were French.

Because the campaign at first was as much diplomatic as military, the powers that be didn't permit our itchy typewriter fingers to delve into things international, which were ticklish enough without our comments. I believe misconceptions at home must have grown out of some missing parts of the picture.

Our position in Africa, although all right for the long run, was not all strawberries and cream by any means.

In Tunisia, for instance, we seemed to be stalemated. The reasons were two. Our army was a green army, and most of our Tunisian troops were in actual battle for the first time against seasoned troops and commanders. It would take us months of fighting to gain the experience our enemies started with.

In the second place, nobody had known exactly how much resistance the French would put up, so we had to bet on full resistance. That meant, when the French capitulated in three days, we had to move eastward at once, or leave the Germans unhampered to build a big force in Tunisia.

So we moved several hundred miles and, with the British, began fighting. But we simply didn't have enough stuff on hand to knock the Germans out instantly. Nobody was to blame for that. I think our army did wonderfully—both in fighting with what we had and in getting more here—but we were fighting an army as tough in spirit as ours, vastly more experienced, and more easily supplied.

At that time our losses in men were not appalling, by any means, but we were losing men. However, an American ship brought a current newspaper from home, and it said only twelve men had been lost in taking Oran. The losses, in fact, were not great, but they were several times twelve times twelve.

Most of our convalescent wounded were sent to England. Some of us thought that if more of the wounded were sent home, it would put new grim vigor into the American people. We felt we weren't the sort of people from whom wounded men had to be concealed.

The biggest puzzle to us who were on the scene was our policy of dealing with Axis agents and sympathizers in North Africa. We took into custody only the most out-and-out Axis agents, such as the German Armistice Missions and a few others. That done, we turned the authority of arrest back to the French. The procedure was that we investigated, and they arrested. As it turned out, we investigated, period.

Our policy was still appeasement. It stemmed from what might be called the national hodgepodge of French emotions. Frenchmen then thought and felt in lots of different directions. We moved softly at first, in order to capture as many French hearts as French square miles. Before long that phase was over. We were in full swing. Here we were occupying countries and pretending not to. We were tender in order to avoid offending our friends, the French, in line with the policy of interfering as little as possible with French municipal life.

We left in office most of the small-fry officials put there by the Germans before we came. We permitted fascist societies to continue to exist. Actual sniping had been stopped, but there was still sabotage. The loyal French saw our tactics and wondered what manner of people we were. They were used to force, and expected us to use it against the common enemy, which included the French Nazis. Our enemies saw it, laughed, and called us soft. Both sides were puzzled by a country at war which still let enemies run loose to work against it.

There was an astonishing number of Axis sympathizers among the French in North Africa. Not a majority, of course, but more than you would imagine. That in itself was a great puzzle to me. I couldn't fathom the thought processes of a Frenchman who preferred German victory and perpetual domination to a temporary occupation resulting in eventual French freedom.

But there were such people, and they were hindering us, and we over here thought you folks at home should know three things: That the going would be tough and probably long before we cleaned up Africa and were ready to move to bigger fronts. That the French were fundamentally behind us, but that a strange, illogical stratum was against us. And that our fundamental policy still was one of soft-gloving snakes in our midst.

There's no doubt that the situation was very involved. The population was all mixed—Arabs, Jews, Spanish and French. And there didn't seem to be much national loyalty. It looked as if the people, being without any deep love of the country, favored whichever side appeared more likely to feather their nest.

Outside the big cities, Algeria hadn't fared badly under the Germans. But the cities had been actually starving, because the Germans bought produce direct from the farms, and the cities couldn't get it.

America promptly contributed shiploads of food to the Algerian people, but for some reason little of it showed up in the public markets. City housewives found the stalls bare as usual, and they muttered about "les Américains."

The Germans had paid high prices to the farmers for their crops, and had paid in French money. They didn't levy the terrific indemnities here that they did in France. Hence the farm population actually prospered, and had almost nothing to kick about.

That winter Algeria had the biggest orange crop since the war started. In distant sections oranges were actually rotting on the trees for lack of transportation. The farmers blamed the Americans for this, and I suppose with some justice. True, we arranged to ship vast cargoes of oranges to England in returning convoys, but we couldn't spare enough transportation to get the whole crop to the docks. As far as I could see, the only way to get the Arab, French, and Spanish farmers on our side was to buy the whole orange crop, even at the high prices the Germans had paid

When the Germans took control they demobilized the French North African Army. That suited the people fine. They didn't want to fight anyway. But after our occupation the army was mobilized again, and people grumbled: "Under the Germans we didn't have to fight. Under the Americans our leaders make us go into the army again."

They were passive about it, but many of them were not happy. There was a deep fascist tinge among some of the officers of the regular army and I tried to find out the reason. As far as I could learn, it was mostly a seeking for an ordered world to live in. The people and the army alike were disillusioned and shattered by the foul mess into which Paris had fallen—the mess that resulted in catastrophe to France. They were bitter against the politicians and the general slovenliness in high places. They wanted no more of it. They wanted things to run smoothly. They wanted security—and they visualized it as guaranteed by the methodical rule of the Axis.

The German propaganda here had been expert. The people had been convinced that Germany would win. Apparently lacking any great nationalistic feeling at that point, they jumped onto whatever seemed to be the leading band wagon, and they thought it was Germany. The same propaganda also had made them think America was very weak. Literally, they believed we didn't have enough steel to run our factories or enough oil for our motors. German propaganda had also drilled into them the glories of the New Order. Those people believed that life for them under German control would be milk and honey, perpetual security and prosperity. They really believed it. Also, our troops made a poor impression, in contrast to the few Germans they had seen. We admittedly are not rigid-minded people. Our army didn't have the strict and snappy discipline of the Germans. Our boys sang in the streets, unbuttoned their shirt collars, laughed and shouted, and forgot to salute. A lot of Algerians misinterpreted this as inefficiency. They thought such a carefree army couldn't possibly whip the grim Germans.

Most of the minor peoples of the world expect discipline. They admire strict rulers because to them strictness is synonymous with strength. The Algerians couldn't conceive of the fact that our strength lay in our freedom.

Out of it all I gathered a new respect for Americans, sloppy though we might be. They may call us Uncle Shylock, but I know of no country on earth that actually is less grabby. In all my traveling both before and during the war I was frequently revolted by the shriveled greediness of soul that inhabits so much of the world. The more I saw of us Americans and British, the more I liked us. And although Germany was our bitter enemy, at least the Germans seemed to have the character to be wholly loyal to their own country.

5. ON THE LAND

THE Arab kids that swarmed the roads around the army camps and near-by villages were a friendly bunch. Our soldiers weren't two days in a new place until every kid in town was able to say in English "chewing gum, chocolate, cigarette, good-bye, okay." They pestered us to death for tidbits, and the soldiers kept giving them away as long as they had any.

The youngsters seemed to have more sense than the pestering child-natives of many countries. Instead of being dumb and surly, they had a nice spark of life about them. If we said we had no chewing gum and smiled at them, they smiled back and then stood around good-naturedly just smiling at us. Their favorite word was "okay." Even some of the grownups adopted it. They yelled it at every passing American. We couldn't walk down the road without being walled in by a surging melody of hundreds of "okays" coming at us from all sides.

Once in a while we saw a light-skinned, clean-gowned, almost sheiklike Arab. But mostly their clothes were unwashed, and their long gowns an unbelievable mass of patches.

At first the Arabs were allowed to roam the airdromes, and they helped the crews fill the planes' big tanks from the countless five-gallon tins.

There were quite a few carriages for hire in the desert towns and soldiers took rides in lieu of anything better to do. If I had been an Arab I know how I would have made a small fortune. I would have bought about ten camels, and rented them out to soldiers to take rides on. I would also have invested in a camera and taken pictures of soldiers on camelback, and sold them for one hundred francs apiece. Apparently no Arab thought of it, but somebody just passed up an opportunity of making about ten thousand bucks awfully easily.

The horse carriages were fancy. The driver sat on a high box up front and was often dressed in bright clothes. One of those carriages provided the funniest sight I had seen since leaving America. It was just before dusk and, by dinner bell and rifle shot, the air-raid signal swept across one of our airdromes. I was standing far out on the field, when suddenly there came dashing out from behind the palm trees one of those Arab carriages.

The driver had brought some soldiers to the field, had heard the alarm and being touchy about raids, as Arabs were, had decided to get the hell out of there in a hurry. He was standing up in his box, coattails flying, whipping his horses for all he was worth. The team was in a dead run. The buggy was bouncing and swaying over the rough desert trail. The horses were going so hard that their bodies were stretched out, their flying feet almost level with their noses, and one was a little ahead of the other, just as on the track.

With the carriage's red wheels and the driver's red coat for color, the scene looked exactly like a Currier & Ives print. The poor, frightened man's pathetic hurry was so comical that we all stopped and laughed till he was out of sight, still going like mad.

Queer little incidents happen in war. Mechanics on the Flying Fortresses kept discovering empty machine-gun shells in the engine nacelles. Where they came from was a mystery. Finally it dawned on somebody. After firing, the boys were dumping the empty shells out of the planes in midair, and they were being carried back by the slipstream, right through the propellers of the following planes, and lodging in the nacelles. You'd think it would have damaged the propellers, but apparently it didn't.

And speaking of freaks, a Fortress gunner came home from a mission with the corner of his pants pocket torn apparently by a piece of flak, although it must have been fairly spent for he didn't know when it hit. Later he put his hand in his pocket and discovered the metal fragment nestling there.

Practically all of our soldiers in North Africa had slept on the ground ever since their arrival. One day I overheard one boy tell about going to Algiers on leave, and sleeping all night in a hotel bed. "I woke up at three o'clock in the morning with a splitting headache, just because the damn' bed was so soft," he said, "and I never did get back to sleep."

I don't know whether much was written at home about our African booklet or not. It was on the same principle as the booklet about England that had been issued to our troops there.

The African booklet was a neat little blue-backed affair of sixteen pages. It had been written before we came here, and consequently was prefaced by the admission that "our welcome by the inhabitants is not known at this time." I might add that after several months of studying the situation I still didn't know what our welcome was.

The booklet described briefly the history and geology of the North African countries. Since it always makes a good impression for a writer to pick out flaws, I'll take the liberty of pointing out a few small errors in our booklet. For instance, it said "little rainfall is experienced along the coast." Some Californian must have written that. If the stuff that came down day after day along the Algerian coast in a piercing, chill, Englandlike downpour wasn't rain, then I must have been shell-shocked.

After they had been wet to the skin for three days at a time and shivering with cold in mud halfway to their knees, I'm afraid you would have had a hard time convincing several hundred thousand soldiers that it hadn't been raining.

The booklet also said that "mirage is of fairly frequent occurrence. It generally occurs early in the morning." Perhaps there would be mirages in summertime, I didn't know. But the only mirage anybody saw that winter would have been one induced by approximately four bottles of cheap wine.

The booklet explained the new issue of American money given us. It added that there would be little to buy over here (and they were right) and advised soldiers to allot at least seventy-five per cent of their pay home. There was so little to spend money on that everybody had more than he knew what to do with. Officer friends of mine said they had never saved so much money in their lives. As for me, I was spending a total of about five dollars a week.

The most interesting part of the book was its "Do's and Don'ts." It warned us never to enter mosques, and never to loiter, smoke, or spit in front of a mosque.

It said that bread was holy to the Moslems, and never to cut it but always break it with the fingers, and not to let any drop on the ground. It said further that we must always eat with our right hand, even if we were southpaws. I asked a French Algerian about this, and he said he never had heard of it before. So I continued to eat left-handed and nothing happened.

The booklet warned us not to give Moslems alcoholic drinks, not to take dogs into a house, and not to kill snakes or birds, since the Arabs believed that the souls of departed chieftains resided in them.

Finally the book said, "Talk Arabic if you can to the people. No matter how badly you do it, they like it." That was good advice but how any American was to go about trying to talk Arabic was more than I knew. Most of us couldn't even learn enough French to get by, and Arabic is an almost impossible language to learn.

The army had put out a few little booklets giving some Arabic words and phrases. I'll give you a few examples of how easy it is to speak Arabic. For instance, if an Arab asked what that thing was hanging from our belt, we were to reply "hundikeeya sughayzara"—which means pistol. After we had talked an hour or two along that line and were ready to call it a day, we were to say to the Arab, "Lailtak syeeda ataimsik behair"—which means "good night."

The book ended by saying that some Arabic sounds were almost impossible for Americans to learn. For example, it said that "kh" resembled the sound made when clearing the throat, and that "gh" was a deep gurgling noise.

If we were to sneeze, cough, whistle, choke and hiccup all at once, that would mean "I love you, baby, meet me in front of Walgreen's right after supper, and leave your veil at home."

Four good soldiers, who had already done more than their share in the war, unexpectedly turned up over here. They were Kay Francis, Martha Raye, Mitzi Mayfair and Carole Landis.

Some people may have taken lightly the contributions of Hollywood folks to the war effort, but I didn't. Those gals worked themselves to a frazzle. They traveled dangerously. They lived and worked under mighty unpleasant conditions. They didn't get a dime. They were losing a lot and they had nothing to gain—nothing material, that is. But surely they went home with a warm inner satisfaction, knowing that they had performed far beyond the ordinary call of duty.

The quartet of stars had been away from America since October of 1942. They had flown the Atlantic by clipper, toured the camps in Northern Ireland and England and, despite the gloomy predictions to the contrary, had come to Africa by Flying Fortress. They had heard bombs fall, and they knew about army stew. They averaged four hours' sleep a night. Each of them had had a bout with the flu. They had done all their own washing, because there was no other way to get it done. Yet if they had chosen they could all have been in California lying on the sand.

When they went out to one of our far desert airdromes they put on their performance on the flat bed of a big wrecking truck out in the midafternoon sun, surrounded by soldiers sitting on the ground. They spoke the first English from a woman's mouth these soldiers had heard in months. To say they were appreciated is putting it mildly.

Half the fun and half the good, I suppose, of such a performance is the opportunity it gives the soldiers in the audience to imagine themselves as great lovers, and the inspiration it provides for the soldiers' own brand of humor.

Kay Francis started it off by saying they'd rather be there than any place in the world. That brought a thunderous cascade of boos. Then she said: "The reason is there's no place else we could be the only women among several thousand men." That brought the laugh. Then she said: "And I know every one of you would protect me, wouldn't you?"

That brought the "Oh yeahs!" and yells and whistles of appreciation.

When Carole Landis came out, something like a great sigh went over the crowd. Carole, as you know, is rather voluptuous. As she finished her song and held out her arms a pathetic, wracked voice came from the far edge of the audience, a lonely guy screaming to the world his comical misery: "I can't stand it!"

Mitzi Mayfair wore a skimpy green spangly thing and did her famous dances. A couple of dozen soldiers perched on the truck's big steel boom above her, and every time Mitzi kicked they pretended to swoon and fall off. Mitzi ended her act by calling for jitterbug volunteers. The boys were bashful, but finally a private was pulled down off the boom. He was no slouch as a jitterbug, but she almost danced him off his feet. She wound up by throwing the exhausted soldier over her shoulder and carrying him off the stage.

Sometimes Mitzi gets herself in a pickle with this stunt. One night in England she had to carry off a guy who weighed 225 pounds. Another time she sprained a shoulder. And in her second performance at the airdrome she almost met her Waterloo.

The show was for flying officers, the ones who actually did the bombing and fighting, and there was nothing bashful about them. When Mitzi called for volunteers, up rose Captain Tex Dallas, a Fortress pilot who didn't give a damn about anything. Tex took off his coat, folded it neatly, and walked challengingly onto the stage. Mitzi whispered instructions to him, but Tex didn't follow instructions very well. Instead of pretending to be exhausted, he had Mitzi on the ropes within a minute. After chasing her around the stage he finally had her hiding behind the piano. The audience went wild.

Eventually, after poor Mitzi had given herself up for lost, Tex relented and let her carry him off the stage.

I had seen Mitzi dance in New York musical comedies. I saw her dance in dust-covered slacks on the African desert, I learned that she had already given a strenuous year and a half of her life to the war and was in it for the duration, and all I can say is, she's a honey.

Martha Raye was really the star of the troupe. The soldiers went for her crazy brand of slapstick. She wound up the program in practically a riot. When it was all over the four girls came out and sang the French, British and American national anthems.

The girls were pretty sore about one thing. It seems one of the American broadcasters in Algiers had broadcast back to America that they wouldn't go to the Tunisian front because they were afraid. He had asked why they were any better than anybody else.

Actually, the girls had begged to go to Tunisia but were turned down. The generals wouldn't let them go because they thought it would be dangerous for troops to be concentrated to see the show. Those girls were not afraid. Carole Landis even wanted to go on a bombing mission.

It's strange, but for some reason or other things seem to get damaged in wartime. Less than two weeks after we landed in Africa an Army Claim Commission had set itself up in each of the big occupied cities and was doling out money to aggrieved citizens whose persons or property had been damaged by our forces. There were twelve officers and thirteen enlisted men in the Oran claims section. They handled 165 cases in the first two weeks. They paid off the first complainant three days after arriving.

Most of the claims were minor ones. A good many were for damage to crops where soldiers marched across fields or camped for the night. The commission brought along an American farmer in order to be able to handle such cases intelligently. He was Major William Johnson, who lived on a 200-acre farm six miles outside of Duluth, Minnesota. Ironically, he had been so busy in the office handling claims that he hadn't had time to get outside of Oran and see any farms.

There were quite a number of traffic accidents. In the first three weeks five people were killed by trucks, and eight or ten mules were killed. The commission paid two hundred dollars for a good work mule. That was more than they'd pay at home, but good mules were harder to get over here. The price for a horse was about the same.

One tough problem the commission faced was how much to pay for destroyed articles that were irreplaceable. One woman, for instance, filed a claim for 375 francs for a radio the army had commandeered. She said she paid 250 francs for it, but was asking 375 because she simply couldn't get another one. The commission agreed with her reasoning and paid her 375 francs.

The head of the commission was Lieutenant Colonel George T. Madison, a tall, gangling, slow-talking lawyer from Bastrop, Louisiana. I can never forget Colonel Madison because he led our little detachment off the boat and behind him I marched into Oran for the first time. Another friend of mine on the commission was Captain John M. Smith of West Memphis, Arkansas. He knew a lot of my friends in Memphis, and relayed news of them that came in his letters.

An army friend of mine, Corporal Jimmy Edwards from Tyler, Texas, used to be a cavalryman before the war, so consequently he went nuts about the Arabian horses he saw here. Being an old horse-hater from way back I refused to look at the beasts, so Jimmy described them to me in his own words: "I can't help but notice how beautiful they are. They've got little feet, slim bodies, well-shaped heads and small ears. I see them hitched to these two-wheeled hacks in the city streets. One owner said I could buy one for about two hundred dollars. That isn't cheap but I'd sure like to have some to put in my pasture back home."

There is one animal in Africa that pleased both Jimmy and me, and that's the burro, or donkey. They're only about two-thirds as big as our southwestern burro, and their hair is slicker, giving them a much neater appearance, but they're still just as droll-looking. Jimmy took the trouble to measure one. It was only thirty-five inches high, and its funny head was half as long as the burro was high. I asked the burro if he knew the Americans had arrived and he shook his head and said he didn't care who was in charge as long as he got fed. He wasn't the only one, either.

The Americans' love for pets never ceases to delight me. As a People, we seem to be fundamentally kind to animals. You'd be surprised at how many nationalities aren't. Our soldiers over here were shocked—I heard them remark on it a hundred times—at the way the Arabs mistreated their dogs and burros.

I had to laugh when I saw the collection of pets at one camp I visited. There were countless dogs, several cats, one gazelle, one monkey, two or three rabbits, a burro, and, believe it or not, half a dozen chickens.

A gazelle, as somebody said, is a cross between a jack rabbit and a moose. Actually it's a tiny, doll-like deer, delicate and dainty, and stands no higher than a big dog. You've heard of the gazelle's speed. They say they've been clocked at sixty miles an hour. They run wild in the mountains over here, and the French hunt them with shotguns. Many of our officers went on gazelle-hunting trips. Personally I could no more shoot one of them than I could a friendly dog.

About the cutest dog on the post was a fuzzy little mongrel called "Ziggie," which belonged to Corporal Robert Pond, of 2147 Marion Street, Denver. He paid 500 francs for Ziggie and would not have parted with him for any money.

I happened to fall in with four young lieutenants of a bomber crew who had recently arrived from America. They had been on three missions in their first ten days, and had got shot up every time. Not shot down—just shot up.

The third time one engine was knocked out, and one rudder fell clear off just as they landed at the home airdrome. They really started getting their thrills in a hurry. I asked them whether this sudden taste of violent adventure pepped them up, or whether they were beginning to wonder. They laughed and said their only feeling was one of regret and annoyance that their plane would be out of commission for a few days.

The four were Pilot Ralph Keele, a Salt Lake City Mormon, Copilot William Allbright, of Western Springs, Illinois, Navigator Robert Radcliff of Richland Center, Wisconsin, and Bombardier Eugene Platek, of Antigo, Wisconsin.

The soldiers grew such a crop of beards that a person would think he had driven into one of our western towns just the week before the annual Pioneer Day celebration. Over here Hollywood could have found every type of beard that ever existed. Some were big and fierce, some blond and curly, some wispy and foppish, some of the sourdough kind, others as prim and sharp as a boulevardier's. Even the old Irish type of jaw whiskers was represented. I let mine grow for two weeks but nobody noticed it, so I gave up.

In all the area near the front there was no such thing as a Post Exchange. Instead, the army issued free such necessities as cigarettes, soap, razor blades, and so on. But at a forward post one day I tried to get some tooth powder, and was told disgustedly by the sergeant that there wasn't any because we weren't in the combat zone.

"Not in the combat zone?" I said with astonishment. "Who says we're not?"

"Some guy at some desk far far away," he said. "I don't know where he expects us to get it, in the first place, and in the second place, I wish he was here a few nights when the bombs start whistling. I'll bet you couldn't get him out of a slit trench all night. Not in the combat zone! Nuts!"

Even if there were no Post Exchanges, there were Military Police. A couple of them happened to be friends of mine and I liked them as much as anybody I knew in the whole army. One day an officer was in my room when they were there. After they left he said to me: "You're the damnedest guy I ever saw. I've been in the army three years and you're the first guy I ever heard of who knew an M.P. personally. Nobody knows any M.P.s."

Maybe not, but if so they're ignorant of one of the finest groups in the army. The Military Police haven't the taint to them that they had in the last war. This time they are a specially picked, highly trained, permanent organization. An M.P. serves throughout the war as an M.P., he is proud of his organization, and he is respected by his fellow soldiers.

One day an officer and I were talking about a barroom brawl the night before in which a drunk had tried to stab an M.P., and the officer said, "Anybody who starts anything with an M.P. is insane. They're picked men, and their training starts where Commandos leave off. They know every method of fighting in the world."

And from the M.P.s I saw, judging by their demeanor and their conduct, I believe that next to Rangers and Paratroopers they are really the pick of the army.

But to get back to my two friends. They were: Corporal Freeland L. Riles, Jr., of 601 Broad Street, Darlington, South Carolina, and Private Thomas Stewart, Route No. 2, Scurry, Texas. Riles went by the nickname "Snip."

Strangely enough they were the same age to the day. Both were born on July 7, 1919. Snip had gone to school only through the eighth grade, Tom through the ninth. Then they both started to work. Both of them talked low and slow and dragged out their words as if they had all day to say a sentence. Snip's was the soft easy drawl of the deep South, while Tom's was the wide, frank drawl of the open spaces. They were as different as day and night.

"Give me open country," said Tom. "I like big country where if you want to holler you can get out and holler."

Tom was a lanky, jointy fellow with a windy-red face. In the respectful fashion of his part of the country, he always referred to his mother as "mamma." Back home, Tom used to be a carpenter.

He liked best to do the interior cabinetwork when a house was about finished and said his specialty was making tables. He made a beauty for the general when he was at Camp Bowie in Texas. Neither he nor Snip made any headway at all trying to learn French.

Snip had been a traveling route agent for a bakery. He used to drive his bread truck 180 miles a day and make as high as sixty dollars a week during tobacco season when people had money. He was a handsome youngster, black-haired and spick-and-span, but very quiet and serious. He had been a star athlete in school. He said he was never homesick at all in England, but in Africa he thought about home a lot.

He knew jujitsu and all the other methods of fighting, but he said he would never use his jujitsu, except on the enemy, since it was too easy to cripple somebody permanently. Both boys told me they had very little trouble. Most soldiers who got to whooping it up in the back room quieted down like mice and walked along peacefully the moment an M.P. showed up.

My friendship with those two fighters did strike me as odd, for I was nearly old enough to be their father, and there was little in companionship I could contribute to them. Yet they came daily and sat and chatted; they said if I ever needed an escort anywhere just to holler and they would take me; they insisted on running errands for me; they bought a special bottle of champagne and brought it to my room on Christmas Eve for us three.

We arranged to take trips together after the war. Snip insisted on taking me on a South Carolina deer hunt, a famous institution where the man who misses his first deer gets his shirttail cut off.

And Tom had a two-week catfishing and cougar-hunting trip down the Nueces River all planned. I agreed to go on the trips although I don't know why, for I've never shot anything bigger than a rabbit in my life, and never intend to.

Tom wanted to get into the border immigration service after the war. Snip thought maybe his M.P. experience would qualify him for some kind of police work, although he was really undecided what he wanted to do.

I noticed that both boys almost always prefaced their after-war plans with "If I live through it . . ." Nobody talked a great deal about that, but it was at the back of everybody's mind. It was even in mine sometimes, despite the nice safety of my noncombatancy. Even a deer hunt looked beautiful away off there in the future.

One night I met Lieutenant Colonel William Clark, a great, tall, gaunt man from Princeton, New Jersey. Since the start of the war he had been in Australia, Africa, and twice in England. He had been in France in the last war, and personally I thought he was having the time of his life in World War II. Colonel Clark was a big shot back home. He was judge of the Third Circuit Court of Appeals in Phila-delphia. He was the guy who declared the Prohibition Amendment unconstitutional. It was beyond his powers, however, to create much "drinkin' liquor" on the continent of Africa.

Judge Clark was liaison officer with the British Army in Tunisia, right up where everything was hottest. He asked me if I'd mention his name in one of my reports so his family would know he was all right. I said sure, and asked him what he wanted me to say about him.

"Oh," he said, "just say you met the damned old fool."

The average American soldier went without eggs for a long time, and I for one can testify that we missed them very much. The prob-lem was alleviated somewhat when we got on the desert. We knew the Arabs had eggs, so we went around and bought them up. We foolish Americans promptly raised the price to five francs apiece (about seven cents), but what did we care? Everybody had too much money anyhow, and when we had reached our state an egg was practically golden.

I went on two egg orgies within a week. One night Major Austin Berry, of Belding, Michigan, bought twenty-nine eggs from an Arab. Major Berry was a young squadron leader, and he had an appetite. We took the eggs to an army kitchen and had them scrambled. Then Major Charles E. Coverley, Captain Jack Traylor, Major Berry and I ate all twenty-nine eggs at one sitting, with nothing else whatever to go with them. That's an average of better than seven eggs apiece. True, I woke up at two in the morning with a historic stomach-ache, but what of it?

Undeterred, I tried it again three days later. Two of my Flying Fortress friends came past about eleven in the morning, and we went to the village market and scoured around sort of speakeasylike until we found a guy with some eggs. We bought two dozen.

That time my fellow gourmands were Lieutenant Bill Cony, of 1001 Oakwood Avenue, Wilmette, Illinois, a bomber pilot, and Lieutenant Bob Wollard, of Clovis, New Mexico, a bombardier. We had the cook hardboil them and then we went to my quarters and gorged ourselves. The three of us ate twenty-four eggs and twenty tangerines in half an hour flat.

Warrant Officer Luke Corrigan, of 816 Hemlock Street, Scranton, Pennsylvania, had a tough experience. It happened that a large bunch of American nurses were headed for the front and had to be outfitted in short order. Mr. Corrigan was in charge of one of the army's big warehouses, so it was his job to outfit the nurses. But army ware-houses, it turned out, didn't carry such things as slips, step-ins, bras-sières, and what not. So Mr. Corrigan had to get himself an interpreter and go blushing all over Oran buying up dozens of those feminine items.

He completed his mission, and dashed to the train just before departure time. One nurse saw what he had, and grabbed at a box. Then others grabbed. The boxes flew open, and the first thing Mr. Corrigan knew he looked like a Christmas tree very much bedecked with panties, undies, and other pink unmentionables. Mr. Corrigan was very ill at ease. And in the midst of his confusion he heard a familiar voice say, "Well, Luke, I'll have to write home and tell your mother how you're fighting the war."

He turned around and it was a Scranton girl who lived just a few blocks from him at home. Her name was Helen Jeffers and she was one of the nurses. Luke had been in the army two years and in all that time Helen Jeffers was the only person from home he had ever run into. And she had to find him like that.

All ain't fair in peace or war.

6. THE MEDICAL FRONT

Wʜᴇɴ I was in England I spent some time with the army's Medical Corps, and witnessed some of our preparations for tending wounded soldiers. The sight of surgeons being taught to operate at the front, of huge warehouses filled to the roofs with bandages, of scores of hospitals built for men then healthy who would soon be wounded—seemed shocking and morbid to me. But I saw all that preparation being put to use. Soon after arriving in Africa, our doctors and nurses and medical aides had had their first battle experience. When I first visited them the hospitals were going full blast, and it didn't seem morbid in actuality, as it had in contemplation.

In the Oran area, where our first heavy casualties occurred, the wounded were in five big hospitals. Three were French hospitals taken over by the army, one was an abandoned French barracks turned into a hospital, and one was a huge tent hospital out in an oatfield.

On one of my first tours of inspection I happened on a friend I didn't know I had. A nurse in an old blue sweater came walking down a muddy street at one of these army hospitals. An army pal with me yelled at her, and stopped and introduced me. And the nurse said, "Well, at last! I've been saving sugar for you for two years, but I never expected to meet you here."

I had never seen the nurse before in my life, so a little inquiring about the sugar business was necessary. Mary Ann Sullivan was a former surgical supervisor in Boston City Hospital. She and her sister nurses were reading my reports two years ago, when I was in London and complaining bitterly in the public prints about not getting enough sugar. So it seems the nurses felt sorry for me and started saving sugar. Whenever a cube was left over they would save it and say, "This one's for Ernie."

Then in the summer of 1941 these nurses joined a Harvard unit and set sail for England. And they carried with them that sugar especially earmarked for me. Their motive was high but it came to naught. For the Germans torpedoed their ship and my sugar went to the bottom of the Atlantic.

The nurses were eventually picked up and taken to Iceland, then to England, and finally to Africa. And there we all were, and wasn't it a small world after all even if my sugar was gone?

Mary Ann felt badly about my sugar being sunk, but she did break out a hospitable commodity which both censorship and the ethics of war forbid me to mention. So our meeting was not without a certain rare delicacy to put in our mouths.

Mary Ann Sullivan's unit came ashore in Africa on the very first morning of the landings. They operated on wounded men for hours, with snipers' bullets still pinging on the walls. It was just the kind of life Mary Ann had been waiting for. She was so steamed up she could hardly wait for the next battle. When I met her she was with a mobile surgical truck, which she called the super commando truck. It was equipped to rush into the thick of things, slam on the brakes, and operate on wounded men for thirty-six hours without replenishments.

I arranged officially with General Headquarters to be wounded in Mary Ann's vicinity.

By then the doctors could be, and were, proud of their work. The nurses had already covered themselves with glory. The wounded had nothing but praise for those who pulled them through.

Our only deaths in the original occupation were those killed outright and those so badly wounded that nothing could have saved them. In other words, we lost almost nobody from infection or from medical shortcomings in the hurly-burly of battle.

You probably read of the miracles wrought by sulfanilamide in the first battles of Africa. Doctors and men both talked about it constantly, almost with awe. Doctors knew it was practically a miracle drug, but they hadn't realized quite how miraculous.

Every soldier was issued a sulfanilamide packet before he left England, some even before they left America. It consisted of twelve tablets for swallowing, and a small sack of the same stuff in powdered form for sprinkling on wounds. The soldiers used it as instructed, and the result was an almost complete lack of infection. Hundreds were alive who would have been dead without it. Men lay out for twenty-four hours and more before they could be taken in, and the sulfanilamide saved them.

It was amusing to hear the soldiers talk about it. Sulfanilamide was a pretty big word for many of them. They called it everything from snuffalide to sulphermillanoid.

There was one sidelight on it—some of the wounded soldiers

didn't have any sulfanilamide left, because they had surreptitiously taken it all to cure venereal diseases. They said a venereal case could be knocked out in four or five days with it, and thus a man didn't have to report in sick.

One doctor told me that most American wounds were in the legs, while most of the French wounds were in the head. The explanation seemed to be that we were advancing and thus out in the open, while the French were behind barracks with just their heads showing. Both sides treated the wounded of the other side all during the battle, and our soldiers were full of gratitude for the way they were treated in the French hospitals. They said the French nurses even stole cigarettes for them.

Morphine was a great lifesaver. Pure shock is the cause of many deaths; but if morphine can be given to deaden the pain, shock cases often pull through. Many officers carried morphine and gave injections right on the field. My friend Lieutenant Colonel Louis Plain of the Marine Corps, who had never given an injection in his life, gave six on the beach at Arzeu.

Many of our wounded men already had returned to duty. Those permanently disabled would be sent home as soon as they were able. Those still recovering were anxious to return to their outfits. I inquired especially among the wounded soldiers about this, and it was a fact that they were busting to get back into the fray again. Morale was never higher.

When a soldier was in a perilous predicament or especially irritated with the rough-and-tumble life of the battle front, he usually pacified himself by thinking, If the folks at home could only see me now!

And if the folks of Charlotte, North Carolina, could only have peeped down out of the African sky and seen their family doctors and nurses in their new kind of life—what a surprise they would have had! A bunch of men and women from Charlotte were operating an American tent hospital set up in North Africa, and they were doing a dramatically beautiful job. They were really like something out of Hollywood, and I visited them time after time just out of fascination.

They were far from any town, set in the middle of a big oatfield, out on the rolling plains. They began setting up the day after troops had battled their way over that very ground. They took in their first patients the next morning. Soon the hospital had more than seven hundred patients, it took four hundred people to run it, and there were more than three hundred tents covering eighty acres of oat stubble. The stubble field was picked so the mud and dust wouldn't be so bad—but they were anyway.

Everything was in tents, from operating room to toilets. Everything was set up in three days. They could knock down and be on the move again in another three days, and they expected it to happen at any moment. They were like a giant medical Ringling Brothers.

They were known as the evacuation hospital. They had been taken into active service in April of 1942, practically denuding the Charlotte Memorial Hospital of doctors and nurses.

They arrived in England in mid-August that same year. They stood off the North African coast with the great overwhelming convoy that brought our occupying troops, and they came ashore in assault boats the morning after the occupation. They jumped immediately to work.

There were fifty Charlotte men in the unit—mostly doctors and surgeons, but there were a few businessmen who did the nonmedical part of running a hospital. There were fifty nurses too. None had ever lived any closer to nature than an occasional hunting trip. But they had become nomads of the desert, living on the ground and under the sky, and they loved it.

Their commanding officer was a Regular Army man—Lieutenant Colonel Rollin Bauchspies. He was a tough, hoarse, friendly guy who cussed continuously, drank hard liquor, drove his own jeep and said to hell with regulations, dying people can't wait. He was a Pennsylvanian and claimed he could lick the whole damned Dixie tribe if he had to, but he didn't have to because the whole outfit vibrated with accomplishment and they were all proud together.

When they arrived in Africa, they were neophytes at living in the field, for that part of their training had been overlooked. Lieutenant Colonel Bauchspies had taken over command while they were on the boat coming from England, and he'd had no time to give them the neglected field training.

So they arrived in the middle of an African oatfield with three hundred tents to set up, and not a soul knew how to put up a shelter-half or drive a tent peg properly. But they soon learned. Colonel Bauchspies, who did know how, being a Regular Army man, got out and drove tent pegs himself. Everybody worked like a slave. Doctors helped dig ditches. Nurses helped unload trucks.

One amateur electrician among the enlisted men started wiring the office tents for lights. A couple of carpenters-by-trade made themselves known, and went to work. A professional sign painter turned up among the first patients, and painted the street signs that helped to give the hospital a civilized touch.

In a few days the veterans had taught the tenderfeet how to make themselves comfortable living in the rough. The tents of officers and nurses were touchingly homelike. There was canvas on the floor, mosquito nets over the cots and framed pictures of wives and children standing on the wooden tables. The Charlotte doctors and nurses were wise enough to bring air mattresses and sleeping bags, and they had never slept more comfortably.

Of course getting up in the cold before daylight and washing in cold water out of a canvas washpan took some getting used to. And yet it grew on them.

Major Paul Sanger was chief surgeon of the hospital. He had been chief surgeon back in Charlotte. He was a highly skilled, well-to-do professional man. He told me, "I never go into town. I feel better out here than I've ever felt in my life. We were all prima donnas back home. We had every comfort that money could buy. We would have been shocked at the idea of living like this. But we love it. We all do. I suppose we'll be making our families live in tents when we get home."

Lieutenant Colonel Preston White, chief medical officer, was from Lexington, Virginia. He was an older man than the others, but he was as enthusiastic as a child over the whole hospital setup. And he too had become an addict of outdoor living.

"We have only a quart of water a day to wash, shave and wash clothes in," he said, "so we don't take many baths. Maybe we don't smell so good, but when we're all in the same boat we don't notice it. And it sure feels good living out like this."

The hospital was already spreading a fame for its food. Anybody in the army knows that a field hospital is the best place to eat. One night we had big juicy steaks for dinner. "Where did these come from?" I asked Colonel Bauchspies.

"Hell, I wouldn't dare ask," he said. "I suppose Stan stole them."

Stan was Captain Stanton Pickens, who had gone along as mess officer. His brother, Lieutenant Colonel Bob Pickens, was a friend of mine in London. Stan set such a good table that the trucks bringing patients from outlying camps always managed to arrive just at lunchtime. And another indication—Stan made arrangements with a local Arab to collect their garbage, for which he was to give the hospital a crate of oranges every three days. But it seems everybody cleaned his plate, and the Arab was getting so little garbage he wanted to give oranges only every four days now.

The hospital's supply officer was Captain William F. Medearis. He was a Charlotte bigwig. They said he owned all of Main Street, plus half the real estate and all the laundries. He was national secretary-treasurer of the Laundry Association. He turned down a lieutenant-colonelcy in Washington in order to go to Africa with his friends.

Captain George C. Snyder, who commanded the nonmedical detachment of enlisted men at the hospital, shared the Coca-Cola honors with Captain Pickens. Between them they had that special gold mine sewed up in Charlotte. But they had nary a bottle of it in Africa.

In the outfit there were two named Captain Otis Jones. They were no relation and never had heard of each other until they joined the army. One was the chaplain, and he was from Bude, Mississippi, near Natchez. The other was a Charlotte obstetrician. Since none of the soldiers was given to having babies, Dr. Jones was registrar for the hospital. So they wisecracked that he "delivered papers" over there.

Seen from the mud road leading across a field, the hospital looked like a dark-green sea of tents. It blended so well with the fields and against the low rolling mountains in the distance that a person could hardly pick it out half a mile away.

Even the first tent had a "going concern" air about it—there was a tidy, painted sign on a stake saying "Headquarters," and a little dirt walk lined with whitewashed rocks led up to it. Inside that tent men worked at crude tables with folding legs. Before them were file cases that folded up into small portable trunks. Field telephones rested in their leather cases. It was the same equipment I had seen in all the camps in England and Ireland, and there in Africa its quickly movable character was being genuinely put to work.

Back of headquarters the tents spread out and formed a city, with streets between the rows. The whole place was laid out just as it had been planned on paper in Washington years before. But the little touches—the street signs, the whitewashed rock borders all over the place—they were additional, and were the volunteer work of the enlisted men.

The officers and nurses lived two in a tent on both sides of a company street—nurses on one side, officers on the other. At the end of the street was a neatly painted sign which read "Carolina Avenue." Under it some Yankee had inscribed "Rebel Street."

The three hundred enlisted men who did the nonmedical work lived in small shelter tents just beyond. They were mostly from New England. They had built a little wall of whitewashed rocks between the two areas, and put up a sign saying "Mason-Dixon Line."

The chief nurse was First Lieutenant Bessie Fullbright. In true southern style everybody called her "Miss Bessie." They even had a small detachment of Negro engineer troops, just to make everybody feel at home. The nurses wore khaki coveralls because of the mud and dust. Doctors went around tieless and with knit brown caps on their heads. Pink feminine panties flew from a line among the brown warlike tents. On the flagpole was a Red Cross flag, made from a bed sheet and a French soldier's red sash.

Doctors, nurses, everyone but the patients, washed outdoors in cold water, and went to a Chic Sale with a canvas wall around it.

They ate and read by lanternlight. They almost never took a bath. They seldom drove the twenty miles into town because they got to like it out there, and they felt so healthy.

They slept on folding cots under mosquito bars, with the tent flaps open. Planes bound for destruction of the Axis roared over the weird city of canvas. At night a trillion stars showered down out of the clear African night.

They were up in the darkness of 6:30 A.M.—boy, was it cold! At first, they sometimes even put off washing their faces till later in the day. The whole crude existence was built around the call of those thousands of men whose lives depended on them—and they realized they were happier than they had been in a long time.

Yes, if the folks back in Charlotte could only have seen them!

At the receiving tent, trucks and ambulances arrived with wounded men transferred from other hospitals, with sick men from incoming ships, with ill and injured from our dozens of camps around the countryside, with airmen stricken at high altitudes.

Those able to walk went down a line of desks, where their history was taken for the files. In the next tent they turned in all their belongings. That tent was stacked high with barracks bags. Rifles and mud-covered bayonets stuck out of the bags. Attendants gingerly accepted hand grenades and gave the owner a receipt.

In the next tent the patient turned in his clothes and got a tag in return. He was given a pair of flannel pajamas and a red corduroy bathrobe. He had to keep his own shoes, for the hospital had no house slippers. Then he went to whatever ward tent his type of illness indicated. His belongings were taken by truck to the opposite end of the hospital a quarter mile away, to await his exit.

The surgical and laboratory tents were in the middle of the big compound. There were three fully equipped surgeries, and they were astonishingly modern. All equipment was brand-new. It was like the newest hospital in New York, except that the floor was canvas-covered dirt, the walls canvas, and the street outside a deeply rutted boghole of red clay.

When an operation was going on, a triple flap was pulled over the tent entrance, and a heavy mosquito bar dropped over that. Inside, the air became stiflingly hot even then; by summer it would be cruel. Patients were brought up the muddy street on a field stretcher running on bicycle wheels. Surgeons wore white robes, white masks, rubber gloves. Everything was white, and I was struck with the vast amount of sheeting, swabs, bandages and towels—all white—around a desert operating table.

The light above the surgeons was fiery bright. The hospital tapped a near-by high-tension line for its operating-room current. If that failed, there was a whole progression downward for emergency—a generator run by a gas engine, a portable battery set, then powerful flashlights, then lanterns, then candles, and finally just matches if it ever came to that.

There was an X-ray room, and a fluoroscope. The darkroom was a tent within a tent. All the new equipment shone and sparkled, sitting incongruously on its dirt floor.

There were more than forty tents of wards. Each tent held twenty men, on folding camp cots. The floor was stubble. It sounds make-shift, but the patients were thoroughly comfortable.

There was also the dentist's office, in one end of a surgical tent. The chair was just a hard green metal one, tilted back. There were no arms to hold to when it hurt. The drill was run by the dentist pumping on an old-fashioned treadle. Yet the dentist, Major Vaiden Kendrick, said he could do anything he did back home in Charlotte. He offered to make me a plate just to prove it, but I gnashed my original teeth at him and fled.

One tent housed a laboratory, filled with basins and test tubes and burners. Another was a drugstore, where thousands of prescriptions were filled from endless bottles on shelves. And all this, mind you, every bit of it from tents to kitchen stoves to anesthetics, had come to Africa on a single boat.

There were a lot of things the Charlotte doctors and nurses hadn't visualized before they set up their big tent hospital there in the field. The natives, for instance. Arabs in their long gowns came wandering across the plains hoping the miraculous Americans could cure their ailments. So the hospital had to set up a separate tent for them. They had local people in there wounded by shrapnel in the first battle. There was one old woman of eighty-one whose arm had been blown off. There were several patients on whom they had done normal operations.

One Arab woman had been shot through the stomach. Her condition was grave, but on the second morning her husband arrived, said he had to go to work and there wasn't anybody to take care of the kids, and for her to get the hell home where she belonged. So she got up and walked out. The doctors didn't think she could have lived through the day. But you know how it is with us Arabs—we don't like our women gadding about when there's work at home.

While I was there a ragged Arab with a long stick came in with his ten-year-old boy. The child had a hideous rash over his neck and face. Through the interpreter, the Arab said he had been praying and praying for the Americans to come, so they could do something for his boy. His belief in us was touching, but the doctors feared the scourge was beyond their ken.

The army's Arabic interpreters, incidentally, were completely accidental. They weren't assigned to the hospital unit by design or anything. It just happened.

One was Private Israel Tabi, of 245 Broome Street, New York City. He was born in Yemen, and had settled in America when he was twenty. He was thirty-five when I met him, and a house painter by profession. So far as he knew his parents were still in Arabia, and who could tell, he might see them someday. He said the Arabic spoken around these parts was quite similar to what he knew. I mentioned that he was performing a very valuable service. Private Tabi was volubly patriotic. He said, "I will do anything for my country. Whatever they ask me to do, I will do. I will work day and night. I love my country. I will do anything for it."

The other interpreter was an Egyptian—Private Abraham Casper Leon Saide (pronounced Sadie). He lived at 343½ Seneca Street, Buffalo, New York. He was a watch repairer by trade. He had been born in Alexandria, Egypt, was thirty-four, and had migrated to America in 1924. He spoke Turkish, Greek, Egyptian and all those exotic languages. It looked as if Private Saide might have a very useful career ahead of him in the army.

The hospital already had handled more than one thousand patients and hadn't lost a one. The doctors ran to the nearest stake and knocked on wood when they said it. The surgeons had performed more than 125 operations.

There was no red tape about whether a patient was legally entitled to enter the hospital or not. They took anybody who came along— soldier, civilian, Arab, Frenchman, anybody. The way they ignored formalities when emergency arose was one of the things that made me feel so warmly toward this battle-front hospital. One day we were looking at the round-bellied iron stoves half buried in the ground in each tent.

"What do you burn in them?" I asked Lieutenant Colonel Bauch-spies.

"Wood," he said.

"Where do you get the wood?" I asked.

"Steal it," he said.

When you were saving lives you didn't requisition and wait; you foraged and borrowed and even stole if necessary. And nobody stood on rank. Once Major General Fredendall made an inspection tour through the hospital. Colonel Bauchspies croaked hoarsely like a frog.

"How did you lose your voice?" asked the general.

"I lost it driving tent pegs," said the colonel.

"Your guard looks nice," said the general. "Where did they get those new rifles?"

"I daren't tell you, sir," said the colonel. The general smiled. And nodded.

The American nurses—and there were lots of them—turned out just as you would expect: wonderfully. Army doctors, and patients too, were unanimous in their praise of them. Doctors told me that in that first rush of casualties they were calmer than the men.

One hospital unit had a nurse they were afraid of. She had seemed neurotic and hysterical on the way down. The head doctor detailed another nurse just to watch her all through the hectic first hours of tending the wounded. But he needn't have. He admitted afterward that she was the calmest of the lot.

The head of one hospital, a full colonel who was a soldier in the last war, worked in the improvised hospitals set up at Arzeu to tend the freshly wounded. He said they worked thirty-six hours without sleep, with wounded men lying around knee-deep, waiting. He said not a soul in the outfit cracked up or got flustered.

"We were so busy we didn't think about its being horrible," he said. "We weren't ourselves. Actually we seemed to become different people. And after it was over, we were thrilled by it. Gosh, I hope I'm not stuck in a base hospital. I want to get on to the front."

The Carolina nurses, too, took it like soldiers. For the first ten days they had to live like animals, even using open ditches for toilets, but they never complained.

One nurse was always on duty in each tentful of twenty men. She had medical orderlies to help her. Most of the time the nurses wore army coveralls, but Colonel Bauchspies wanted them to put on dresses once in a while, for he said the effect on the men was astounding. The touch of femininity, the knowledge that a woman was around, gave the wounded man courage and confidence and a feeling of security. And the more feminine she looked, the better.

Only about one hundred of the hospital's seven hundred patients were wounded men. The others were just sick with ordinary things such as flu, appendicitis, sprains. They had a whole tentful of mumps, and a few cases of malaria and dysentery.

At the far end of the hospital, behind an evil-looking barricade of barbed wire, was what Colonel Bauchspies called "Casanova Park." Back there were a hundred and fifty soldiers with venereal disease.

"What's the barbed wire for?" I asked. "They wouldn't try to get out anyhow."

"It's just to make them feel like heels," the colonel said. "There's no damned excuse for a soldier getting caught nowadays unless he just doesn't care. When he gets a venereal he's no good to his country and somebody else has to do his work. So I want him to feel ashamed, even though at the same time he does get the finest medical treatment."

Many of the wounded soldiers were then able to be on their feet. On warm days they went out in their bathrobes and sat for hours in the sun, out in the stubble field. Most of them were getting a good tan. At night they played cards on their bunks, by the light of lanterns hanging from the ridgepoles. The usual bunkhouse profanity was strangely absent from those tents, for there was always a nurse around.

The boys liked to talk about their experiences. I spent much time with a tentful of men wounded in the harbor battle at Oran, and they recounted the fight by the hour.

The deafened soldier I mentioned a while back, Sergeant Ralph Gower—was in this model hospital. I called on him several times. He grew more remarkable every time I saw him. I didn't know what the boys would do without him when he left. They called him "the wee sergeant." They picked up the "wee" when they were training in Scotland, and it had been tagged onto him ever since. One day he said, with his dead-pan Arkansas expression, "I'm glad I'm deaf so I won't have to listen to that damned 'wee sergeant' stuff any more."

Although wounded veterans by then, and alive only by a miracle, those patients were just the ordinary American boys they had always been, friendly and enthusiastic and sensible. Only occasionally was there one who seemed affected by his experiences—one officer brooded over having lost so many of his men, another deafened boy stayed by himself and refused to try to learn lip reading. But on the whole they were just as normal as if nothing had happened. They hadn't been paid and they couldn't get trace of their friends and they didn't know where they would be sent, but still they didn't complain much, and they said calmly that they guessed it was enough just to be alive.

7. TURNS AND ENCOUNTERS

I HAD a slight bout with the African flu, and I must tell you about the aggregation of plumbers, professors, horse doctors, and traveling salesmen who were delegated by the army to pull me back to life.

First there was Private Henry R. Riley, who walked in one day with his arms full of laboratory apparatus, and said he was ready to give me the inhalation treatments necessary to clear my throat and chest of its awful load. Private Riley was a jockey by trade! He was one of those good old boys from Oklahoma, good-natured and slow-talking. He was born in Pawhuska, and had been riding horses ever since he could remember.

His nickname was "Beans." He said he was Leading Rider of America in 1930, booting home 187 winners that year. He rode for Mrs. Harry Payne Whitney's Greentree Stables. Beans had to give up racing in 1933 when his weight got up to 132 pounds and he couldn't do anything with it. He weighed 145 pounds when I met him, was thirty years old, and felt wonderful.

After he quit riding, Beans went into the medical end of race-horse training. He said he worked under the finest veterinarians in the business. He was still making the race-track circuits with the training stables right up to wartime. He had a wife and stepson.

I thought it necessary to make a little joke about a horse doctor being put into the Army Medical Corps and set to doctoring people, but Beans saw no inconsistency in it at all. He was happy in his work, and said he'd rather be in the Medical Corps than any other branch of the army, even the cavalry.

"Doctoring people and doctoring horses is exactly the same," said Beans very seriously, "except you give a horse from twelve to sixteen times as much. There's a difference of opinion. Some say twelve, some say sixteen. I always hold to twelve myself, to be on the safe side."

70

Beans's treatment worked all right with me. But from that day onward I was never able to look upon myself as anything more than one-twelfth of a horse.

Then there was the pleasant young man who brought my meals—a redheaded, nice-looking fellow perpetually ready to break out into a grin. He was Private Thomas Doyle, 1422 Woodward Avenue, Lakewood, Ohio. He answered to either Tom or Red, so I called him Red to remind me of the days when I had hair and it was red.

On the second meal Red came beaming in behind his tray and said, "I know you now. I thought at noon I ought to know your face and I've been thinking ever since and finally I've got it. We read your column all the time at home in Cleveland."

From then on Red would bring my meals and then sit down and light a cigarette and hold conversation while I was eating. Red used to be an asbestos worker. "What on earth is an asbestos worker?" I asked. "We put asbestos around pipes," he said.

Like the other boys, Red didn't mind being in the army. At first he was an infantryman, and then in England they made a fireman out of him, on the grounds that he knew about asbestos, I suppose. And then when he got to Africa they converted him into a waiter on tables. Red's colonel was a pretty tough egg, not much given to compliments. But on the third day of Red's dining-room career the colonel complimented him on his prowess.

"That was pretty nice," Red said, "but I had to laugh at getting complimented on being a waiter when I don't want to be a waiter. Oh, it's all right, but I'm going to try to get transferred, because I'd hate to have to say I fought the whole war with a serving tray."

One of the saddest parts about getting well was the end of the nice mealtime conversations with Red Doyle, the Asbestos Kid.

Another sawbones who aided me to victory was a young Boston doctor named Lieutenant Albert Deschenes. He and I had happened to be on a couple of trips together before I fell ill, consequently we already knew each other by our first names. Thus the doctor's bedside manner was all that the most plaintive patient could ask. Furthermore, I was the first of my breed that he had ever seen, and he felt it would be a bad omen to lose his first correspondent. So Dr. Deschenes leveled his full professional skill in my direction and thus preserved one more lousy newspaperman for posterity.

The army took no pay for medical services rendered, of course, so my only hope was to keep on surviving all and sundry foreign germs for the duration, and wind up in Boston some beautiful day in 1944 (I hope) and buy Dr. Al Deschenes a drink. He'll need it by then.

Another of the medical corpsmen who came to render services at my bedside was Corporal William C. Barr—a high-school teacher by profession. Barr lived at 1314 Logan Avenue, Tyrone, Pennsylvania, and had taught arithmetic, history, and English in the Tyrone High School before going into the army. He was a bachelor.

Barr had a degree from Muskingum College at New Concord, Ohio, and had been working on his master's at Penn State. You'd think it would be pretty devastating on a fellow of Barr's background to swing into the rough-and-tumble life of the army. But he said he had no trouble adjusting himself. He actually enjoyed his work in the Medical Corps, even though some of it was pretty menial. He said he preferred it to any other branch of the army. He even went so far as to say he met a lot of interesting people.

One advantage in being sick was that people kept bringing me things. Sergeant Chuck Conick, from Pittsburgh, took an airplane trip to a neighboring country and brought me back bananas, grapefruit, and lemons. Major Raleigh Edgar, of Columbus, Ohio, barged in one evening with two cans of American oyster stew. And Major James W. Smith gave forth with a big slice of old-fashioned fruitcake, direct from Mrs. Smith's personal oven in Greenville, Mississippi.

The Red Cross sent me books to read. The sentries downstairs sneaked up with cups of hot coffee late at night, coffee which I didn't want at all but which I drank hungrily out of deep gratitude for their thoughtfulness. Even a general wandered in one night and sat on my bed and talked a while, thinking he was in somebody else's room, I presume.

One afternoon Lieutenant Duncan Clark of Chicago, one of the press censors, came past to help cheer me up, and since I was busy killing flies with a folded-up French newspaper, he contributed a little item on fly-killing technique. Lieutenant Clark said he had discovered, in some earlier research, that flies always take off backwards. Consequently if a person aimed about two inches behind them, he would always get his fly on the rise. So for the next few days I murdered flies under this scientific system. And I must say that I never missed a fly as long as I aimed behind it.

Everybody who landed in North Africa with the army was issued a special desert kit. The main item in our kit was a dust mask. It was a frightful-looking contraption. It consisted of a big black rubber schnozzle that covered the nose and half the face. To this were attached two circular devices, about saucer size, which looked like wheels and which hung over each jaw. Apparently the theory was to scare the dust away.

For dust glasses, we were given a pair of old-fashioned racetrack goggles, the kind that strap around the head and have fuzz around the edges of the eyepieces. They were tinted slightly brown to act also as sunglasses. Further than that, each of us was given a dozen isinglass eyeshields, to be used largely for gas attack, but which could double for dust protectors as well.

If the day ever came when we had to put on our gas mask, dust mask, gas eyeshields, dust goggles, and steel helmet all at once, they promised to give a medal to the last man to choke to death.

Actually, nobody used or needed his dust equipment at that season. It was raining a good part of the time, and some kind of duckfoot attachment for our shoes would have been much more appropriate than a dust mask. But soon it would blow, and from what the people said, it would blow until we almost went insane. Even then, after a few rainless days, we noticed a thin film of dust on the furniture. We really couldn't sense dust in the air, but some was there.

The doctors said this invisible dust, plus the rapid drop in temperature at sundown, was responsible for what we called, or at least I called, "sundown throat." Almost everybody I knew got a sore throat just about sundown. It was a strange, seemingly unaccountable thing. It came on just after the sun went behind the hills and the evening chill started coming down. Our throats got so sore we could hardly swallow. It was gone next morning. If our general health was good, nothing came of this "sundown throat." But if we were run down, one of those African flu bugs might come along, and then our sore throat turned into the African flu, as happened to me.

Our desert kit also held two little bottles of pills for purifying drinking water when we were in the country. We put one pill in our canteen, let it sit half an hour, put in the other pill and waited a few minutes, then drank the water. Pill No. 1 killed all the germs in the water, and Pill No. 2 killed the nasty taste left by Pill No. 1. In addition we had a can of mosquito paste, and pills to take for malaria. But in Algeria and at that season, there wasn't much need for those. I had yet to see a mosquito, although once in a while a malaria case turned up at one of the army hospitals.

The local people considered December, January, and February their winter. They said they stopped taking quinine on the first of December, and started again in March. Right there, it seemed the last place on earth where anyone would get malaria—it simply didn't look like malaria country. For although it was Africa, it was still as far north as Norfolk, and it was not the steaming jungle you may be thinking of that was a thousand miles south.

Our malaria pills were not quinine, but a substitute known as atabrin. We were warned not to take them without doctor's instructions. Personally I decided never to take mine. I had talked to one doctor from the South, a malaria specialist, who took his and thought he was going to die. He said he'd rather have malaria and get it over with.

Africa was not clean, and we knew we could expect a good bit of disease before we finally got out. Our sore throats and flu were known to the doctors as "winter respiratory diseases." The malaria, dysentery, and stuff we'd have come spring would be known as "summer intestinal disturbances."

The large and small diseases that infected the ragged carcass of this sad correspondent at all seasons and in all climes were known medically as "Puny Pyle's Perpetual Pains."

The staff of the army newspaper *Stars and Stripes*, then being published regularly in Africa, as well as in England, was probably the most compact little family among all our troops abroad. By sticking together and using their noodles, they just about whipped the miseries of African life.

There were eighteen of them. Their big boss was Lieutenant Colonel Egbert White, a gray-haired, lovable man who spoke quietly and made sure that the boys under him were well cared for. Colonel White, incidentally, spent a week at the front one time, wandered around until he got behind the German lines, and got himself shot at.

The actual working editor of *Stars and Stripes* in Africa was Lieutenant Bob Neville. He was promoted from sergeant shortly after we landed. Like all others commissioned in the field, he had a terrible time getting himself an officer's uniform. Colonel White gave him a blouse, which fitted perfectly. A correspondent gave him a cap. He bought a pair of pants from another officer. He picked up his bars here, there, and everywhere. He cut the stripes off his overcoat and pretended it was from Burberry's. But, as somebody said, the rules at the front were pretty elastic, and how you looked didn't matter much.

The *Stars and Stripes* had its editorial offices in the Red Cross building, a beautiful brand-new structure of six stories in downtown Algiers. It was just as modern as New York, except that the acoustics engineer must have been balmy: if you dropped a pin on the first floor it sounded like New Year's Eve in a boiler shop on the fifth floor.

The staff of the *Stars and Stripes* worked and lived in this building. On the top floor they had a huge front room, which served as both dormitory and clubroom. At first they slept on the hard tile floor. But later the Red Cross dug up French iron cots for them, so there they were almost as comfortable as at home.

They had big steel cupboards to use as shelves, and a large table where they wrote letters and played cards. There was always a huge basket of tangerines sitting on the table. The windows were blacked out, so they could have lights at night. They bought an oil stove for the center of the room, so they had the unspeakable winter climate whipped and tied.

A dozen of the staff wrote and edited the paper, half a dozen did the mechanical work. They made an arrangement with a local newspaper for using its composing room, but the American soldiers did all their own mechanical work.

There were four linotype operators on the staff. The boss man was Private Irving Levinson, of Stamford, Connecticut. He was a good-natured genius at getting work done in a foreign country.

He had to get out a paper in a French composing room in which not a soul spoke English, and Irv spoke not a word of French. But his native good humor worked so well that within two weeks all the French printers were addressing him by the familiar "tu," they were having him out to their homes for dinner, and the paper was coming out regularly.

Two of the other lino operators were Private First Class William Gigente, of Brooklyn, and Corporal Edward Roseman, of Pleasantville, New Jersey. The fourth was Private Jack Wentzel of Philadelphia, and his was the funniest case of all. He hadn't run a linotype since he joined the staff of *Stars and Stripes*. He hadn't, because he had been too busy cooking.

Private Wentzel never had cooked a meal in his life, outside of helping his mother a little when he was a kid. But the *Stars and Stripes* decided to set up its own mess right in its own building, and by drawing straws or something, Private Wentzel became the cook.

Before many meals passed, the staff discovered they had a culinary wizard in their midst. Wentzel sort of liked it himself. So by acclamation they made him permanent cook.

The three other linotype operators had to work overtime, doing his composing-room work for him, so he could remain as cook. As they said, it wasn't quite in line with union rules, but right there they didn't happen to be under union jurisdiction.

At any rate, the staff contributed to the mess fund out of their own pockets, for various local delicacies in addition to the regular army rations. So they wound up with what was unquestionably the best army mess in the Algiers area. The food was so good that Lieutenant Neville and by-this-time Captain Harry Harchar, the circulation manager, who were supposed to eat at some officers' mess, ate most of their meals with the men instead.

The whole shebang was about the nearest thing in spirit to a genuine newspaper office back home that I could conceive of.

Every army headquarters anywhere in the world has what is called a "Message Center." It is run by the Signal Corps, and through it goes all the vast flow of communications necessary to keep an army running.

From Africa some of my stuff went home by wireless, some went part way by air and the rest by wireless, some went all the way home by air. I had to trust blindly to the boys in the Message Center to get my reports headed in the right direction and by the right means, and especially trust them to get them started immediately, and not let them lie around for days under a stack of papers. I found out that for a while there bits of my immortal prose had been bottle-necked somewhere along the route. But I was sure the delay hadn't been at the fountainhead of literature for the boys at the Message Center and I had a system, to wit: I was to put their names in the copy if they treated me nice and handled my copy well; they would treat me nice and handle my copy well if I put their names in the copy. It sounds like collusion, and undoubtedly was. At any rate, the boys did their part, so now I'll pay off. The boys were:

Lieutenant Gordon Carlisle, of 14 Cass Street, Exeter, New Hampshire, was still in college when he joined the army. They called him the boy from "Cow College," the nickname for the University of New Hampshire. Coming from up north he was a fresh-air fiend, and kept the boys frozen stiff by having the windows open all the time.

Private Frank T. Borezon, of 631 Payne Avenue, Erie, Pennsylvania, said the worst part of being in Africa was that he couldn't find a bowling alley. He was a champion back home.

Private Julius Novak, of 1613 Avenue V, Brooklyn, New York, was so quiet the boys couldn't tell me a thing about him.

Private First Class Doomchin, of 1944 Unionport Road, the Bronx, said the great mystery of the war was how the *Saturday Evening Post* got along without him. He used to sell it at home.

Private Gerald Kelly, of 22 Central Street, Elkins, West Virginia, was a cheerful, good-looking young fellow who used to be an athletic director for the Y.M.C.A.

Corporal A. C. Moore, came from Mobile, Alabama. His mother always called him "A.C.," which was slurred into "Ace" in the army. In the slack hours late at night, the boys passed the time by drawing up court-martial charges against Ace. He was a printer by trade. His wife was waiting for him out in Lufkin, Texas.

Private William J. Harrington of 908 Greenfield Avenue, Pittsburgh, was jovially known in those parts as "Fill-'er-up Phil." It seems his glass was always getting empty.

Private Jacob L. Seiler, of Covington, Louisiana, or "Jake the Fake," as the boys called him, said to put down that he was a "mixologist" before the war—in other words, a bartender.

Private George Murphy, of 172 Grand Street, Lowell, Massachusetts, spent years as a textile mill's traveling salesman, and couldn't seem to stop traveling.

Sergeant John D. Taylor, of Temple, Texas, was a big husky who had been a football and baseball letter-man at the University of Alabama.

Corporal Jack Price, of Bellefontaine, Ohio, said he grew up in a poolroom. His father owned one. Jack spoke only about twice a day, and then it was always something that rolled the other boys in the aisles.

Private Ed Sailor, of 2542 North 31st Street, Philadelphia, said to put down that he was a former postal clerk and well-known Strawberry Mansion pinball player. I asked him what Strawberry Mansion was. He said anybody in Philadelphia would know.

Private First Class Thomas C. Buckley, of Newhebron, Mississippi, was called the "Mississippi Mud Hen." He used to jerk sodas way down South. He celebrated Christmas and his first wedding anniversary the same day.

Corporal Russell W. Harrell, of 902 East Burlington Street, Fairfield, Iowa, had been everything—farmer, building constructor, hardware salesman—so nothing surprised him any more.

Private Primo de Carlo lived at 255 North 7th Street, Steubenville, Ohio. The boys gave him more Italian nicknames than Musso himself, the main one being Signor Vaselino. The signor just grinned. Primo was once an opera singer. He went to school for three years in Milan, and then wound up selling beer in Steubenville. He wondered if he wouldn't eventually get back to Milan, after all.

One day Mrs. Sara Harvey of 227 Natchez Place, Nashville, Tennessee, wrote a letter to me, and it finally found its way over here. Mrs. Harvey asked me to look up her husband in England, and tell him to hurry up and get the war won and get back home to her.

Lots of people wrote me letters like that. Unfortunately the world is a big place and our troops were scattered. Only once in a blue moon did I happen to be in the vicinity of the husband or sweetheart asked for. But the Harvey case turned out just right. When Mrs. Harvey wrote, both her husband and I were in England. When the letter arrived we were both in Africa, and Mrs. Harvey's ever-loving was right under my nose. All I had to do was walk through a bunch of palm trees and across a little sand, and there he was.

He was Sergeant Benson Harvey, radioman with a fighter squadron. He was playing catch with a baseball right after supper when I found him. Harvey and another fellow lived in a pup tent just big enough to hold their blankets. Their private slit trench was a jump away. A small tinted picture in a glass frame hung on the tiny pole at the back of the tent. The picture was of Mrs. Harvey.

Sergeant Harvey was a young fellow. Back in Nashville he used to be janitor, telephone operator and all-around flunky at an apartment house. He was quiet, friendly, sincere, slow-speaking—you'd almost know he came from Tennessee. His captain thought a lot of him. He was one of four brothers scattered all over the world. Major Robert Harvey was a doctor then on his way overseas, probably to Africa. James was a chief petty officer in the navy. He had been through Pearl Harbor and the Solomons battles, and was somewhere at sea.

Once his wife received a notice telling of his death; but someone had made a mistake. The fourth brother was Frank, an aviation machinist's mate, who had been on the *Wasp* when she went down.

Sergeant Harvey said it was bound to be tough when they got home, for they'd all want to tell their lies at the same time. Harvey had been in the army two and a half years. He had things pretty nice, as things went over here. I was glad Mrs. Harvey had written me about him.

While we were roaming around, Sergeant Harvey took me into the squadron's little dispensary and hospital. It was a big hole in the ground, about four feet deep—all tented over. It was about the nicest improvised operating room around there. We got to talking with Sergeant Burt Thompson of 3660 East 151st Street, Cleveland, Ohio. He used to be a production clerk in a hydraulic-equipment factory in Cleveland. Being in the medical section and hanging around doctors so long, he'd started inventing things—medicos are great ones for inventions.

The Air Forces made up a medical kit for pilots to take with them on their missions, a zippered canvas case which was placed behind the pilot's seat. All well and good if a man could get to it, but a wounded fighter pilot couldn't always reach it. So Sergeant Thompson had assembled a smaller kit, which a pilot could carry right in the map pocket on his trousers leg. It was packed in the little tin box our dust goggles came in—about the size of a Nabisco-wafer box. It had everything in it from bandages to a half grain of morphine. It even had a tourniquet, wrapped around the outside. Sergeant Thompson gave me one of them.

"Are you going to issue these to pilots?" I asked.

"We'd like to, but some new regulation has to come from headquarters first," he said.

"That'll take months," I said. "Why don't you just issue them?"

"That's what we intend to do," said Sergeant Thompson with a little grin.

At that time, there started to grow up among the soldiers a little feeling of resentment at, and superiority over, the soldiers back in the States. I was sorry to see this, for I thought it unfair. Few soldiers had the slightest control over whether they were to be in Africa or in Florida. Soldiers didn't choose; they were sent. The ones back home weren't cowards, and were no doubt itching to get abroad.

There was one thing concerning home life that soldiers were absolutely rabid on: that was strikes. Just mention a strike at home to either soldier or officer, living on monotonous rations in the mud under frequent bombing, and you had a raving maniac on your hands.

8. IN THE AIR

OUR airmen had been dishing it out to the Germans; on the other hand, they had been taking it too. Our ratio of losses was vastly lower than that of the enemy, yet our boys had to fly constantly against terrible opposition. It made quick veterans out of them. They went through more in Africa than they ever did on missions to Europe from English bases.

It was generally agreed among airmen that the bombing runup over Bizerte was one of the hottest spots in the world to fly through. It lasted less than a minute, but they had to fly straight and steady through an absolute cloudburst of noise and black smoke puffs— little black puffs of death everywhere they looked—and after a few of those something began to jump inside them.

There was no lack of bravery among our bomber and fighter pilots. But also they were human beings, and I doubt if there was one among them who wouldn't have liked to be sent home. The English had long had a system of resting aircrewmen after a certain number of missions over enemy territory. This consisted of transferring such men to noncombatant flying for several months, after which they went back for another tour of combat duty. Rumors were rampant among our fliers that we would soon have such a system.

Many of our pilots had executed as many as twenty-five missions, and were certainly due for a rest of some kind soon. They banked all their hope in a belief that they would be transferred back to America. Wishfulness became almost fact, and I heard pilot gunners say, "I've got half enough trips now to go home" or "I've got two-thirds enough."

The fact was that no permanent system of posting the men for leave or transfer had been worked out at that time. But some crews were going home before long. They were going back for a much-deserved respite from combat, and to train and organize new crews. After several months they would probably return and start a second tour of combat missions. Many British pilots were then on their third tour of combat duty.

It was unlikely that our air crews would ever have a system whereby a certain number of missions would earn a one-way ticket home. It would have been wonderful for them to know they could quit the front forever after thirty missions and spend the rest of the war working at home, but airmen were needed too badly to permit that. It was more likely that some crews would be sent home just for a while and that others would take their rest periods in Africa.

There were discussions of rest camps in the mountains, and recreation centers staffed in such a way as to give the men some American female companionship—that being one of the most important lacks of the soldiers on foreign soil. But whatever the system, and whatever the number of missions before posting, there would be a wild rush for the planes when that magic last mission came up. If we were working our men hard we could take comfort from the fact that the Germans were working theirs hard too.

New bombers and fighters arrived several times a week, in little groups. We heard reports that absolute floods of planes were on the way, that planes were backed up all along the route clear to Miami. I talked to one crew that was ready to go into action only six days after leaving Connecticut.

Also, specialists from Washington popped in on quick flying trips, stayed a few days, and headed back across the ocean to give firsthand information on war needs at the front. I am sure that what they saw must have made their eyes pop out of their heads. Things were being done over here that just weren't possible on paper.

The airdromes were full of stories about freakish escapes from death, but the strangest story I heard was that of an airplane and its whole crew that disappeared in mid-air.

This was a veteran Flying Fortress crew. Its members had been heroes on many missions over Europe. They were leading a flight of three on their bombing run over a Tunisian port. The two wing planes were flying close on either side, the pilots following the lead plane, and suddenly it disappeared right before their eyes.

What happened was a matter of conjecture. But it seemed very likely that an antiaircraft shell made a direct hit on the plane's bomb load, and that the whole plane blew to tiny bits instantly and just vanished. Nothing was ever seen except a little cloud of black smoke where the plane had been. Then the two other ships were flying on alone. One airman happened to be taking a picture at the very moment of the disappearance. The film showed two planes and a puff of smoke between.

A direct hit setting off a plane's bomb load had never happened before in the American or British forces. I think it must have happened to the Germans, however, for I remember a British artillery officer telling me two years ago of a high-flying German bomber disappearing in a flash while he was looking at it through field glasses.

Fellow fliers of the ill-fated American crew were naturally pretty blue over the accident. But, as they said, when anything as freakish as that got you your number was just up regardless. And they went on with the war as usual.

When the boys told about it they said, "Well, at least they never knew what happened to them, it was so quick."

Once more I met up with the House of Jackson—the bomber crew of which I was so fond. We followed each other around so much that our reunions got to be commonplace.

They were out on a mission when I arrived at their remote airdrome. So I went out to their plane's parking place, and was waiting when they came back. The first man to drop out of the plane was Lieutenant Malcolm Andresen, of Hixton, Wisconsin, the navigator. We were good friends, and I hadn't seen him for weeks, but he just grinned and said, "Hi, Ernie," and didn't even shake hands, just as if I'd been there all the time.

The House of Jackson was still perking, but the inevitable perils and shiftings of war were starting to whittle it down. The skipper was Captain Jack Traylor, of Wollaston, Massachusetts. He had been promoted to ground work in an operations job, and took the faithful old plane on its mission only once in a while.

He hated office work; just wasn't the type. But when I asked him if he didn't chafe at being on the ground so much he said, "Hell no. If I never go on another mission it'll suit me all right." But later I noticed he was begging the squadron leader to let him go on one.

The bombardier was temporarily out of the crew too. He got a piece of flak in his left hand, and was going around proudly with his arm in a sling. He was Lieutenant Joe Wolff, of Omaha. He would be flying again in a few days, but the boys kidded him about maybe he would get a ticket home, since he had been wounded. Joe laughed too, but he wished they weren't just kidding.

There was no laughter about the ball-turret gunner, Sergeant John D. Wadkins of Coolidge, Arizona. For he was dead. He loved his ball turret so much he even wanted to be in it while the plane took off; loved it so much he wouldn't let anybody else get inside it.

His death was a brave one. When the Germans came over the airdrome one night Wadkins jumped from the trench, where he was safe, and dashed to the nearest Fortress and began shooting at the enemy planes from the upper turret. A bomb landed near by, and a small fragment tore through the side of the plane and went through his heart.

I was on the field that night, and the rest of the crew were asking their officers if they could take up a collection and send his body home. It was impossible, but they marked his grave well, and maybe after the war the reinterment could be arranged.

The Air Forces have a language all their own. One old expression was increasing in popularity until it began to substitute for about fifty per cent of ordinary verbs. The expression was "sweating out." They "sweat out" a mission, or they "sweat out" the weather, or they "sweat out" a promotion. It meant they waited, or they fought, or they did anything hard that took some time.

Another much used expression was "rugged." When they had been living in mud, that was "rugged." When the flak over Bizerte had been especially bad, that was a "rugged" trip. Anything extraordinarily tough was "rugged."

In the village near one of the airdromes there was a terribly crippled Arab boy about ten or twelve years old. He couldn't walk, and he used to crawl on his stomach all over town through the dirt and filth.

And what did our soldiers do? Why, they took the wheels off a battery carrier at the airdrome, and made a little wheeled platform for the kid to lie on, so he could roll along the streets instead of crawl.

One night in Central Tunisia I was sitting in the room of Lieutenant Colonel Sam Gormly, a Flying Fortress commander from Los Angeles. We were looking over a six-weeks-old copy of an American picture magazine, the latest to reach us. It was full of photos and stories of the war; dramatic tales from the Solomons, from Russia, and right from our own African front. The magazine fascinated me and,

when I had finished, I felt an animation about the war I hadn't
felt in weeks.

For in the magazine the war seemed romantic and exciting, full
of heroics and vitality. I knew it really was, and yet I didn't seem
capable of feeling it. Only in the magazine from America could I
catch the real spirit of the war over here.

One of the pictures was of the long concrete quay where we
landed in Africa. It gave me a little tingle to look at it. For some
perverse reason it was more thrilling to look at the picture than it
had been to march along the dock itself that first day. "I don't know
what the hell's the matter with me," I said. "Here we are right at the
front, and yet the war isn't dramatic to me at all."

When I said that, Major Quint Quick of Bellingham, Washington,
rose up from his bed onto his elbow. Quick was a bomber squadron
leader and had been in as many fights as any bomber pilot over here.
He was admired and respected for what he had been through. He
said, "It isn't to me either. I know it should be, but it isn't. It's just
hard work, and all I want is to finish it and get back home."

So I didn't know. Was war dramatic, or wasn't it? Certainly
there were great tragedies, unbelievable heroism, even a constant
undertone of comedy. But when I sat down to write, I saw instead:
men at the front suffering and wishing they were somewhere else,
men in routine jobs just behind the lines bellyaching because they
couldn't get to the front, all of them desperately hungry for somebody to talk to besides themselves, no women to be heroes in front
of, damned little wine to drink, precious little song, cold and fairly
dirty, just toiling from day to day in a world full of insecurity, discomfort, homesickness, and a dulled sense of danger.

The drama and romance were here, of course, but they were like
the famous falling tree in the forest—they were no good unless there
was somebody around to hear. I knew of only twice that the war
would be romantic to the men: once when they could see the Statue
of Liberty and again on their first day back in the home town with the
folks.

I passed up my only opportunity of being dramatic in the war. It
was a tough decision either way. As you know, correspondents finally
were allowed to go along on bombing missions. I was with a bomber
group that I'd known both in England and in Africa, and many of
them were personal friends by then. They asked if I cared to go along
on a mission over the hot spot of Bizerte.

I knew the day of that invitation would come, and I had dreaded it.
Not to go branded a man as a coward. To go might make him a
slight hero or a dead duck. Actually I never knew what I'd say until
the moment came. When it did come, I said, "No, I don't see any

sense in my going. Other correspondents have already gone, so I couldn't be the first anyhow. I'd be in the way, and if I got killed my death would have contributed nothing. I'm running chances just being here without sticking my neck out and asking for it. No, I think I won't go. I'm too old to be a hero."

The reaction of the fliers astounded me. I expected them to be politely contemptuous of anyone who declined to do just once what they did every day. But their attitude was exactly the opposite, and I could tell they were sincere and not just being nice.

"Anybody who goes when he doesn't have to is a plain damned fool," one of them said.

"If I were in your shoes I'd never go on another mission," another pilot said.

A bombardier with his arm in a sling from flak said, "You're right. A correspondent went with us. It wasn't any good. He shouldn't have done it."

A lieutenant colonel, who had just got back from a mission, said, "There are only two reasons on earth why anybody should go: either because he has to or to show other people he isn't afraid. Some of us have to show we're not afraid. You don't have to. You decided right."

I put this all down with such blunt immodesty because you may be wondering when I'm going to describe a bombing mission, and if not, why not. I'm not going to, and the reason is that I rationalized myself into believing that for one in my position the sole purpose in going on such a mission would have been to perpetuate my vanity. And I decided to hell with vanity.

It happened that my best flying friends were bomber men, but I wish somebody would sing a song, and a glorious one, for our fighter pilots in Africa. They were the forgotten men of our aerial war.

Not until I went up close to the African front did I realize what our fighter pilots had been through and what they were doing. Somehow or other we didn't hear much about them, but they were the sponge that was absorbing the fury of the Luftwaffe over here. They were taking it and taking it and taking it. An everlasting credit should be theirs.

In England, the fighters of the RAF got the glory because of the great Battle of Britain in 1940. But in America our attention had been centered on the bombers. The spectacular success of the Flying Fortresses when they went into action made the public more bomber-conscious.

There was still rivalry between the fighters and the bombers, as there always had been. That in itself was probably a good thing. But after a time it had sort of slipped out of the category of rivalry—it had developed into a feeling on the part of the fighter pilots that they were neglected and unappreciated and that they were taking a little more than their share on the nose. Their ratio of losses was higher than that of the bombers, and their ratio of credit was lower.

There had been exaggerations in the claims that the Fortresses could take care of themselves without fighter escort. Any number of bomber pilots told me they were deeply grateful for the fighter cover they had in Africa, and that if they had to go without it they would feel like very naked men on their way to work.

Our heavy bombers then were always escorted by Lockheed Lightnings (P-38s). It was their job to keep off German fighters and to absorb whatever deadliness the Nazis dealt out. It meant longer trips than fighters had ever made before. Sometimes they had to carry extra gas tanks, which they dropped when the fight started. They mixed it with the enemy when they were already tired from long flying at high altitudes. And then if they were crippled they had to navigate alone all the way home.

The P-38 is a marvelous airplane, and every pilot who flew it loved it. But the very thing that made the Lightning capable of those long trips—its size—unfitted it for the type of combat it faced when it got there.

If two Lightnings and two Messerschmitt 109s got into a fight, the Americans were almost bound to come out the little end of the horn, because the Lightnings were heavier and less maneuverable.

The ideal work of the P-38 was as an interceptor, ground strafer, or light hit-and-run bomber. It would have been a perfect weapon in the hands of the Germans to knock down our daylight bombers. Thank goodness they didn't have it.

Convoying bombers was monotonous work for the fighter pilot who lived on dash and vim. Those boys sometimes had to sit cramped in their little seat for six hours. In a bomber they could move around, but not in a fighter. The bomber had a big crew to do different things, but the fighter pilot was everything in one. He was his own navigator, his own radio operator, his own gunner. When I heard the pilots tell of all the things they had to do during a flight I was amazed that they ever found time to keep a danger eye out for Germans.

Although our fighters in North Africa had accounted for many more German planes than we had lost, still our fighter losses were high. I chummed with a roomful of five fighter pilots for a week. By the seventh night two of those five were gone.

It is hard for a layman to understand the fine points of aerial combat as practiced in North Africa. It was hard even for the pilots themselves to keep up, for there were changes in tactics from week to week.

We would have some new idea and surprise the Germans with

it. Then they would come across with a surprise maneuver, and we would have to change everything to counteract it. But basically it can be said that everything depended on teamwork. The lone dashing hero in this war was certain to be a dead hero within a week. Sticking with the team and playing it all together was the only guarantee of safety for everybody.

Our fighters waited in groups with the bombers, ranging the sky above them, flying back and forth, watching for anything that might appear. But if they saw some Germans in the distance nobody went after them. That would have been playing into the enemy's hands. Our fighters stuck to their formation above the bombers, making an umbrella.

The Germans had two choices—to dive down through them, or to wait until somebody was hit by flak and had to drop back. If anyone dropped back, they were on him in a flash. When that happened the fighters attacked but still in formation. Keeping that formation always and forever tight was what the flight leaders constantly drilled into the boys' heads. It was a great temptation to dash out and take a shot at some fellow, but by then they had seen too many cases of the tragedy of such actions.

One group leader told me, "If everything went according to schedule we'd never shoot down a German plane. We'd cover our bombers and keep ourselves covered and everybody would come home safe."

The fighter pilots seemed a little different from the bomber men. Usually they were younger. Many of them were still in school when they joined up. Ordinarily they might be inclined to be more harum-scarum, but their work was so deadly and the sobering dark cloud of personal tragedy was over them so constantly that it seemed to have humbled them. In fact, I think it made them nicer people than if they had been cocky.

They had to get up early. Often I went to the room of my special friends at nine-thirty in the evening and found them all asleep. They flew so frequently they couldn't do much drinking. One night when one of the most popular fighter pilots had been killed right on the home field, in an accident, some of the boys assuaged their grief with gin. "Somehow we feel it more when it happens right here than when a fellow just doesn't come back," they said.

When they first arrived, I frequently heard pilots say they didn't hate the Germans, but I didn't hear that for long. They lost too many friends, too many roommates. Soon it was killing that animated them.

The highest spirits I saw in that room were displayed one evening after they had come back from a strafing mission. That was what they liked to do best, but they got little of it. It was a great holiday from escorting bombers, a job they hated. Going out free-lancing to shoot up whatever they could see, and going in enough force to be pretty sure they would be superior to the enemy—that was utopia.

That was what they had done that day. And they really had had a field day. They ran onto a German truck convoy and blew it to pieces. They laughed and got excited as they told about it. The trucks were all full of men, and "they flew out like firecrackers." Motorcyclists got hit and dived forty feet before they stopped skidding. Two Messerschmitt 109s made the mistake of coming after our planes. They never had a chance. After firing a couple of wild bursts they went down smoking, and one of them seemed to blow up.

The boys were full of laughter when they told about it as they sat there on their cots in the dimly lighted room. I couldn't help having a funny feeling about them. They were all so young, so genuine, so enthusiastic. And they were so casual about everything—not casual in a hard, knowing way, but they talked about their flights and killing and being killed exactly as they would discuss girls or their school lessons.

Lieutenant Jack Ilfrey was a fine person and more or less typical of all the boys who flew our deadly fighters. He was from Houston, Texas, and his father was cashier of the First National Bank there. The family home was at 3122 Robinhood Street. Jack was only twenty-two. He had two younger sisters. He had gone to Texas A. & M. for two years, and then to the University of Houston, working at the same time for the Hughes Tool Company. He would soon have been in the army two years.

It was hard to conceive of his ever having killed anybody, for he looked even younger than his twenty-two years. His face was good-humored, his darkish hair was childishly uncontrollable and popped up into a little curlicue at the front of his head. He talked fast, but his voice was soft and he had a very slight hesitation in his speech that somehow seemed to make him a gentle and harmless person. There was not the least trace of the smart aleck or wise guy about him. He was wholly thoughtful and sincere. Yet he mowed 'em down.

In Africa, Ilfrey had been through the mill. He got two Focke-Wulf 190s one day, two Messerschmitt 109s another day. His fifth victory was over a twin-motored Messerschmitt 110, which carried three men. And he had another kill that had not been confirmed. He hadn't had all smooth sailing by any means. In fact, he was very lucky to be alive at all. He got caught in a trap one day and came home with 268 bullet holes in his plane. His armor plate stopped at least a dozen that would have killed him.

Jack's closest shave, however, wasn't from being shot at. It happened one day when he saw a German fighter duck into a cloud. Jack figured the German would emerge at the far end of the cloud, so he scooted along below to where he thought the German would pop out, and pop out he did—right smack into him, almost. They both kicked rudder violently, and they missed practically by inches. Neither man fired a shot, they were so busy getting out of each other's way. Jack said he was weak for an hour afterward.

There was nothing "heroic" about Lieutenant Ilfrey. He wasn't afraid to run when that was the only thing to do. He told me about getting caught all alone one day at a low altitude. Two Germans got on his tail.

"I just had two chances," he said. "Either stay and fight, and almost surely get shot down, or pour on everything I had and try to get away. I ran a chance of burning up my engine and having to land in enemy territory, but I got away. Luckily the engine stood up."

Ilfrey, like all the other men, had little in the way of entertainment and personal pleasure. I walked into his room late one afternoon, after he had come back from a mission, and found him sitting there at a table, all alone, killing flies with a folded newspaper.

Our pilots really led lonely lives. There was nothing on earth for them to do but talk to each other. In two weeks a guy was talked out and after that it was just the same old conversation day after day.

The boys hung around the field part of the day, when they were not flying; then they would go to their rooms and lie on their bunks. They had read themselves and talked themselves out. There were no movies, no dances, no parties, no women—nothing. They just lay on their bunks.

"We've got so damn' lazy we hardly bother to go to the toilet," one of them said. "We're no damn' good for anything on earth any more except flying."

And yet people said being an ace was romantic.

Although our fighter pilots were shooting down more German planes than we were losing, still they had a deep and healthy respect for the German airmen.

"They apparently brought their very best men to Africa," one of the boys said, "because the newcomers sure know their business. There are no green hands among them."

American fliers who had been captured, and then escaped, reported that there seemed to be a sort of camaraderie among airmen—not in the air, but on the ground. There was no camaraderie at all in the air—it was fight to the death and nothing else.

One night the boys were recalling stories from the last war. They had read how Allied and German fighters would shoot up all their ammunition and then fly alongside each other and salute before starting home. There was none of that stuff in North Africa.

Flying a fighter plane was not comfortable. There was so much to do, a man was so cramped, and strained so constantly watching for the enemy. Also, fighter cockpits were not heated. The pilots got terribly cold at 25,000 and 30,000 feet. They didn't wear electrically heated suits. In fact, they couldn't even wear too heavy flying clothes, for their bulk would have made it impossible to twist around in the cockpit. They wore only their ordinary uniforms with coveralls on top of those, plus flying boots and gloves. And they couldn't even wear really heavy flying gloves.

"Our bodies don't get so cold, it's our hands and feet," one of them said. "Sometimes they get so cold they're numb."

"It's funny," said another, "but we're never cold when we're in a fight. We actually get to sweating, and when it's over our underwear is all wet in back. Of course that makes us get all the colder afterwards."

It was interesting to sit in with a bunch of pilots in the evening after they had returned from their first mission. They were so excited they were practically unintelligible. Their eyes were bloodshot, they were red-faced with excitement, and they were so terrifically stimulated they couldn't quiet down. Life had never been more wonderful. They told the same story of their day's adventure over and over two dozen times before bedtime. One boy couldn't eat his supper. Another one couldn't go to sleep.

The older boys listened patiently. They had been that way not so long before. They knew that battle maturity would come quickly.

I had the unusual privilege of seeing about two hundred miles of Africa from the front of an airplane, up where the view was worth $8.80 a seat.

We were in what the army calls a C-47, but which flying people at home know as the Douglas DC-3, and which all laymen know as one of the great silver airliners that ply all the airlines of America in peacetime—and even today, I suppose. But in Africa they were no longer silver; they were a drab brown, and covered with mud at that. The soft easy seats were gone; on each side was just a long tin bench, with panlike depressions for parachutists to sit on wearing their chutes.

No longer was there a carpet on the floor, and a hostess at the back. The bare floor was covered with mud, and the hostess was a sergeant who hadn't shaved for two weeks. These once luxurious airliners were the work horses of war. They were making a saga for themselves They flew anywhere, at any time, doing impossible jobs under impossible conditions.

They held to a daily schedule between all our big headquarters in North Africa; they ran in big fleets carrying supplies and men right to the front; they carried everything from jeeps to generals; they paid little attention to danger, and not much heed to weather. They were doing in a way what the spectacular TACA airline did in the jungles of Central America.

These C-47s were over here by the hundred. Their pilots were sometimes looked upon patronizingly by the combat fliers, but it was an unfair attitude and they sure had the acclaim of everybody else.

In the last few years I had got to the point, after fifteen years of flying, where I wouldn't get into a plane unless it was one of the regularly scheduled airlines. Yet that day I climbed in with those fellows and flew around over the mountains and deserts of a strange continent with almost the same feeling of safety I used to have on the airlines.

My skipper on that special trip was Captain Bill Lively, from Birmingham. Alabama. He already had eleven hundred hours in the air, which was a lot for a young army pilot. He said he used to fly low over here, just for fun, but the Arabs got to throwing rocks and shooting at him, so he had learned to keep at a respectable altitude.

Ours was the lead plane of a formation of three Douglases, with two Spitfires as escort. The Douglases flew very close together, and the Spitfires ranged above and to the side of us, sometimes crossing over and wandering around for a good look into the sky. Every now and then the pilot would glance around to check on them.

"Have you ever been shot at?" I asked Captain Lively.

He peered all around the cockpit. "Where's some wood?" he asked. He finally found some back of his seat, and knocked on it. "Never yet," he said.

But some of the others had. "This is one of the best airplanes in the world, isn't it?" I asked.

"It's got my money," Captain Lively said. "It has a big load with twenty-six thousand pounds gross, but I've taken off thirty-two thousand out of a field only about half as long as we'd look at back home. I don't think there's anything these planes won't do. If a Civil Aeronautics inspector came over here he'd go nuts."

We flew over bare, rugged mountains, through passes where the going was rough, out over the desert, over oases and lonely little adobe villages, over dry lakes and dust storms. We didn't see anything more exciting than an occasional lone Arab working his fields.

When we finally got to where we were going, Captain Lively asked me to have lunch with him and his crew. He dug underneath the benches where we'd been sitting, and got out about fifteen cans of soup, beans, sausages, jam and pears. Next came two big loaves of bread, and then a little stove that sounded like a blowtorch when it was lighted. Within fifteen minutes we were dining in style out of mess kits, with sand blowing into our mouths. That's the way life was on the desert. As soon as we'd finished, they got back into the plane and flew off across the mountains.

There was one bunch that was the most traveled squadron of American Flying Fortress crews in existence. The guys were such confirmed sightseers they all wanted to go into the tourist business after the war.

This squadron actually took form in India in the spring of 1942, from crews that already had fought on several fronts. For nearly a year then it had been a "bastard" squadron, as the boys said, shifted hither and yon like the thistle. It was still subject to striking out for some weird new place before dawn any day. Those men had fought in the Philippines, Java, Australia, Burma, China, India, Palestine, Egypt, Eritrea, Libya, Tripoli, and Tunisia.

Some of them started out by flying across the Pacific, and if they could just fight their way across the Atlantic they would have been around the world. And that wasn't just a dream either, for some of them had so many missions under their belts they would undoubtedly get to go home before long.

In Burma the squadron was based only sixty miles from the Japs. In India they had lived through the dreadful summer heat that killed one man and put fifteen out of one hundred and fifty of them in the hospital with heat prostration. But through it all they kept sight-seeing. They were authorities on the Holy Land. They had seen the pyramids of Egypt and the Taj Mahal of India. They had been to such places as Cyprus, Syria, and Lebanon. They had lived in luxury in India, with half a dozen servants apiece, and they had lived on the ground under tents in the midst of suffocating sandstorms.

Of all the places they had been, they like Palestine best. When they started talking about Palestine there was no stopping them. They said it was just like California—fresh and green and strictly up-to-date. They said the most modern hotels in the world were there.

They had been through so much heat that the chill of North Africa made them suffer badly. Their losses had been heavy, but they had wreaked such devastation that they'd lost track of the figures. The total of ships sunk got beyond their count in October, when they were operating over the Mediterranean out of Egypt.

They bombed Greece, Crete, and the Dodecanese Islands. They had the credit for stopping Rommel's supply lines just before the British Eighth Army started its drive in the fall of 1942. They said the German flak thrown up over Tobruk and Bengazi was the most deadly they had ever known, even surpassing the hail of metal that floated above Bizerte.

The leader of this squadron was Captain J. B. Holst, of Savannah, Georgia. The boys said that practically the entire population of Savannah who went into the Air Forces was right there on our front. Lieutenant Donald Wilder, one of the squadron's bombardiers, rattled off the names of at least a dozen Savannah boys he had met since arriving from Egypt.

Lieutenant Clarence E. Summers, of Lincoln, Nebraska, said that if all the Savannah boys were here, then apparently all the Phi Gam fraternity members were too. He ate one night with six fliers he hadn't known before, and five of them turned out to be Phi Gams.

Some of the navigators on those well-traveled ships had navigated as much as 200,000 miles since they left home. They had already been on missions far beyond the total that might eventually be set up for "posting" our flying crews for a rest.

Probably the oldest and most experienced pilot in the squadron was Captain James Anderson, of Dahlonega, Georgia. He had thirty-five missions under his belt—not little short missions, but mostly ten-hour ones. Lieutenant Grady H. Jones, of Bremen, Georgia, his navigator, had been on thirty-seven missions. That was far more than the bomber boys who came from England had made.

This seasoned outfit found the going not too tough over Tunisia.

They said, "My God, this is the first time in our whole year's action we've ever had fighter escorts. Fighters are a luxury to us."

For an international touch, they had a pet monkey. Sergeant Pittard of Athens, Georgia, got her in India, and she had flown all the way with them. She had three hundred flying hours to her credit.

She just wandered around the plane during flights, making herself at home. When they got high where it was cold, the monkey burrowed herself between two parachute cushions to keep warm. If somebody came along and lifted one cushion, the monkey frowned and squealed and motioned for them to put the cushion back and go away.

That monkey was smart. She could tell Americans from Englishmen, Arabs, French or Indians. She didn't like anybody but Americans. I made it plain that she had better not start liking me. I knew all about monkeys, and I detested them. Even heroic monkeys.

In the summer of '42 I met a bunch of American fighter pilots training in Ireland. They were the first fliers to arrive in Ireland, and their comment on the Irish weather was: "When you can see the hills, it's going to rain; when you can't see the hills, it's raining."

Well, I ran smack into that same bunch down here in Africa. They had sure been through the mill. Already one squadron was veteran enough so that some were due to go home, and they had all been moved back to take a rest.

For five weeks they had lived and fought in a special kind of hell on the Tunisian front. Their field was bombed on an average of every two hours. The pilots took to the air at a moment's notice, several times a day. They averaged between four and five hours in the air daily, and practically all of it was fighting time.

They started with twenty-one planes and twenty-two pilots. They lost six planes and three pilots. But on their scoreboard they were credited with eleven victories, two probables, and fourteen damaged.

They had had enough thriller-diller experience to fill a book. Lieutenant Ed Boughton of New York had a typical one. His plane was shot all to pieces, and the glass canopy that shut him into the seat was damaged so that he couldn't get it open. Consequently he couldn't jump, and simply had to land the plane or die. Miraculously, he got it back to the field and crash-landed it. The plane was nothing but junk—Lieutenant Boughton wasn't hurt. When they finally got him out, they discovered that the jammed canopy had saved his life. His parachute was shot half away, and if he'd jumped he would have fallen like a plummet.

The squadron commander was Major James S. Coward, of Erwin, Tennessee. Lieutenant Colonel Graham West of Portland, Oregon, was the executive officer of the whole group, but he had spent the entire time at the front with this one squadron. He was still with them, seeing that they rested as hard as they fought.

West's nickname was "Windy." He and Jim Coward were typical of the Air Forces. They were both young, both extremely pleasant to be around, both high in rank for their age. When I had seen Windy West in Ireland he was a captain. A few moments out to denote the passage of time, and he showed up in Africa as a lieutenant colonel.

West was a black-haired, black-mustached fellow who could easily be called "dashing," although he'd no doubt resent it. His clothes were always spick-and-span, and so was his mustache. He played good poker and was always hurrying somewhere. He had been in the army eight years, and if the army hadn't got him the theater should have.

I went into his room one morning. He was standing in the middle of the floor, drinking a cup of coffee he had brewed on his own little French burner. He was fully dressed on the upper half— shirt, tie, flying jacket and everything. But on the lower half he had nothing but shorts and leather boots. Jaunty flying boots that flared at the top. He was a picture of Captain Kidd—a modern Captain Kidd of the air.

When the squadron was at the front everybody had to live out in the open. It was wet and cold at the start, wet and cold at the end.

The ground crew of eighty-five men really went through hell. For they were bombed by day, miserably wet and cold by night, and constantly overworked. When the pilots flew their Spitfires back to a desert airdrome for their much-deserved rest, their main concern was for their ground crews, who had been left up front to care for the replacement squadron.

"We're all right," I heard at least a half a dozen pilots say. "We can use the rest, but we're not in bad shape. It's those ground men that really need it and deserve it."

So Windy West went to work, and a few days later six big transports flying in formation landed at the field, and out of them climbed the eighty-five weary ground men. Replacements had arrived for them. They could begin their rest.

It was a long jump from teaching grade school in Indiana to leaping out of an airplane eleven thousand feet over some African mountains, but Tom Thayer made it. He hoped his next jump would be right back to an Indiana farm, and there he would stay.

Tom Thayer was "the hope of Hoosierdom," as the boys called him. He was from Hope, Indiana. Tom was twenty-seven, weighed two hundred pounds, taught the fifth and sixth grades for five years at Clifford, Indiana, and was the navigator of a Flying Fortress when I met him. They said he was the best celestial navigator in his squadron.

One day a bunch of Fortresses started a bombing trip to Bizerte. Over the mountains they ran into stormy, freezing weather. The ship Tom was navigating iced up and went out of control. Over the intercommunication phone, the captain gave the order for the crew to put their parachutes on and get ready to bail out. A minute later he gave the order to jump. Lieutenant Thayer was first on the list. He opened the escape hatch, and out he went.

Now, in the next few seconds some things happened. The other men didn't jump immediately, because they couldn't get the ball-turret gunner out of his turret. While they were pulling and tugging at him, the captain got some control over the plane. Then he ordered the bombs salvoed—which means dropped so they won't explode—and that gave him still more control. Then he counter-manded the order to jump. But poor Tom was already halfway to earth. The plane returned safely to base in less than an hour. It took Tom four days.

After his parachute opened, Tom said, he could still see the plane but it seemed to be below him instead of above. He thought he must be falling up. He couldn't figure it out.

He dropped through several thousand feet of clouds, still holding his pulled ripcord, for he knew if he saved it he would become a member of some club, although he couldn't remember its name—it's the Caterpillar Club. Anyhow his hand finally got so cold he threw the ripcord away.

The mountains where he landed were very rocky. His head struck as he came down, and he bled a good deal. He was conscious, but couldn't get up for about five minutes.

He says the mountains were full of Arabs, working in the fields, and finally he walked a short way and spoke to one of them. They tried to talk, but not knowing each other's language they didn't get far. So the Arab took him to a village and they went to a stone house, apparently the home of the village chief. The whole village clustered around to stare at him.

The chief was friendly and brought Tom a mattress, and also gave him an Arab nightgown to keep him warm. It was only 4:30 in the afternoon, but Tom lay down and went to sleep. Pretty soon the Arab brought in what Tom supposed was tea, though he wasn't sure. Then he went to sleep again. About 8:30 the Arab came in with dinner—goat meat. It wasn't too good.

Four other Arabs slept on the floor in the same room with Tom that night. Their snoring kept him awake. So did the fleas—he's still got the welts. A sheep slept in the same room too. Tom didn't sleep a wink all night.

Next morning they fed him three fried eggs and some fried potatoes, and wound a turban around his injured head. Then they went
out and killed the sheep that had slept in the same room. They
butchered it and cooked its heart in the same coals where the
Arabs had been warming their feet. They gave the heart to Tom
and he figured then that he was safe for sure.

After all this they got six donkeys, lashed the sheep's carcass
onto one of them, put Tom on another, and started out. The donkeys over here are very small, and Tom is very big. When they
would ride along the edge of a chasm, on a little shelf just wide
enough for a donkey, Tom could feel his long legs itching for the
ground.

He finally got home after four days. He tried to pay the Arabs,
but they wouldn't take anything. However, the photographs in his
wallet fascinated them, and they indicated their desire for some,
so Miss Mary Scott of Shelbyville, Indiana, will be interested to
know that her photograph now reposes, for all I know, next to some
Arab's heart.

Tom says he's going to marry Mary the day he gets back home
and then start farming and never stop.

For a while Tom was pretty mad about the others' not jumping,
but he was all over it by the time he got back to the airdrome. They
say he's the best-natured guy in the outfit. Nobody had ever seen
him really mad, so they decided to rib him plenty when he got in.

One of them came rushing up to him and said:

"Tom, the captain didn't say to bail out. He just said, 'Look at
the hail out.'"

They had him fooled for a minute, but not for long.

Tom's dad used to be county auditor back home. He had one term
and then got defeated last fall for re-election, by only 133 votes. The
boys told Tom that if he'd only had the gumption to make his
spectacular jump a couple of months earlier, his dad no doubt would
have been re-elected on the strength of it.

I ran on to nine American boys who had a unique baptism of war.
They had left America shortly before on a bomber, bound for the
African front. They arrived a little later, by camelback, after a series
of incredible adventures, including a battle with German fighter
planes.

A Flying Fortress, commanded by Lieutenant Harry Devers of
Martinsburg, West Virginia, took off from America and flew without
incident across the Atlantic and to the coast of Africa. Devers's
crew of eight was composed of Lieutenant Richard Banning, of Britt,
Louisiana, copilot; Lieutenant Charles Watt, Jacobsburg, Ohio,

navigator; Lieutenant Victor Coveno, 11002 Woodland Avenue, Cleveland, Ohio, and five sergeant-gunners—W. K. Thames, Fayetteville, North Carolina; Joseph Obradovich, Lacrosse, Wisconsin; Richard Hasbrough, Brooklyn, New York; Harry Alsaker, Montana, and Robert Oheron, Cresline, Ohio.

After landing in Africa they took off one morning and formed up with two other Fortresses for the last lap of their journey to war. They headed for the designated airdrome at the front where they were to report for action. They flew all day, and when they arrived where they thought the field should be they couldn't find it. So they flew on and kept hunting. The afternoon wore on and dusk grew near.

Suddenly, out of a blank sky, two fighters dived on them. Bullets began to spatter. That was how those youngsters, fresh from America, discovered that they had wandered into enemy territory. What a fine way to start their war!

Devers's crew began shooting back, but the fighters switched to one of the other Forts, which soon circled downward and disappeared, apparently shot down. It has not been heard from since.

The two remaining planes lost the Germans in the dusk. Then one of the American planes made a crash landing. Devers circled over it and was given a signal not to land. Several days later American reconnaissance planes discovered this Fortress being towed along the road, headed for Italian territory. They dived at it, guns going and set it afire.

The third plane was then alone in the air and they headed back west to get away from the enemy. It was dark, and they still couldn't find the airdrome to which they were being sent, so they flew far south to make sure of getting away from the mountains. They went up to eleven thousand feet, flew until their gas was gone, and then bailed out. They had a box of vitamin pills aboard, and they each ate a handful of pills just before jumping. Coveno grabbed a .45 automatic in one hand and a flashlight in the other, and jumped that way, carrying them all the way down.

One of the sergeants tucked an orange under his right arm. And then while plunging through space he had to reach up and get the orange in his left hand so he could free his right hand for pulling the ripcord. He saved the orange then, but later he let it drop somehow. He was still cussing about it.

Coveno sang all the way down. He didn't remember what he sang, but he just sang because he was so damned happy about that parachute. However, it oscillated badly and he got seasick.

Devers had given them all instructions. They were flying south and he would be the last man out, so he would start walking north and all the others were to head south. The plan worked. Eight of the nine found each other within half an hour. Lieutenant Coveno landed in a gully half a mile away from the meeting place and spent the night there, rejoining the others next morning.

That first night they all slept on the ground, wrapped in their parachutes. They didn't know whether they were in enemy territory or not.

At dawn an old Arab came wandering past. He was a nomadic shepherd, and he spoke neither English nor French. But he was wonderful to the boys. He led them northward, and they walked all day, covering twenty miles. Again that night they slept in their chutes. They didn't sleep much; it was too cold. Both the first and second nights Devers appointed guards, for they still weren't sure where they were.

The second morning they came across a caravan of fifteen camels. In charge of them was an Arabian enlisted man in the French Army. He was touring the desert buying camels for the French. This Arab took the boys along with him. They learned later that he thought they were Italian parachutists and that he was capturing them.

They rode camels for two days—and they never wanted to see another camel. They had to ride bareback, and they said a camel's back would make an excellent razor blade. They rode till they couldn't bear it any longer, and then got off and walked. But the sand was so deep they couldn't walk either, so they had to get back on their desert chariots.

Parachutes in the war zone were packed with chocolate rations, and the boys had stuffed a few additional rations in their pockets before stepping off. On the ground, Lieutenant Devers ordered them to cut their rations to half portions, in case they should be in the desert a long time. As it turned out, their parachute rations were still untouched when they finally reached an American airdrome. They ate goat meat all the time with the Arabs. They didn't care much for goat meat.

The Arab, like most of his tribe, naturally was a wizard at finding water holes, and the boys filled their canteens regularly. They always remembered to put in their pills too.

During the day, when riding razorback camels in utmost agony, they all sang that Bing Crosby-Bob Hope song, "The Road to Morocco." They were a long way from Morocco but they felt that the song sort of fitted into their background.

The old Arab who first picked them up was a spectacular character, a true nomad moving from day to day with his family and his herd of goats. He was eighty years old, had only one eye and no teeth.

They talked to him in sign language. He told them he had heard their plane the night before. The boys tried to give him money when they parted. He wouldn't take it, but he did accept some knives. The boys forgot to find out his name, but the Arab would be taken care of anyhow when the French found him, for the American Army would reward him.

Coveno said, "Boy, I've seen one beautiful Arab girl. She's this old fellow's granddaughter, and she's really beautiful."

But the lieutenant had heard how the Arabs felt about their women, so he didn't make eyes at her.

For two of the days and nights they traveled by camelback across the bare sands. There were no trails, no roads. On the morning of the fourth day they came upon a French desert garrison and there they were able to identify themselves for the first time, as Devers speaks some French. The French officers put them to bed and arranged for a truck to take them to a meeting place with an American truck. So, finally, at the end of the fifth day, they arrived at the airdrome they had hunted so desperately five nights before.

They were tired, but not in bad shape. They were still animated, and willingly told the story over and over. We finally had to make them go to bed, at ten o'clock.

A good sleep was too much for them. The next morning they felt washed out and weary. Some of them were even sick at their stomachs. But in a day or two they were normal again, when their excitement over being alive quieted down a bit.

Lieutenant Watt was the only one in the bunch who saved his ripcord. Several of the crew arrived carrying specimens of a peculiar rock, picked up from the sands. It was called desert rose, and was a hard sandstone. It really looked like a rose. It was a souvenir they would always keep.

All of them lost everything they had on the plane. When they arrived they naïvely said, "We want to go to the quartermaster in the morning and get some new outfits."

Everybody laughed loudly, and an officer said, "We don't get new outfits here. We wear just what we've got on, and keep on wearing it for months and months."

Those boys felt miserable about bungling their trip and losing a brand-new ship. They were humble about it. And they were almost worshipful in the presence of the veterans who had seen so much action. But they would get a new ship, and in a few months they would be able to talk like veterans to other new arrivals.

Everything around a fighter-bomber airdrome was important, but there was nothing more important than the repair section. It was vastly different from airplane shops or garages back home, where nothing more than a little inconvenience resulted from the long layup of a plane or car. Here in Africa there were just so many planes. With us and Germany teeter-tottering for air superiority over Africa, every single one was as precious as if it had been made of gold. Every plane out of action was temporarily the same as a plane destroyed.

It was the job of the repair section to take the shot-up planes and get them back into the air a little faster than was humanly possible. And that was what they were doing.

At one of our desert airdromes the repair section was in charge of Major Charles E. Coverley, of Palo Alto, California. His nickname was "Erk," and he had been one of my fellow travelers from England.

His right arm was a quiet mechanical genius named Walter Goodwin, of Grove City, Pennsylvania—a Regular Army sergeant, just promoted on the field to warrant officer. The men worshiped him and every officer on the field accepted as final his judgment on plane damage.

The repair section operated under a theory that seemed outlandish after coming from the peacetime business world. Its motto was to give away everything it could. Instead of hoarding their supplies and yelling that they were snowed under with work, they went around the field accepting every job imaginable, fulfilling every pilot's request, donating from their precious small stock of spare parts to any line mechanic who asked for something. For only by doing it that way would planes get back into the air a few hours sooner.

In the repair section were two hundred and fifty master craftsmen. They were happy and sincere and proud. I've never seen greater willingness to work beyond all requirements than those men showed.

Let me give an example of how the section worked. After a little to-do with the enemy, fourteen of our planes had been found to be damaged. Some needed only skin patches; others had washtub holes through the wings and were almost rebuilding jobs. Major Coverley and the squadron engineers surveyed the situation all morning, driving in a jeep from one plane to another. I rode with them, and when noon came and not a plane had been moved over to the repair area, I thought to myself that it was a mighty slow way to win a war. But I changed my mind a little later.

It took that long to estimate all the damage, plan out the program, distribute the men and machines over the huge field, and get things rolling. But once rolling——

Two days later I checked on their progress. Five of those wrecked planes had been ready for missions that first evening. Three more were delivered the following day. On the third day four more were just about finished. That made twelve. The other two had been turned into salvage, for spare parts.

Under peacetime conditions at home, it would have taken perhaps two months even in the finest shops to get all those planes back into the air. But there they were fighting again within three days. A man can do the impossible when he has to.

This field operated with a dearth of spare parts, as probably did all our fields at the far ends of the earth. So this crew provided its own spare parts by scrapping the most badly damaged planes, and using the good parts that were left. It happened to about one of every fifteen planes that were shot up. Those condemned planes were towed to the engineering section, and there they gradually disappeared. Finally they were skeletons—immobile, pathetic skeletons, picked bare by the scavenging mechanics.

The salvage planes were nicknamed "hangar queens." Five of them were sitting on the line when I was there. As you know, every bomber has a name painted on its nose. One of those hangar queens was called "Fertile Myrtle." Another was "Special Delivery." And a third was "Little Eva."

All plane work was done right outdoors. The only shops were tents where small machine work was done. The tents were three-sided, the fourth side being open. The door was sand. When the wind blew the men had to wear goggles. Beside every tent, almost within one-jump distance, was a deep slit trench to dive into when the enemy bombers came. Theirs was real war work, and no one could say they were much safer than the airmen themselves, for they were subject to frequent bombing.

They said their main hope was that no experts from the factories back home showed up to look things over. The experts would have told them a broken wing couldn't be fixed this way, a shattered landing gear couldn't be fixed that way. But these birds knew damned well it could be, for they were doing it.

It was late afternoon at our desert airdrome. The sun was lazy, the air was warm, and a faint haze of propeller dust hung over the field, giving it softness. It was time for the planes to start coming back from their mission, and one by one they did come—big Flying Fortresses and fiery little Lightnings. Nobody paid a great deal of attention, for this returning was a daily routine thing.

Finally they were all in—all, that is, except one. Operations reported a Fortress missing. Returning pilots said it had lagged behind and lost altitude just after leaving the target. The last report said the Fortress couldn't stay in the air more than five minutes. Hours had passed since then. So it was gone.

Ten men were in that plane. The day's accomplishments had been great, but the thought of ten lost friends cast a pall over us. We had already seen death that afternoon. One of the returning Fortresses had released a red flare over the field, and I had stood with others beneath the great plane as they handed its dead pilot, head downward, through the escape hatch onto a stretcher.

The faces of his crew were grave, and nobody talked very loud. One man clutched a leather cap with blood on it. The pilot's hands were very white. Everybody knew the pilot. He was so young, a couple of hours before. The war came inside us then, and we felt it deeply.

After the last report, half a dozen of us went to the high control tower. We went there every evening, for two things—to watch the sunset, and to get word on the progress of the German bombers that frequently came just after dusk to blast our airdrome.

The sunsets in the desert are truly things with souls. The violence of their color is incredible. They splatter the sky and the clouds with a surging beauty. The mountains stand dark against the horizon, and palm trees silhouette themselves dramatically against the fiery west.

As we stood on the tower looking down over this scene, the day began folding itself up. Fighter planes, which had patrolled the field all day, were coming in. All the soldiers in the tent camps had finished supper. That noiseless peace that sometimes comes just before dusk hung over the airdrome. Men talked in low tones about the dead pilot and the lost Fortress. We thought we would wait a few minutes more to see if the Germans were coming over.

And then an electric thing happened. Far off in the dusk a red flare shot into the sky. It made an arc against the dark background of the mountains and fell to the earth. It couldn't be anything else. It had to be. The ten dead men were coming home!

"Where's the flare gun? Gimme a green flare!" yelled an officer.

He ran to the edge of the tower, shouted, "Look out below!" and fired a green rocket into the air. Then we saw the plane—just a tiny black speck. It seemed almost on the ground, it was so low, and in the first glance we could sense that it was barely moving, barely staying in the air. Crippled and alone, two hours behind all the rest, it was dragging itself home.

I was a layman, and no longer of the fraternity that flies, but I could feel. And at that moment I felt something close to human love for that faithful, battered machine, that far dark speck struggling toward us with such pathetic slowness.

All of us stood tense, hardly remembering anyone else was there. With all our nerves we seemed to pull the plane toward us. I suspect a photograph would have shown us all leaning slightly to the left. Not one of us thought the plane would ever make the field, but on it came—so slowly that it was cruel to watch.

It reached the far end of the airdrome, still holding its pathetic little altitude. It skimmed over the tops of parked planes, and kept on, actually reaching out—it seemed to us—for the runway. A few hundred yards more now. Could it? Would it? Was it truly possible?

They cleared the last plane, they were over the runway. They settled slowly. The wheels touched softly. And as the plane rolled on down the runway the thousands of men around that vast field suddenly realized that they were weak and that they could hear their hearts pounding.

The last of the sunset died, and the sky turned into blackness, which would help the Germans if they came on schedule with their bombs. But nobody cared. Our ten dead men were miraculously back from the grave.

And what a story they had to tell! Nothing quite like it had happened before in this war.

The Tripoli airdrome, which was their target, was heavily defended, by both fighter planes and antiaircraft guns. Flying into that hailstorm, as one pilot said, was like a mouse attacking a dozen cats.

The Thunderbird—for that was the name of their Fortress—was first hit just as it dropped its bomb load. One engine went out. Then a few moments later the other engine on the same side went. When both engines went out on the same side it was usually fatal. And therein lay the difference of that feat from other instances of bringing damaged bombers home.

The Thunderbird was forced to drop below the other Fortresses. And the moment a Fortress dropped down or lagged behind, German fighters were on it like vultures. The boys didn't know how many Germans were in the air, but they thought there must have been thirty.

Our Lightning fighters, escorting the Fortresses, stuck by the Thunderbird and fought as long as they could, but finally they had to leave or they wouldn't have had enough fuel to make it home.

The last fighter left the crippled Fortress about forty miles from Tripoli. Fortunately, the swarm of German fighters started home at the same time, for their gas was low too.

The Thunderbird flew on another twenty miles. Then a single German fighter appeared, and dived at them. Its guns did great damage to the already crippled plane, but simply couldn't knock it out of the air.

Finally the fighter ran out of ammunition, and left. Our boys were alone with their grave troubles. Two engines were gone, most of the guns were out of commission, and they were still more than four hundred miles from home. The radio was out. They were losing altitude, five hundred feet a minute—and then they were down to two thousand.

The pilot called up his crew and held a consultation. Did they want to jump? They all said they would ride the plane as long as it was in the air. He decided to keep going.

The ship was completely out of trim, cocked over at a terrible angle. But they gradually got it trimmed so that it stopped losing altitude.

By then they were down to nine hundred feet, and a solid wall of mountains ahead barred the way homeward. They flew along parallel to those mountains for a long time, but they were then miraculously gaining some altitude. Finally they got the thing to fifteen hundred feet.

The lowest pass was sixteen hundred feet, but they came across at fifteen hundred. Explain that if you can! Maybe it was as the pilot said: "We didn't come over the mountains, we came through them."

The copilot said, "I was blowing on the windshield trying to push her along. Once I almost wanted to reach a foot down and sort of walk us along over the pass."

And the navigator said, "If I had been on the wingtip, I could have touched the ground with my hand when we went through the pass."

The air currents were bad. One wing was cocked away down. It was hard to hold. The pilots had a horrible fear that the low wing would drop clear down and they'd roll over and go into a spin. But they didn't.

The navigator came into the cockpit, and he and the pilots navigated the plane home. Never for a second could they feel any real assurance of making it. They were practically rigid, but they talked a blue streak all the time, and cussed—as airmen do.

Everything seemed against them. The gas consumption doubled, squandering their precious supply. To top off their misery, they had a bad headwind. The gas gauge went down and down.

At last the navigator said they were only forty miles from home, but those forty miles passed as though they were driving a horse and buggy. Dusk, coming down on the sandy haze, made the vast flat desert an indefinite thing. One oasis looked exactly like another. But they knew when they were near home. Then they shot their red flare and waited for the green flare from our control tower. A minute later it came—the most beautiful sight that crew had ever seen.

When the plane touched the ground they cut the switches and let it roll. For it had no brakes. At the end of the roll the big Fortress veered off the side of the runway. It climaxed its historic homecoming by spinning madly around five times and then running backwards for fifty yards before it stopped. When they checked the gas gauges, they found one tank dry and the other down to twenty gallons.

Deep dusk enveloped the field. Five more minutes and they never would have found it. The weary, crippled Fortress had flown for the incredible time of four and one-half hours on one pair of motors. Any pilot will tell you it's impossible.

That night, with the pilot and some of the crew, we drank a toast. One visitor raised his glass: "Here's to your safe return."

But the pilot raised his own glass and said instead, "Here's to a God-damned good airplane!"

And the others of the crew raised their glasses and repeated, "Here's to a God-damned good airplane!"

Perhaps the real climax was that during the agonizing homeward crawl that one crippled plane shot down the fantastic total of six German fighters. The score was officially confirmed.

The Fortress crew was composed of men who were already veterans of the war in the air. They had been decorated for missions over Europe. They already had two official kills and several probables to their credit. The Tripoli mission, which only by a miracle was not their last, was their twenty-second.

The skipper of the prize crew was 23-year-old Lieutenant John L. Cronkhite, of St. Petersburg, Florida. They called him Cronk. He was short, with a faint blond mustache and a very wide mouth, from which the words came in a slow drawl. His shoulders were broad, his arms husky. Usually he didn't wear a tie. He said he wasn't married because nobody would have him.

When the Fortress finally reached home, Cronkhite decided to go through the copilot's window onto the wing. As he stepped onto the wing his feet hit some oil and flew out from under him, and he went plummeting off the high wing onto the hard ground. The doctors thought he had been wounded, and picked him up and put him into an ambulance.

Cronkhite didn't want to be picked up. "I wouldn't have given a damn if I had broken a leg when I fell off the wing, I was so glad to be on the ground again. I just felt like lying there forever."

Cronk's father was a St. Petersburg florist. He had three pictures of his mother and father in his room. I spent the evening with Cronk and his copilot and navigator after their return from the dead.

When he walked into the room Cronk picked up something from the bed.

"Hell, I can't be dead," he said. "Here are my dog tags. I forgot to take them with me. I can't be dead, for they wouldn't know who I was."

He and his copilot were bound by an unbreakable tie then, for together they had pulled themselves away from death.

The copilot was Lieutenant Dana F. Dudley, of Mapleton, Maine. This is a little town of eight hundred, and Dud said he was the only pilot who ever came from there. He was a tall and friendly fellow, who got married just before coming overseas. His wife was in Sarasota, Florida. Dud said one of the German fighters dived toward his side of the plane, and came on with bullets streaming until it was only a hundred feet away. At that moment, what might have been his last thought passed through Dud's head: Gee, I'm glad I sent my wife that $225 this morning.

The navigator was Lieutenant Davey Williams, 3305 Miller Street, Fort Worth, Texas. He too had been recently married. The pilots gave Davey all the credit for getting them home. He was about the busiest man on the trip, navigating with one hand and managing two machine guns with the other. When they thought they were done for, Davey said to the pilots, "I'll bet those guys back home have got our stuff divided up already."

He said he thought mainly about how he was going to get word to his family that he was a German prisoner, and he felt sore that friends of his would soon get to go home to America while he'd have to spend the rest of the war in a prison camp.

9. SHERMAN HAD A WORD
FOR IT

THERE is nothing lighthearted about the imminence of death at the moment it is upon a man, but the next morning it can be very funny. It was worth a small fortune to be around an American camp on the morning after an aerial attack. Soldier comics had fertile ground then, and they went to work in the old vaudeville fashion of getting a laugh by making fun of themselves.

One morning I sat in a tent with a dozen airplane mechanics and heard Sergeant Claude Coffey of Richmond, Virginia, say:

"I hear there's one man who says he was not scared last night. I want to meet that man and shake his hand. Then I'll knock him down for being a damned liar.

"Me, I was never so scared in my life. As soon as those bombs started dropping I started hunting a chaplain. Boy, I needed some morale-building. A big one came whistling down. I dived into the nearest trench and landed right on top of a chaplain. Pretty soon I had an idea. I said, 'Chaplain, are you with me?' He said, 'Brother, I'm ahead of you.' So we went whisht out of the ditch and took off for the mountains.

"Anybody who says a scared man can't make fifty miles an hour uphill doesn't know what he's talking about. Me and the chaplain can prove it. Now and then we'd slow down to about thirty miles an hour and listen for a plane, and then speed up again. But in the moonlight the Jerries picked us out and came down shooting. I dived into an irrigation ditch full of water and went right to the bottom. After a while I said, 'Chaplain, you still with me?' And he said, 'With you? Hell, I'm under you.'

"It never occurred to me till this morning what damned fools we were to get out of that ditch and run in the moonlight. It won't happen again. After this, from six P.M. on, my address will be the top of that farthest mountain peak."

The reactions of the American soldiers to their first bad bombings were exactly what you would expect of them. They took it in a way to make you proud. The following figures aren't literal for any certain camp or particular bombing, but just my own generalization, which I believe a real survey would have authenticated. Let's say there was a camp of five thousand men, and they went through a dive-bombing and machine-gun strafing. One man out of that five thousand would break completely and go berserk. He might never recover. Perhaps twenty-five would momentarily lose their heads and start dashing around foolishly. A couple of hundred would decide to change trenches when the bombs seemed too close, forgetting that the safest place was the hole where they were. The four thousand seven hundred and seventy-four others would stay right in their trenches, thoroughly scared, but in full possession of themselves. They would do exactly the right thing. The moment it was over they would be out with shovels and tools helping to put out fires, working just as calmly as in the safety of broad daylight.

Our bombings here have proved that deep trenches are fully satisfactory as shelters. I've seen a crater big enough to put a Ford car in, within forty feet of an open trench full of men. An uprooted palm tree fell across the trench, and the men were covered with flying dirt, but not one was scratched. Their tents were mangled. One boy had just received a two-pound tin box of candy from his girl. Shrapnel slashed it wide open.

During the melee some running soldiers found one guy dead drunk in a ditch. He was sound asleep and snoring away. It was so funny they paused in their flight to laugh and envy him. Some men didn't hear the alert and had to dive into trenches in their underwear and bare feet. One boy showed me his steel helmet with bullet holes front and back. I foolishly asked, "Did you have it on?" Obviously he hadn't.

Where German machine-gun bullets hit the ground around their tents, soldiers described the result as looking like snake holes. At first the boys searched for pieces of shrapnel as souvenirs to take home, but within a few days shrapnel was so common they didn't bother to pick it up.

To top it all off, every morning at sunrise the dirt started flying and the trenches went a little deeper.

The American soldier is a born housewife, I've become convinced. I'll bet there's not another army in the world that fixes itself a "home away from home" as quickly as ours does. I've seen the little home touches created by our soldiers in their barns and castles and barracks and tents all over America, Ireland, England and Africa. But nowhere was this sort of thing given such a play as here at one of our desert airdromes.

The reason was twofold: First, the climate was so dry that something could be fixed up with a fair certainty that it wouldn't be washed away in the morning. Second, because of the constant danger of a German bashing, the boys dug into the ground to make their homes, and the things they could do with a cave were endless, as every farm boy knows.

The basic shelter was a pup tent, but the soldiers dug holes and set their tents over those. And the accessories inside provided one of the greatest shows on earth. Wandering among them was better than going to a state fair. The variations were infinite.

There were a few fantastically elaborate two- and three-room apartments underground. One officer had dug his deep slit trench right inside his tent, at the foot of his bed. He even lined the trench with blankets so he could lie six feet below ground under canvas and sleep during a raid. The finest homes were made by those who were lucky enough to get or borrow the covered-wagon ribs and canvas from a truck. They dug a hole and planted the canopy over the top.

Some of them had places fixed like sheiks' palaces. On the dirt floors were mats bought from Arabs in a near-by village. Some had electric lights hooked to batteries. One man bought a two-burner gasoline stove from some Frenchman for $3.20. On it he and his buddies heated water for washing and fried an occasional egg. Furthermore, they rigged up a shield from a gasoline tin and fitted it over the stove so that it channeled the heat sideways and warmed the tent at night.

An officer whose bedroll lay flat on the ground dug a hole two feet deep beside this "bed" so he could let his legs hang over the side when he sat on the bed. Many dugouts had pictures of girls back home hanging on the walls. A few boys papered their bare walls with Arab straw mats.

One evening I stuck my nose into the dugout of Sergeant Ray Aalto, 4732 Oakton Street, Skokie, Illinois. He was an ordnance man, caring for the guns on airplanes, but before the war he had been a steam-boiler man. Aalto had one thing nobody else in camp had. He had built a fireplace inside his dugout. He tunneled into one end of the dugout, lined the hole with gasoline tins, and made a double-jointed chimney so that no sparks nor light could show. He wished his wife could see him.

The deepest and most comfortable dugout I saw was built by four boys in the ground crew of a fighter squadron. It was five feet deep, and on each side they left a ledge wide enough for two bedding rolls, making two double beds. The entrance was a long L-shaped trench, with steps leading down the first part of the L. At the door was a double set of blackout curtains. Inside they had rigged up candles and flashlights with blackout hoods.

Most of the soldiers went to bed an hour or so after dark, because the camp was blacked out and there was nothing else to do. Only those with blackout lights in their dugouts could stay up and read or play cards or talk. Those four boys had dug a square hole in the wall of their dugout and fitted into it a gasoline tin with a door lock, making a perfect wall safe for cigarettes, chocolates, etc. Their dugout was so deep they could stay in it during a raid. In fact, they didn't even get out of bed.

It took the four of them three days, working every minute of their spare time, to dig their hole and fix it up. The four were Private Neil Chamblee, of Zebulon, North Carolina, Private W. T. Minges, Gastonia, North Carolina, Sergeant Robert Cook, Montpelier, Indiana, and Sergeant Richard Hughes, Weiner, Arkansas. Sergeant Hughes was especially pleased that I came around, because his mother had written him that I was in Africa and that she hoped our paths would cross, but he never supposed they would.

I believe a character analyst could have walked around that camp and learned more about the boys than a thousand filled-out questionnaires could reveal. Hundreds of the boys had done nothing at all to their tents, but I believe at least half of them had added some home touch. And a fellow didn't think of those things and work his head off on his own time creating them unless he had a lively ingenuity in him.

War coarsens most people. Men live rough and talk rough, and if they didn't toughen up inside they simply wouldn't be able to take it. But an officer friend of mine, Lieutenant Leonard Bessman of Milwaukee, told me two incidents of a battle that touched him deeply.

One evening he and another officer came up to a tiny farmhouse, which was apparently empty. To be on the safe side he called out, "Who's there?" before going in. The answer came back, "Captain Blank, and who the hell wants to know?"

They went in and found the captain, his clothes covered with blood, heating a can of rations over a gasoline flame. They asked if they could stay all night with him. He said he didn't give a damn. They started to throw their blankets down, and the captain said, "Look out for that man over there."

There was a dead soldier lying in a corner.

The captain was cooking his supper and preparing to stay all night alone in that same room. The blood and fury of death about him that day had left him utterly indifferent both to the companionship of the living and the presence of the dead.

The other incident was just the opposite. Another captain happened to be standing beside Bessman. It was just at dusk and they were on the desert. The night chill was coming down. The captain looked to the far horizon and said, sort of to himself, "You fight all day here in the desert and what's the end of it all? Night just closes down over you and chokes you."

A little later Bessman got out a partly filled bottle of gin he had with him and asked this same sensitive captain if he'd like a drink. The captain didn't even reach out his hand. He simply asked, "Have you got enough for my men too?"

He wouldn't take a drink himself unless the enlisted men under him could have some.

All officers are not like that, but the battlefield does produce a brotherhood. The common bond of death draws human beings toward each other over the artificial barrier of rank.

It didn't get much below freezing when I was in Central Tunisia, but we all suffered agonies from the cold. The days were sunshiny, and often really warm, but the nights were almost inhuman.

Everybody wore heavy underwear and all the sweaters he could find, plus overcoat and gloves and knitted cap. And still he was cold. There was snow on the mountains there.

The soldiers somehow resented the fact that so many of the folks at home thought just because we were in Africa that we must be passing out with the heat. Any number of soldiers showed me letters from their families full of sympathy because of the heat prostrations they must be suffering.

I'll tell you, in one little incident, just how cold it was, and also how little money meant compared to bodily necessities. One day, along the road, I ran into a soldier in a half-track who had a kerosene stove—the old-fashioned kind they used to heat the schoolroom with. I offered him $50 for it—back home it would have been worth about $3. He didn't hesitate a second. He just said, "No, sir," and that was the end of that.

It would have been just the same if I'd offered him $500. He couldn't use the money, and without the stove he would have been miserable.

Our soldiers at the front learned quickly how to keep their stomachs filled during emergencies. Ordinarily, the soldier's food was prepared for him in army mess kitchens, but at the front many things could happen. Small parties went out for days at a time and had to carry their own rations. On the battle front, kitchen trucks came up only at night and sometimes not even then. With our mobile armies on the move it wasn't always possible for kitchen trucks to be in the right place at the right moment, and as a consequence every soldier learned how to feed himself. Every vehicle from jeep to tank had a few spare cans of rations hidden away somewhere.

Soldiers cooked their own meals when on the move. They made a fire in one of two ways, each involving the use of gasoline: For a short fire they dug a hole about the size of a man's hand, poured gasoline into it, sprinkled sand over the gasoline, and then threw in a match. The sand kept the gas from burning too quickly. On a small fire like that they could heat a canteen or cup of coffee. For a bigger fire, they filled a small can with gasoline and buried it even with the surface of the ground. They piled rocks around to set their cooking utensils on, and then tossed a match at the gas.

I never saw a real skillet, pan or stewpot. The soldiers made their own utensils out of those famous five-gallon gasoline tins. I don't believe there's anything in the world that can't be made out of a five-gallon gasoline tin.

The soldiers also learned not to be lax about keeping their mess kits clean, for they found out by bitter experience that a dirty mess kit was the quickest way to violent nausea through poisoning. To wash their mess kits they scoured them with sand and then polished them with toilet paper—the best dishrag I've ever found.

Despite their primitive forms of cooking, the soldiers did eat well. They got either British or American rations, or a mixture of the two. Soldiers who were traveling actually preferred the British "compo"

to our own famous C ration. The reason being that the C ration had
so little variety that after three meals a man could hardly look a C
can in the face.

The British compo was more diverse. It had such things as sausage,
puddings, chocolate bars, salt, jam, butter, and cheese. It even included toilet paper.

Although a general order was issued against buying food from the
Arabs, in order to avoid using up their supply, we bought it anyhow.
Mess sergeants scoured the country and came back with eggs,
sheep and chickens. You might say we lived partly off the country.

Of course ridiculous prices were paid to the Arabs, which infuriated
the Europeans in North Africa because it ran up the prices for them
too. But the Americans' attitude was usually expressed something
like this: "Well, money means nothing to us here, and from the looks
of most of the Arabs a few extra francs won't hurt them."

We had more eggs right at the front than anywhere else in the
whole European and African theaters of war. The love of Americans
for eggs has become almost a legend. Along the roads over which our
motor convoys were passing constantly, Arabs stood by the score,
even out on the limitless desert, holding up eggs for sale. The natives
paid one franc for an egg. Mess sergeants paid three francs when
buying in bulk, and individual soldiers paid five francs an egg.

One day I was at a command post in a farmyard in a prosperous
irrigated valley. The grounds were full of officers and soldiers who
had just arrived. All of a sudden across the barnlot there came plod-
ding a huge white hog.

It was touching and funny to see the wave of desire that swept
over the soldiers. Everybody looked longingly at that hog. Everybody
had some crack to make.

"Oh, you big juicy blankety-blank! How I'd like to eat you!"

Another soldier said, "I never stuck a hog in my life, but I'll bet I could find his jugular vein with my bayonet."

Another, obviously a city man, said, "But how could we skin him?"

A truck driver answered scornfully, "You don't skin hogs. We'd boil him in scalding water and scrape him."

A year before none of us would have looked twice at a hog. But then the mere grunting passage of a swine across a barnlot brought a flood of covetous comment.

When I first met Charles P. Stone on a Tunisian hillside he was a major. Within two hours he was a lieutenant colonel. The promotion consisted of nothing more than his regimental commander walking up and telling him about it. Stone was a West Pointer and a Regular Army man. So had his father been before him.

"I beat my father by thirteen years," he said proudly. "He was forty when he got his lieutenant-colonelcy."

Colonel Stone went by the name of Charlie, and he called his officers by their first names. He was tall and slender, his hair was short in a crew cut, and he had a front tooth missing. He had had a one-tooth bridge but it came out in battle and he lost it.

Stone carried a couple of dozen big snapshots of his wife back home in New Brunswick, New Jersey. He wrote one letter a day no matter where he was and managed to shave every three or four days. Despite his rank he slept on the ground in the open, with only one blanket.

He was friendly, but his decisions were quick and positive. And he was a hard man to rattle. Anyone could see that the whole complicated battle area and its hourly confusing changes were as clear as crystal in his mind.

Sergeant Jack Maple, who hailed from Culver City, California, was one of those funny guys. The boys of his infantry company said Maple was about a hundred and twenty per cent. He was the kind who made himself the butt of his own jokes. When a visitor showed up the others gathered around just to hear him perform. Sergeant Maple said he fully intended to be a hero every time he was in a battle but somehow there was always so much suction in his foxhole that he couldn't get out of it. He also said he expected to be the Sergeant York of World War II, but since he had been a little slow in starting he had nicknamed himself Sergeant Cork.

Cork said he had all the hard luck. He pulled a tiny piece of shrapnel out of his pocket. It was paper-thin and about the size of a pinhead. "That's my souvenir," he said. "It landed on top of my hand and didn't even break the skin."

And then he continued, mimic-like, "Cork Maple, you unfortunate s.o.b., if it had been anybody else in the company it would have gone clear through his hand and he'd have got the next hospital boat home. But you can be smothered by 88s and they won't even draw blood on you."

Major Charles Miller of Detroit had a Rolleicord camera and ten rolls of film that he bought from an English-speaking Italian prisoner. When he offered to buy it the prisoner was aghast: "Why, I'm a prisoner. It's yours. You don't buy it, you take it." But Major Miller told him we didn't do it that way, and he gave the Italian three times as much as the price the prisoner finally proposed. At home the same camera would have cost $200.

We weren't the only ones who liked to collect enemy gear. The Germans did the same. German prisoners showed up with American mess kits and with tommy guns, and even wearing pieces of American uniforms.

The Germans worked up a terrific respect for the uncanny accuracy of our artillery. It was so perfect it had them agog. They told of one German officer, taken prisoner, who when brought into camp said, "I know you're going to kill me, but before you do would you let me see that automatic artillery of yours?"

We didn't kill him, of course, and neither did we show him our automatic artillery, because we didn't have any. We were just crack shots, that's all.

A fighter pilot I knew—a squadron leader—sent close to two hundred Germans to their doom. He was homeward bound from a mission and flying right on the deck—in other words, just above the ground. He zoomed over a little rise, and there straight ahead, dead in his sights, was the evening chow line behind a German truck.

It all happened in a second. There wasn't time for the Germans to duck. The pilot simply pressed the button, cannon shells streamed forth, and Germans and pieces of Germans flew in all directions.

The squadron leader barely mentioned it in his report when he got back. He said it almost made him sick. Killing was his business, but it was killing an opponent in the air that he liked. I'm not even giving his name, because he felt so badly about it.

A big military convoy moving at night across the mountains and deserts of Tunisia is something that nobody who has been in one can ever forget.

Late one afternoon the front-line outfit I was visiting received sudden orders to move that night, bag and baggage. It had to pull out of its battle positions, time the departures of its various units to fit into the flow of traffic at the first control point on the highway, and then drive all night and go into action on another front.

All the big convoys in the war area moved at night. German planes would have spotted a daytime convoy and played havoc with it. It was extremely difficult and dangerous, this moving at night in total blackness over strange and rough roads. But it had to be done.

Our convoy was an immense one. There were hundreds of vehicles and thousands of men. It took seven and a half hours to pass one point. The convoy started moving at 5:30 in the evening, just before dusk. The last vehicle didn't clear till one o'clock the next morning.

I rode in a jeep with Captain Pat Riddleberger, of Woodstock, Virginia, and Private John Coughlin, Manchester, New Hampshire. Ahead of us was a small covered truck which belonged to Riddleberger's tank-destroyer section. We made a little two-vehicle convoy within ourselves. We were to fall in near the tail end, so we had half the night to kill before starting. We stood around the truck, parked in a barnlot, for an hour or two, just talking in the dark. Then we went into the kitchen of the farmhouse which had been used as a command post and was then empty. There was an electric light, and out of boxes we built a fire in the kitchen fireplace. But the chimney wouldn't draw, and we almost choked from the smoke.

Some officers had left a stack of copies of the New York *Times* for October and November lying on the floor, and we read those for an hour or so. We looked at the book sections and the movie ads. None of us had ever heard of the new books or the current movies. It made us feel keenly how long we had been away and how cut off we were from home. "They could make money just showing all the movies over again for a year after we get back," one of the boys said.

We finished the papers and there were still three hours to kill, so we got blankets out of the truck and lay down on the concrete floor. We were sleeping soundly when Captain Riddleberger awakened us at 1:00 A.M. and said we were off.

The moon was just coming out. The sky was crystal-clear, the night bitter cold. The jeep's top was down. We all put on all the clothes we had. In addition to my usual polar-bear wardrobe, which included heavy underwear and two sweaters, that night I wore a pair of coveralls, a heavy combat suit that a tank man lent me, a pair of overshoes, two caps—one on top of the other—and over them a pair of goggles. The three of us in the jeep wrapped up in blankets. In spite of all that, we almost froze before the night was over.

We moved out of the barnlot, and half a mile away we swung onto the main road, at the direction of motorcyclists who stood there guiding the traffic. Gradually our eyes grew accustomed to the half-darkness, and it wasn't hard to follow the road. We had orders to drive in very close formation, so we kept within fifty feet of each other.

After a few miles we had to cross a mountain range. There were steep grades and switchback turns, and some of the trucks had to back and fill to make the sharper turns. There was considerable delay. French trucks and buses would pass and tie up traffic, swinging in and out. And right in the center of these tortuous mountains we met a huge American hospital unit, in dozens of trucks, moving up to the front. They were on the outside of the road, and at times their wheels seemed about to slide off into the chasm.

We had long waits while traffic jams ahead were cleared. We shut off our motors and the night was deathly silent except for a subdued undertone of grinding motors far ahead. At times we could hear great trucks groaning in low gear on steep grades far below, or the angry clanking of tanks as they took sharp turns behind us.

Finally the road straightened out on a high plateau. There we met a big contingent of French troops moving silently toward the front we had just vacated. The marching soldiers seemed like dark ghosts in the night. Hundreds of horses were carrying their artillery, ammunition and supplies.

I couldn't help feeling the immensity of the catastrophe that had put men all over the world, millions of us, to moving in machinelike precision throughout long nights—men who should have been comfortably asleep in their warm beds at home. War makes strange giant creatures out of us little routine men who inhabit the earth.

Our jeep was almost at the tail end when we started, but before many hours had passed we had overtaken so many slow-moving vehicles that we worked our way well up into the convoy. As we droned along through the night it was hard to realize that we were part of such a fabulously long string of war machines. Vehicles stretched ahead of us for scores of miles, but of course we couldn't see them, and our only companionship was five or six red taillights ahead of us. We all drove without headlights, but did have taillights so we could see when the fellow ahead was stopping.

Occasionally we smoked, and I lit cigarettes for the others. We didn't try to hide the flare of the match, for it was only a flash and then quickly gone. Once in a while we overtook a truck with a dead engine, or a big wrecker towing a half-track. But our American machines were good ones, and of the hundreds of vehicles in that great convoy only a handful had trouble during the long journey.

Our convoy was as complete as a circus. There were ammunition trucks, kitchens, repair shops, trucks carrying telephone switchboards and generators for camp lighting, trucks carrying bombs. There were jeeps carrying generals, and there were great wreckers capable of picking up a whole tank. It was quite a contrast to the Arabs we passed in the night, with their heavily loaded camels and burros.

The moon gave us enough light to drive by, but how the bulk of the convoy, which started long before the moon came up, ever got over the mountain range is beyond me. They had to drive in total blackness. Guides went ahead to study the road. They spotted all the sharp turns and steep banks, and they indicated the direction of traffic with their hooded flashlights.

About every hour and a half we stopped for the truck driver's traditional stretch. At one of these stops the drivers checked their mileage. We had been on the road three hours and come exactly twenty-seven miles. Snaking a huge convoy over a mountain range in the dead of night was a slow business.

But open country lay ahead, and when we reached that we stepped up to thirty-five and forty miles an hour. The night wind began to cut more cruelly. We didn't talk much, for it was too cold. My goggles kept steaming inside, and I had to lift them off and wipe them. Finally all of us except the drivers pulled blankets over our heads and dozed a little. But not much, for holes in the gravel roads were hard to see and often the jeep would do a backbreaking hurdle.

At the rest stops the soldiers got out and ran up and down the road, or stood in one spot jitterbugging in an effort to warm their feet. The ones I felt sorriest for were the infantrymen, packed like sardines in open trucks with no protection from the bitter cold. It seemed that the infantry always got it in the neck.

Several hours after midnight the convoy got itself into a ridiculous snarl. During a rest stop apparently some driver far ahead had gone to sleep and forgotten to start on again. We waited for half an hour. Then impatient drivers pulled out and started passing. That was fatal. The first thing we knew two lines of traffic choked the road. At every gully and every turn they snarled up and one line had to stop. Eventually it got just like those awful holiday jams at home where you move a few feet at a time. "I'm amazed that such a thing could be allowed to happen," I said to Captain Riddleberger. "This strikes me as being the perfect way not to win the war."

We agreed, but I was sorry for my remarks later. In an hour or so everything straightened itself out. We were clear of the mountains then. We passed through silent little Arab villages, and drove across treeless prairies.

About four o'clock Riddleberger and I changed places with two soldiers riding in the back end of the truck ahead. We lay down on barracks bags and pulled blankets over us, thinking we'd snatch a little sleep. Pretty soon Riddleberger said, "These blankets smell so bad I can't sleep."

Mine didn't smell exactly like perfume either.

"Well, hell," the captain said. "The poor guys never have a chance to take a bath."

Apparently it didn't occur to him that he and I never took baths either. I wonder how we smelled to others.

My feet were so cold and achy that at last I took off my overshoes and shoes and held my cold toes in my hands, trying to warm them. After half an hour or so they quit hurting. Eventually I went to sleep. When I came to there was a faint light in the sky. It was just seven o'clock. I had been dead to the world for two hours. It was hard to believe, for the truck had been jolting and bouncing and stopping and starting all that time. Weariness is a great cure for insomnia, or maybe I had been anesthetized by those blankets.

Just after daylight the members of our little party changed places again. Captain Pat Riddleberger got behind the wheel of the truck on which we had snatched a couple of hours' sleep. I went back to relieve one of the half-frozen soldiers in our jeep. When we started again we were all wide awake and vividly alert, for the hour of danger was upon us. We still had hours to go in daylight, and it was a magnificent chance for the Germans to destroy us by the hundreds— with strafing planes.

The sun came up slowly over the bare mountain ridges. The country was flat and desertlike. There was not a tree as far as we could see. It looked like West Texas. We passed Arabs blue with cold, shepherding their flocks or walking the roads. There was hoarfrost on the ground, and sometimes we saw thin ice in the ditches.

At daylight our vehicles, acting on orders and through long experience, began to spread out. Now we were running about two hundred yards apart. As far as we could see across the desert, ahead and behind, the road was filled with drab brown vehicles.

Sergeant James Bernett, 1541 Cheyenne Street, Tulsa, Oklahoma, was driving our jeep. I rode up front with him. Private John Coughlin sat in the back. He unsheathed a machine gun and mounted it on a stanchion between us. We kept a careful lookout for planes. After a while we saw trucks ahead stopping and soldiers piling out like ants, but I was in such a daze from cold and fatigue that I didn't sense at first what that meant. Neither did the others.

Then all of a sudden Coughlin yelled, "Watch it! Watch it!"

And we knew what he meant. By now all the men ahead were running out across the desert as fast as they could go. Bernett slammed on the brakes—and a man can stop a jeep almost instantly. I was so entangled in blankets that it took a few seconds to get loose. Coughlin couldn't wait. He went out right over my head before the jeep had stopped. He caught a foot as he went, and it threw him headlong. He hit the road flat, and skidded on his stomach in the gravel. He hurt one knee, but he limped the fastest limp I've ever seen.

We beat it out across the desert until we found a little gully a hundred feet from the road. We didn't get into the gully, but stopped and took our bearings. None of us could see or hear anything. We

was a part of the Chemical Warfare Service, but instead of dealing out poisonous gases they dealt out harmless smoke that covered up everything when raiders came over. By the nature of their business they worked all night and slept all day. They took their various stations in little groups in a big semicircle around the city, just before dusk, and stayed there on the alert till after daylight. At midnight a truck made the rounds with sandwiches and hot coffee. Captain Todd himself also made a four-hour tour of the little groups each night, ending about 2:00 A.M.

Their assignment had been permanent enough to justify their fixing up their camp in a homelike way. They had taken old boards from the dock area and built about three dozen small cabins, sort of like tourist-camp cabins back home. They had board floors, board side walls, and canvas roofs.

They had built bunks for their bedrolls, hung up mosquito nets, hammered boards together for chairs, made tables, and put little steps and porches in front of their cabin doors. They named their cabins such things as "Iron Mike's Tavern," "African Lovers," "The Village Barn," "The Opium Den."

Lieutenant Kesner had a sign hanging outside his door that said, "Sixty-Five Hundred Miles from Deep in the Heart of Texas." The heart was drawn instead of spelled out.

Captain Todd had a wife back home named Marigene and a daughter named Paulagene. He left when his daughter was four weeks old, nearly a year and a half before. But he kept himself well reminded of his family, for tacked on the wall of his cabin were thirty-four pictures of his wife and baby. He was the picture-takingest man I ever met.

The hundred men in that camp were just like a clan. They had all been together a long time and they had almost a family pride in what they were doing and the machinery they were doing it with.

One of the boys in the kitchen said he'd read my stuff in the Cleveland *Press* for years. He was Corporal Edward Dudek, of 8322 Vineyard Avenue, Cleveland. Before the war he had been a chemical worker. The army clicked long enough to put him into the Chemical Service, but then a cog slipped somewhere and now he had become a cook instead of a chemical worker. But I suppose he could make his own fumes when he got homesick by spilling a little grease on the stove.

We spent a comfortable night with this outfit and tarried around a couple of hours the next morning, just chatting, because everybody was so friendly. Then they gassed us up without our even asking, and we finally left feeling that we'd visited the nearest thing to home since hitting Africa.

10. BULLETS, BATTLES, AND

RETREAT

WHEN our infantry went into a certain big push in Tunisia, each man was issued three bars of D-ration chocolate—enough to last one day. He took no other food. He carried two canteens of water instead of the usual one. He carried no blankets. He left behind all extra clothes except his raincoat. In his pockets he might have a few toilet articles. Some men carried their money, others gave it to friends to keep.

In the days that followed the men lived in a way that is inconceivable to anyone who hasn't experienced it. They walked and fought all night without sleep. Next day they lay flat in foxholes, or hid in fields of freshly green, knee-high wheat. If they were in the fields they dared not even move enough to dig foxholes, for that would have brought the German artillery. They couldn't rise even for nature's calls. The German felt for them continually with his artillery. The slow drag of those motionless daylight hours was nearly unendurable. Lieutenant Mickey Miller of Morgantown, Indiana, said that lifeless waiting in a wheatfield was almost the worst part of the whole battle.

The second evening after the attack began, C rations and five-gallon cans of water were brought across country in jeeps, after dark. One night a German shell landed close and fragments punctured fifteen cans of water. The men ate in the dark, and they couldn't see the can from which they were eating. They just ate by feel. They made cold coffee from cold water.

Each night enough canned rations for three meals were brought up, but when the men moved on after supper most of them either lost or left behind the next day's rations, because they were too heavy to

123

carry. But they said when they were in battle and excited they sort of went on their nerve. They didn't think much about being hungry.

They fought at night and lay low by day, when the artillery took over its blasting job. Weariness gradually crept over them. What sleeping they did was in daytime. But it was never very much, for at night it was too cold and in daytime too hot. Also the fury of the artillery made daytime sleeping next to impossible. So did the heat of the sun. Some men passed out from heat prostration. Many of them got upset stomachs from the heat. But as the third and fourth days rolled on, weariness overcame all obstacles to sleep. Men who sat down for a moment's rest fell asleep in the grass. There were even men who said they could march while asleep. Lieutenant Colonel Charlie Stone actually went to sleep standing up talking on a field telephone—not when he was listening, but in the middle of a spoken sentence.

When sometimes they did lie down at night the men had only their raincoats to lie on. It was cold, and the dew made the grass as wet as rain. They didn't dare start a fire to heat their food, even in daytime, for the smoke would attract enemy fire. At night they couldn't even light cigarettes in the open, so after digging their fox-holes they got down and made hoods over their heads with their rain-coats, and lighted up under the coats. They had plenty of cigarettes. Those who ran out during battle were supplied by others. Every night new supplies of water and C rations were brought up in jeeps.

You can't conceive how hard it was to move and fight at night. The country was rugged, the ground rough. Everything was new and strange. The nights were pitch-black. The men groped with their feet. They stepped into holes, and fell sprawling in little gullies and creeks. They trudged over plowed ground and pushed through waist-high shrubs. They went as a man blindfolded, feeling unsure and off balance, but they kept on going.

Through it all there was the fear of mines. The Germans had mined the country behind them beyond anything ever known before. Our troops simply couldn't take time to go over each inch of ground with mine detectors, so they had to discover the mine fields by stumbling into them or driving over them. Naturally there were casualties, but not as many as you might think—just a few men each day. The greatest damage was psychological—the intense watchful-ness our troops had to maintain.

The Germans had been utterly profligate with their mines. The Americans dug four hundred from one field. They found so many fields and so many isolated mines that they ran out of white tape to mark them with. But still they went on.

Most of the preliminary battles between Axis and American troops in Tunisia were for possession of mountain passes leading to Eastern

Tunisia. In one of those battles our men had worked their way up to the mouth of a pass on one side and the Italians had done the same on the other side. There they lay, well dug in, not more than two hundred yards apart. They were separated by previously laid mine fields over which neither dared to pass. So they just stayed there, each side waiting for the other to act.

The Italians began sending over notes to the Americans. I've heard many stories of such happenings in the last war, but it was rare in this one. The Italians sent over one note telling the Americans they were badly outnumbered and didn't have a chance and had better surrender. The Americans sent back a note saying, "Go to hell, you lousy spaghetti eaters. We'll tear your ears off before this is over."

Similar notes, with perfect incongruousness, were carried back and forth through the mine fields by a small Arab boy who happened to wander past and took on the job for a few francs.

One day we drove past a big bivouac of supply trucks a few minutes after some German planes had dive-bombed and strafed them. The soldiers all took to foxholes and nobody was hurt, but three trucks were set afire. The soldiers got two fires out immediately, but the third was hopeless, for it was a big truck loaded with scores of five-gallon tins of gasoline. These began exploding and scattered flaming debris.

Then suddenly there was a bigger explosion and one lone gasoline tin went shooting straight up into the air. That can rose majestically to a height of about four hundred feet, gradually slowed down until it seemed to pause motionless for a moment in the sky, then came plunging straight down. Its explosive flight had been so straight up and down that when it fell it grazed the side of the truck not five feet from where it had started.

Some little thing like that—the uncanny straightness of a tin can's war journey—often stays in the mind for ages after the memory of horror or bravery has dimmed and passed.

After living with our troops at the Tunisian front for some weeks I came to the conclusion that the two dominant things in their minds were hatred of the cold and fear of attack from the air. I have already written a great deal about the cold. You can sympathize there, for you all know what it feels like to be cold. But you don't know—can never know, without experiencing it—the awful feeling of being shot at by speeding enemy planes.

If our soldiers were meticulous about any one thing it was about watching the sky. Nobody had to tell them to be cautious. After just one attack, caution became a sort of reflex action. They never let a plane pass without giving it a good looking over. The sound of a motor in the sky was a sign to stop whatever they were doing long enough to make sure.

Of course aerial attack was at its worst in actual battle, when Stukas were diving on our troops; that was a nightmare, but it was not only in battle that they got it. They got it also in bivouacs, and on the roads. They were subject to it all the time—not in great or blanket amounts, to be sure, but the danger was always there, like a snake hidden somewhere along the path.

As a result, camouflage became second nature. Near the front no one ever parked a jeep without putting it under a tree. If there were no trees, we left it on the shady side of a building or wall. If there was no cover at all we threw a camouflage net over it. As we neared the front we folded our windshield down over the hood and slipped a canvas cover over it so it wouldn't glint and attract a pilot's eye.

German pilots liked to sneak up from behind, and it's incredible how difficult it was to spot a hostile plane. Once some army friends of mine never knew there was a plane within miles until one swooped overhead and 20-millimeter shells splattered on all sides of them.

Every day somebody got strafed on the roads, yet it was really the tiniest fraction of one per cent of our men that ever saw a German plane when on a trip. I drove hundreds of miles over Central Tunisian roads in convoy but saw relatively few strafings.

It was the stealthiness of the thing, the knowledge that this sudden peril was always possible, that got a man. There were thousands of Americans over here who were calm under ground fire but hated strafing planes. Soldiers in camp lost no time in hitting their slit trenches and soldiers on the road flowed like water out of their vehicles every time a plane was sighted. Nine times out of ten it turned out to be one of our own, but if we had waited to make sure we might have been too late. More than once I quickly slowed down and then realized the approaching plane was only a soaring bird.

As I drove along roads in the frontal area I met hundreds of vehicles, from jeeps to great wrecker trucks, and every one of the hundreds of soldiers in them would be scanning the sky as if they were lookouts on a ship at sea.

Once when a friend and I were coming back from the front lines in our jeep we met a great convoy of supply trucks making a suffocating cloud of dust. Our first intimation of danger was the sound of ack-ack shells exploding in the sky behind us. We stopped in nothing flat, and piled out. I remember looking back and saying, "There are two dozen of them coming right at us!"

We ran out across the fields about fifty yards to a small ditch, and stopped there to look again. My two dozen enemy planes were actually just the black puffs of our ack-ack shells. We couldn't see the planes at all. That shows how deceptive our senses were when we got excited. We learned to hate absolutely flat country where there were no ditches to jump into or humps to hide behind. We even made jokes about carrying collapsible foxholes for such country.

In camp I often saw soldiers sitting in their slit trenches, completely oblivious of the presence of anyone around them, and cussing the German planes and rooting for our ack-ack to get one, just as if they were at a football game.

The commandant of one outfit which had been at the front for two months told me they had been strafed and dive-bombed so much they couldn't hear even a motor without jumping. I knew one American outfit that was attacked by Stukas twenty-three times in one day. A little of that stuff goes a long way.

If we had ack-ack to shoot back, it lessened the soldiers' fear greatly; if our own fighters were in the sky, the men felt almost no uneasiness at all.

Yes, the cold and the Stukas were the bugaboos of the average guy over here. But with the spring the cold would disappear, and we all hoped the Stukas would take the hint also.

One fine day a pal and I drove our jeep under a tree, camouflaged it by covering it with limbs, and then walked up the side of a hill for about five hundred yards. Half a mile to the south of us the battle for Ousseltia Pass in Central Tunisia was going on. We stopped in what is known as a forward command post, from which a battle is directed. This one consisted of a tent twenty feet square, hidden under a tree. However, the whole tent had been dropped down and simply lay like a tarpaulin covering the officers' bedrolls and bags. All the work was being done around two field telephones lying in their leather cases on the ground ten feet from the tent.

The rocky hillside was covered with little bushes and small fir trees. The sun was out and the day was rather warm. There were no papers or desks or anything—just three or four officers standing and sitting on a hillside near two telephones on the ground. One officer had a large map case. That's all the paraphernalia there was for directing the battle.

Our troops were on top of a ridge about a quarter of a mile above us. The enemy was in the valley beyond, and on a parallel ridge a mile farther on. We could walk up and look over, but we couldn't see anything. Both sides were hidden in the brush.

Every minute or two our near-by artillery would fire, and then half a minute or so later we could hear faintly the explosion of the shells far away. "Nobody's doing much damage right now," an officer said, "but at least we're getting in ten shots to their one."

Now and then a louder and much nearer blast interrupted us. When I asked what size gun it was, an officer said it wasn't a gun— it was enemy mortar shells exploding. I supposed they were three or four miles away, but he said they were falling only eight hundred yards from us.

Once in a while we could hear machine-gun fire in the distance. A young second lieutenant stood near the phones and did all the talking over them. In fact, he appeared to be making all the decisions. And he impressed me as knowing his business remarkably well.

The highest officer around was a lieutenant colonel, but he seemed to leave everything to his lieutenant, and at every signal of approaching planes he ran to a foxhole and stayed there till the planes had gone. Other officers commented about him in terms not meant for mixed company, but the young lieutenant said nothing.

The phone rang every few minutes. Other command posts were calling in to report or to ask instructions. Now and then the chief post, some fifteen miles back, called and was given reports. Officers and enlisted men kept appearing from down below or over the hill, asking about things. One sergeant came to inquire where a certain post was, saying he had two jeep tires and a tire for an antitank gun that he was supposed to deliver.

Another sergeant, wearing an overcoat, came up the hill, saluted formally, and reported that a certain battery setup was ready to fire. They told him to go ahead. A phone rang. The captain of an ack-ack battery said the enemy had his range and asked permission to move. Permission was granted. All the conversation was informal and unexcited.

A phone rang again. A captain at another command post requested a decision on whether to move forward. The young lieutenant, apparently not wishing to give direct orders to a higher officer, solved the problem by putting his words in the form of advice, sprinkling two or three "sirs" in every sentence. I thought he handled it beautifully.

Every now and then the lieutenant phoned some other post.

The afternoon sun went over the hill and the evening chill began to come down. Officers who had been in the battle all day started wandering in through the brush on foot, to report. They were dirty and tired but the day had gone well, and they were cheerful in a quiet sort of way.

A Medical Corps major came up the hill and said, "Those blankety-blanks! They've knocked out two of my ambulances that were trying to get the wounded back. A hell of a lot a Red Cross means to them!"

Nobody said anything. He went back down the hill, as mad as a hornet.

The officers kept talking about three fellow officers who had been killed during the day, and a fourth one who was missing. One of the dead men apparently had been a special favorite. An officer who had been beside him when it happened came up with blood on his clothes. "We hit the ground together," he said. "But when I got up, he couldn't. It took him right in the head. He felt no pain."

"Raise up that tent and pack his stuff," an officer told an enlisted man.

Another one said, "The hell of it is his wife's due to have a baby any time now."

Just then a sergeant walked up. He had left the post that morning with the officer who was now missing. "Where's Captain So-and-so?" they all asked.

The sergeant said he didn't know. Then he said he himself had been captured. "Captured?" the officers asked.

"Yes," he said. "The Italians captured me and then turned me loose."

The sergeant was Vernon Gery, 305 West Navarre Street, South Bend, Indiana. He was a married man, and had been a lawyer before the war. He was a young and husky fellow. He didn't appear to be very much shaken by his experience, but he said he never was so scared in his life.

Sitting there on the ground he told me his experience. He and the missing captain and a jeep driver had gone forward at nine-thirty in the morning to hunt for the body of a popular officer who had been killed. They parked the jeep, and the captain told them to stay there till he returned. They covered the jeep with brush and then hid in the bushes to wait while the captain went on alone. As they were lying there the driver yelled to Sergeant Gery, "Look they're retreating!"

He saw eight soldiers coming toward them. He thought they were French, but actually they were an Italian patrol. The driver's shout attracted their attention and they began shooting. The two Americans fired back. The jeep driver was hit and killed instantly. Gery said the driver yelled just once when he was hit. "I'll be hearing that yell for a long time," he said.

In a moment the Italians had Gery. Apparently they were on a definite mission, for seven of them went on, leaving one guard to watch Gery. They had taken his rifle, searched him, and given back his identification cards, but they kept his cigarettes, pipe, tobacco, chewing gum, and message book.

"Did they take your money?" I asked.

"I didn't have any," Gery said. "I haven't been paid in three months. I haven't had a cent in my pocket for weeks."

For an hour the one Italian sat ten feet from Gery with his rifle pointed at him. Gery says the Italian must have been well-acquainted with the American rifle, for he passed the time taking it apart and putting it together, and did it rapidly and correctly. The Italian didn't try to talk to Gery.

Suddenly our artillery began dropping shells close to where they sat. That was too much for the Italian. He just got up and disappeared into the bushes. And Gery started home.

As Gery finished his story, the commanding colonel came back from his afternoon's tour. He sat down on the ground, and the officers gathered around to hear his reports and get their instructions for the night. The colonel, a tall, middle-aged man, wore glasses and had a schoolteacherly look. But he cussed a blue streak and made his decisions crisply. I could tell he was loved and respected. He called all his men by their first names. He wore a brown canvas cap, without any insignia at all. Officers at the front tried to look as little like officers as possible, for the enemy liked to pick them off first.

Somebody asked if the colonel would like a cup of tea. He said he would. An order was yelled, and out of the bushes came a Chinese boy in uniform and helmet, carrying a teapot covered with a rag.

Planes came over again, and several officers ran to foxholes, but the colonel acted as if he didn't see them. The rest of us stayed and continued the conversation. The officers told him about the three members of his staff who had been killed.

"Christ!" he said. "Well, we're in a war. We've got to expect it. We must try not to feel too bad about it." And then he gave his instructions. "We are being relieved at eleven-thirty tonight. Jim, you start taking up your phone wire, but nothing else moves a foot before daylight. Joe, you keep on firing up to leaving time, so they won't know we are pulling out. We've got 'em on the run, and I wish we could stay, but we've got our orders."

Everybody left to carry out his new duties, and we correspondents went back down the hill to our jeep.

On the morning in February the big German push started against the American troops in Tunisia, our forward command post in that area was hidden in a patch of cactus about a mile from the town of Sidi bou Zid. The post had been there more than a week and I had visited there myself only three days previously. I had spent a lot of time with our forward troops in the hills, and I knew most of the officers.

A command post is really the headquarters of a unit. In this case a brigadier general was in command. His staff included Intelligence and S3 (planning) officers, unit commanders, a medical detachment, kitchens, and various odds and ends.

A command post of that size has several score vehicles and two or three hundred men. Its work is all done in trucks, half-tracks or tents. It was always prepared to move, when at the front. And it does move every few days, so the enemy won't spot it. This special command post was about ten miles back from the nearest known enemy position. Our artillery and infantry and some tanks were between it and the enemy.

That Sunday morning hordes of German tanks and troops came swarming out from behind the mountains around Faid Pass. We didn't know so many tanks were back there, and we didn't know so many Germans were either, for our patrols had been bringing in mostly Italian prisoners from their raids.

The attack was so sudden nobody could believe it was in full force. Our forward troops were overrun before they knew what was happening. The command post itself didn't start moving back till after lunch. By then it was too late—or almost too late.

Command cars, half-tracks and jeeps started west across the fields of semicultivated desert, for by then the good road to the north was already cut off. The column had moved about eight miles when German tanks came charging in on the helpless vehicles from both sides.

A headquarters command post is not heavily armed. It has little with which to fight back. All those men and cars could do was duck and dodge and run like hell. There was no such thing as a fighting line. Everything was mixed up over an area of ten miles or more. It was a complete melee. Every jeep was on its own. The accompanying tanks fought till knocked out, and their crews then got out and moved along on foot. One tank commander, whose whole crew escaped after the tank caught fire, said that at least the Germans didn't machine-gun them when they jumped from the burning tank.

Practically every vehicle reported gasoline trouble that afternoon. Apparently there was water in the gas, yet nobody felt that it was sabotage. They said there had been similar trouble before, but never so bad.

A friend of mine, Major Ronald ("Satch") Elkins, of College Station, Texas, had his half-track hit three times by German shells. They were standing still, cleaning a carburetor filter, when the third shell hit. It set them afire. Some of the crew eventually got back safely, but others were missing. Major Elkins said they could have got clear back with the car "if the damned engine had only kept running."

The Germans just overran our troops that afternoon. They used tanks, artillery, infantry, and planes dive-bombing our troops continuously. Our artillery was run over in the first rush. We were swamped, scattered, consumed, by the German surprise.

Twilight found our men and machines straggling over an area extending some ten miles back of Sidi bou Zid. Darkness saved those who were saved. During the night the command post assembled what was left of itself in another cactus patch about fifteen miles behind its first position. Throughout the night, and for days afterward, tired men came straggling in afoot from the desert.

That night the Germans withdrew from the area they'd taken, and next morning we sent trucks back to bury the dead and tow out what damaged vehicles they could. But by next afternoon the battle was on again.

On the morning of the Germans' surprise break-through out of Faid Pass, I was up in the Ousseltia Valley with another contingent of our troops.

Word came to us about noon that the Germans were advancing upon Sbeitla from Faid. So I packed into my jeep and started alone on the familiar 85-mile drive south to Sbeitla. It was a bright day and everything seemed peaceful. I expected to see German planes as I neared Sbeitla, but there was none, and I drove into my cactus-patch destination about an hour before sundown. I checked in at the Intelligence tent to see what was going on, and found that things were dying down with the coming of dusk. So I pitched my tent and went to bed right after supper.

Next morning I got up before daylight and caught a ride, just after sunrise, with two officers going up to the new position of our forward command post. We drove very slowly, and all kept a keen eye on the sky. I didn't have a gun, as correspondents are not supposed to carry arms. Occasionally we stopped the jeep and got far off the road behind some cactus hedges, but the German dive bombers were interested only in our troop concentrations far ahead.

Finally we spotted a small cactus patch about half a mile off the road. We figured this was the new home of the forward command post, and it was. The cactus patch covered about two acres. In it were hidden half a dozen half-tracks, a couple of jeeps, three light tanks, and a couple of motorcycles—all that was left of the impressive array of the traveling headquarters that had fled Sidi bou Zid eighteen hours before.

The commanding general had already gone forward again, in a tank, to participate in the day's coming battle. The remainder of the command post were just sitting around on the ground. Half their comrades were missing. There was nothing left for them to work with, nothing to do.

When I came into this cactus patch the officers that I knew, and had left only four days before, jumped up and shook hands as if we hadn't seen each other in years. Enlisted men did the same thing. I thought this was odd, at first, but before long I knew how they felt. They had been away—far along on the road that doesn't come back—and now that they were still miraculously alive it was like returning from a voyage of many years, and naturally we shook hands.

Captain Jed Dailey of Sharon, Massachusetts, got back safely in his jeep after the German break-through, but he had a horrible time. He was beating it to the rear across the desert, along with the rest of the command post's personnel, when suddenly he saw a Mark IV tank staring him in the face not a hundred yards away. The tank was stopped, the crew had the turret door open, and a German was just standing there, looking at Captain Dailey as cold as ice. It was enough to give a man the creeps.

Jed swung the jeep around—and there was another Mark IV staring at him. He kept turning and dodging, but everywhere he turned he was looking smack at the front end of a Mark IV. They just seemed to appear from nowhere, and there they were suddenly, until he felt like a mouse trying to get out of a roomful of silent cats.

Finally Jed did the only thing left to do. He took his heart in his hand and drove right between two German tanks, with their crews sitting there at the guns and looking at him as he passed fifty yards away. They didn't shoot, and to this day he doesn't know why they didn't.

He stepped on that jeep and went soaring across the desert, flying over irrigation ditches normally crossed in low gear. German artillery got after him. They dropped an 88 on his right, and then one on his left, and then one in front of him. They had him pocketed. When artillery does that, the next shot always finishes the job. But they never fired a fourth shell. He had no idea why. It was a kind of miracle.

Finally it got dark, and a sort of safety came. But it wasn't complete safety, for German patrols were out scouring the desert for stragglers. Jed finally got away by driving the jeep straight up over the top of a mountain and down the other side. He just missed driving over several sheer cliffs. From then on he hated Germans. He swore he would get the German who was probably sleeping in his bedroll. Jed also lost his camera and a dozen rolls of film he had been taking for months. One of them was a foolish picture, the sort in which the soberest of adults sometimes indulges. He had picked some desert flowers, stuck them behind his ears, and posed for the camera making a silly face. "The Germans will develop those films for what information they can get," he said. "And when they come to the one of an American officer with flowers behind his ears, they'll probably tell Goebbels to put it out on the radio that Americans are sissies."

Most of the men who survived the Germans' surprise breakthrough on that first day of the Sbeitla battle lost everything they had. Major "Satch" Elkins came out with only the clothes on his back. But he resented most losing three hundred razor blades to the Germans.

One soldier was sore because the day before he had overcome his inertia and accomplished the job of writing six long overdue letters home. But the Germans captured them, and he had that writing job to do all over again.

Another soldier told me his most vivid impression of the afternoon was seeing ten brand-new tires burning up on the wheels of a huge American truck. "With rubber so short at home, and tires rationed," he said, "it seemed awful to see those brand-new ones burning."

"Why, you damn' fool," a pal of his jeered. "Here's the sky full of planes, and the country full of tanks, and 88s dropping all around you, and you're worrying about tires!"

Lieutenant Colonel George Sutherlin of Shreveport, Louisiana, and Lieutenant Robert Simons, Jr., of Columbus, Ohio, walked twenty-nine miles across the desert that night. They had a compass, and it saved them. We had been talking about them while they were missing. "George will show up," one officer said. "I'll bet any amount of money on it. Hell, the Germans will turn him loose after two days, to get rid of him before he talks them to death."

And show up he did. He and Junior Simons said they considered the compass the most valuable piece of equipment the army issued. They had one horrible experience that night, though. An Arab they encountered in the desert ran them almost into the hands of a German patrol. They escaped only by lying deathly still, hardly breathing, for an hour, while the Germans hunted within a few yards of them. But another Arab balanced the account by getting out of bed to give them drinking water. They were so thirsty that they didn't take time to purify it with the pills they carried, but when last I saw them they were still feeling fine.

Most men who walked to safety through the desert that night and the following night were helped by Arabs. I've heard of only two cases where Arabs refused to help Americans. One put "Satch" Elkins into a ditch, and covered him with a long rope from a well, and another Arab walked twenty-five miles leading some enlisted men to safety. Many soldiers traded their overcoats for Arab burnooses to disguise themselves. There was much discussion of the Arabs among our men, and the average soldier seemed to have a feeling that an Arab couldn't be trusted as far as you could throw him by the tail of his burnoose. But figures don't lie, and the statistics of those awful nights of fleeing, crawling and hiding from death show that Arabs were ninety-nine per cent with us. Many hundreds of grateful Americans wouldn't be alive today if the Arabs hadn't helped them.

During the next few hours there in the cactus patch I listened to dozens of personal escape stories. Every time I got within earshot of another officer or enlisted man he'd begin telling what had happened to him the day before. Talk about having to pull stories out of people—I couldn't keep these guys from talking. There was something pathetic and terribly touching about it. Not one of them had ever thought he'd see the dawn, but he had seen it and his emotions had to pour out. And since I was the only newcomer to show up since their escape, I made a perfect sounding board.

The minute a man started talking he began drawing lines on the ground with his shoe or a stick, to show the roads and how he came. I'll bet I had that battleground scratched in the sand for me fifty times during the forenoon. It got so I could hardly keep from laughing at the consistency of their patterns.

By all rights, that morning should have been a newspaperman's dream. There were fantastic stories of escape, intimate recountings of fear and elation. Any one of them would have made a first-page feature story in any newspaper. Yet I was defeated by the flood of experiences. I listened until the stories finally became merged, overlapping and paralleling and contradicting, until the whole adventure became a composite, and today it is in my mind as in theirs a sort of generalized blur.

The sun came out warmly as if to soothe their jagged feelings, and one by one the men in the cactus patch stretched on the ground and fell wearily asleep at midday. And I, satiated with the adventures of the day, lay down and slept too, waiting for the new day's battle to begin.

When the Americans counterattacked during the battle of Sidi bou Zid, which eventually resulted in our withdrawal, I witnessed the biggest tank battle fought until then in that part of the world. I had a talk with the commanding general some ten miles behind the front lines before starting for the battle scene. He took me into his tent and showed me just what the battle plan was for the day. He picked out a point close to the expected battle area and said that would be a good place from which to watch. The only danger, he said, would be one of being encircled and cut off if the battle should go against us. "But it won't," he said, "for we are going to kick hell out of them today and we've got the stuff to do it with."

Unfortunately, we didn't kick hell out of them. In fact, the boot was on the other foot.

I spent the forenoon in the newly picked, badly shattered forward command post. All morning I tried to get on up where the tanks were but there was no transportation left around the post and their communications were cut off at noontime. We sat on the ground and ate some British crackers with jam and drank some hot tea. The day was bright and mellow. Shortly after lunch a young lieutenant dug up a spare jeep and said he'd take me on up to the front.

We drove a couple of miles east along a highway to a crossroads which was the very heart center of our troops' bivouacs. German airmen had been after this crossroads all morning. They had hit it again just a few minutes before we got there. In the road was a large crater and a few yards away a tank was off to one side, burning.

The roads at that point were high and we could see a long way. In every direction was a huge semi-irrigated desert valley. It looked very much like the valley at Phoenix, Arizona—almost treeless with patches of wild growth, shoulder-high cactus of the prickly pear variety. The valley was spotted with cultivated fields and the tiny square stucco houses of Arab farmers, and the whole vast scene was bounded with slightly rolling big mountains in the distance.

As far as we could see, out across the desert in all four sections of the "pie" formed by the intersecting roads, was American equipment—tanks, half-tracks, artillery, infantry—hundreds, yes, thousands of vehicles extending miles and miles and everything standing still. We were in time; the battle had not yet started.

We put our jeep in superlow gear and drove out across the sands among the tanks. Ten miles or so east and southeast were the Germans but there was no activity anywhere, no smoke on the horizon, no planes in the sky. It all had the appearance of an after-lunch siesta, but no one was asleep.

As we drove past tank after tank, we found each crew at its post inside—the driver at his control, the commander standing with his head sticking out of the open turret door, standing there silent and motionless, just looking ahead like the Indian on the calendars.

We stopped and inquired of several what they were doing. They said they didn't know what the plan was—they were merely ready in place and waiting for orders. Somehow it seemed like the cars lined up at Indianapolis just before the race starts—their weeks of training over, everything mechanically perfect, just a few quiet minutes of immobility before the great struggle for which they had waited so long.

Suddenly out of this siestalike doze the order came. We didn't hear it for it came to the tanks over their radios but we knew it quickly, for all over the desert tanks began roaring and pouring out blue smoke from the cylinders: Then they started off, kicking up dust and clanking in that peculiar "tank sound" we had all come to know so well. They poured around us, charging forward. They weren't close together—probably a couple of hundred yards apart. There weren't lines or any specific formation. They were just everywhere. They covered the desert to the right and left, ahead and behind as far as we could see, trailing their eager dust tails behind. It was almost as if some official starter had fired his blank pistol. The battle was on.

We were in the midst of the forward-rushing tanks, but didn't know what the score was. So I pulled the jeep to the side, gradually easing a way out. We decided to get to a high spot and take a look at what was happening, before we got caught. We bounced over gullies and ditches, up the side of a rocky hill.

There—in a hidden gully—we found the commanding colonel, standing beside a radio half-track. We stood close enough to the radio to hear the voice of the battalion commander, who was leading the tank attack. At the same time, through binoculars, we watched the fantastic surge of caterpillar metal move forward amidst its own dust.

Far across the desert, in front of us, lay the town of Sidi bou Zid. Through the glasses we could see it only as a great oasis, whose green trees stood out against the bare brown of the desert. On beyond were high hills, where some of our troops were still trapped after the surprise attack of the day before.

Behind our tanks, leading the attack, other armored vehicles puffed blue smoke. New formations began to move forward swiftly. The artillery went first, followed by armored infantry in half-tracks and even in jeeps. The entire desert was surging in one gigantic movement.

Over the radio came the voice of the battalion commander: "We're in the edge of Sidi bou Zid, and have struck no opposition yet."

This peaceful report from our tank charge brought no comment from anyone around the command truck. Faces were grave: it wasn't right—this business of no opposition at all; there must be a trick in it somewhere. . . .

Suddenly, brown geysers of earth and smoke began to spout. We watched through our glasses. Then, from far off, came the sound of explosions. Again the voice from the radio: "We're getting shelled, but can't make out where it's coming from." Then a long silence, while the geysers continued to burst . . . "I'm not sure, but I think it's artillery along the road north of town . . . Now there is some from the south."

We looked, and could see through our glasses the enemy advancing. They were far away, perhaps ten miles—narrow little streaks of dust, like plumes, speeding down the low sloping plain from the mountain base toward the oasis of Sidi bou Zid. We could not see the German tanks, only dust plumes extending and pushing forward.

Just then I realized we were standing on the very hill the general had picked out for me on his map that morning. It was not good enough. I said to the young lieutenant, "Let's get on up there."

"I'm ready," he replied.

So we got into the jeep, and went leaping and bounding up toward what was—but we didn't know it then—the most ghastly armored melee that had occurred until then in Tunisia.

It was odd, the way we went up into the thick of the battle in our jeep. We didn't attach ourselves to anybody. We didn't ask anybody if we could go. We just started the motor and went. Vehicles ahead of us had worn a sort of track across the desert and through irrigated fields. We followed that awhile, keeping our place in the forward-moving procession. We were just a jeep with two brown-clad figures in it, indistinguishable from the rest.

The line was moving cautiously. Every now and then the procession would stop. A few times we stopped too. We shut off our motor to listen for planes. But, finally, we tired of the slow progress. We dashed out across the sand and the Arabs' plowed fields, skirting cactus fences and small farmyards. As we did this, a sensation of anxiety—which had not touched me before—came over me. It was fear of mines in the freshly dug earth; one touch of a wheel and we could so easily be blown into little bits. I spoke of this to the lieutenant, but he said he didn't think they had had time to plant mines. I thought to myself, Hell, it doesn't take all night to plant a mine.

We did not—it is obvious to report—hit any mines.

The battlefield was an incongruous thing. Always there was some ridiculous impingement of normalcy on a field of battle. There on that day it was the Arabs. They were herding their camels, just as usual. Some of them continued to plow their fields. Children walked along, driving their little sack-laden burros, as tanks and guns clanked past them. The sky was filled with planes and smoke burst from screaming shells.

As we smashed along over a field of new grain, which pushed its small shoots just a few inches above earth, the asinine thought popped into my head: I wonder if the army got permission to use this land before starting the attack.

Both sides had crossed and recrossed those farms in the past twenty-four hours. The fields were riddled by deep ruts and by wide spooky tracks of the almost mythical Mark IV tanks. Evidence of the previous day's battle was still strewn across the desert. We passed charred half-tracks. We stopped to look into a burned-out tank, named Texas, from which a lieutenant-colonel friend of mine and his crew had demolished four German tanks before being put out of commission themselves.

We passed a trailer still full of American ammunition, which had been abandoned. The young lieutenant wanted to hook our own jeep to it as a tow when we returned, but I talked him out of it. I feared the Germans had booby-trapped it during the night.

We moved on closer to the actual tank battle ahead, but never went right into it—for in a jeep that would have been a fantastic form of suicide. We stopped, I should judge, about a mile behind the foremost tanks.

Behind us the desert was still alive with men and machines moving up. Later we learned that some German tanks had maneuvered in behind us, and were shooting up our half-tracks and jeeps. But, fortunately, we didn't know that at the time.

Light American tanks came up from the rear and stopped near us. They were to be held there in reserve, in case they had to be called into the game in this league which was much too heavy and hot for them. Their crews jumped out the moment they stopped, and began digging foxholes against the inevitable arrival of the dive bombers.

Soon the dive bombers came. They set fires behind us. American and German tanks were burning ahead of us. Our planes came over, too, strafing and bombing the enemy.

One of our half-tracks, full of ammunition, was livid red, with flames leaping and swaying. Every few seconds one of its shells would go off, and the projectile would tear into the sky with a weird whang-zing sort of noise. Field artillery had stopped just on our right. They began shelling the German artillery beyond our tanks. It didn't take long for the Germans to answer. The scream of an approaching shell is an appalling thing. We could hear them coming. Then we could see the dust kick up a couple of hundred yards away. The shells hit the ground and ricocheted like armor-piercing shells, which do not explode but skip along the ground until they finally lose momentum or hit something.

War has its own peculiar sounds. They are not really very much different from sounds in the world of peace. But they clothe themselves in an unforgettable fierceness, just because born in danger and death. The clank of a starting tank, the scream of a shell through the air, the ever-rising whine of fiendishness as a bomber dives—these sounds have their counterparts in normal life, and a person would be hard put to distinguish them in a blindfold test. But, once heard in war, they are never forgotten.

The memory of them comes back in a thousand ways—in the grind of a truck starting in low gear, in high wind around the eaves, in somebody merely whistling a tune. Even the sound of a shoe, dropping to the floor in a hotel room overhead, becomes indistinguishable from the faint boom of a big gun far away. A mere rustling curtain can paralyze a man with memories.

The night after our tank defeat at Sidi bou Zid I drove back to our cactus patch near Sbeitla. There I pitched my shelter tent at the same hole where I had dug in a couple of nights before. Things were tense around the command post. Nobody quite knew what the day's score was, for full reports hadn't come in. It seemed that we would try to stand on a new line around Sbeitla. Our cactus patch was two miles west.

There was artillery fire east of Sbeitla when I went to bed. I didn't expect we would get much sleep, and we didn't. At one o'clock in the morning Corporal William Nikolin shook my bedroll aside, and aroused the whole camp. He told me to get my jeep packed, ready to go. A guy is awfully sleepy in the middle of a cold night, even in wartime. I peeked out and saw that the headquarters commandant's tent was not down yet. I knew I could get my little tent down and packed faster than he could, so I rolled over and just lay there—too dopey to have sense enough to be excited.

In about ten minutes, when Corporal Nikolin came back, he said just five words, "German tanks are in Sbeitla."

Brother, I had that tent down and my jeep packed in world-record time. But still the final order to move didn't come. Everybody was ready, so we just stood around in the darkness, waiting. The cactus patch, and the empty holes where the tents had been, looked strange in the dim moonlight. Then, suddenly, a giant flame scorched up into the dark eastern sky. We had set off our gasoline dump. In a minute red flares began to shoot out from the glow—that was the ammunition dump.

We knew then it was all over at Sbeitla. All that ammunition that had traveled so far, at such expense and so much human toil—there it was, shooting off impotently into the sky, like a Fourth of July celebration. Shells exploded continuously. It sounded like a terrific battle. We watched, talking little, walking around to keep warm.

After a couple of hours the evacuation order still hadn't come. So I pulled my bedroll off the jeep, unrolled it on the ground beside the front wheels, crawled in and pulled the mackinaw over my head to keep the accumulating frost off my face. I never slept sounder in my life than during the next three hours.

When I awakened, it was just dawn. Trucks were rolling past the edge of our cactus patch. The continuous line headed out toward the highway. It seemed that we had started the withdrawal. Such things as kitchen trucks and supply trains went first.

Our combat teams were holding this side of Sbeitla, so there really was plenty of time. But we expected a terrific battle to develop right under our chins during the forenoon. The outlook seemed dark. A major I knew came past. He said, "Why don't you and I go to the toilet right now? We won't have another chance today." So we went.

With full daylight came the planes, just as we expected. But they were our planes that time. They were overhead all morning, and all afternoon. We had the sky that day.

Finally, it became obvious that our withdrawal was going to be accomplished without too much opposition from the Germans. The major and I would see another sunset after all.

Then word came that hard fighting was going on at Feriana, forty-five miles west. I forthwith started the jeep, waved a last good-bye downvalley at Sbeitla, and slipped into the slow stream of vehicles headed west. The day was miserably dark and cold. Just as I started it began to hail.

Yes, hail in Africa—even the skies pelting us in our retreat.

The withdrawal of our forces from the vast Sbeitla Valley, back through Kasserine Pass, was a majestic thing in a way. It continued without a break for twenty-four hours. It had no earmarks whatever of a retreat, it was carried out so calmly and methodically. It differed in no way, except size, from the normal daily convoys of troops and supplies. Vehicles were so well-spaced that it was not difficult for me to pass them on the wide gravel road. And, since I was not required to keep line, I could go forward and back to get a good view of the entire movement.

So far as I have heard, the Germans did not do a single road-strafing job on our withdrawing columns. They missed a magnificent opportunity. Why they didn't try is still a mystery to me.

Our great brown vehicles rumbled past—one about every thirty seconds—for twenty-four hours. First, before daylight, came the kitchen trucks and engineers to prepare things ahead. Then came rolling guns, and some infantry to set up protection along the roads. Then the great vast bulk of long supply trains, field hospitals, command posts, ammunition wagons, infantry, artillery, and finally —when night came again—the tanks started and moved on until the next dawn. The whole thing was completely motorized. Nobody was walking.

It simply could not have been done better. Military police patrolled the road with jeeps and motorcycles to see that there was no passing, no traffic jamming, no loitering. Not many of our American trucks broke down; and those that did were immediately taken in tow. There were almost no accidents.

It was hard to realize, being a part of it, that it was a retreat— that American forces in large numbers were retreating in foreign battle, one of the few times in our history. We couldn't help feeling a slight sense of humiliation. Yet, while it was happening, that humiliation was somewhat overcome by our pride in the orderliness of the accomplishment.

The withdrawal from Feriana and Thelepte airdrome was separate, and smaller than ours. They were evacuated in the dawn hours. Ammunition dumps were set off, and all gasoline that could not be moved was set ablaze. Planes that took off that morning on dawn missions did not return to the field but landed elsewhere. All planes that could not get off the ground, because of minor damage or needed repair, were burned.

There never was anything built aboveground at Thelepte, because the field had to take too much bombing. Everything was underground—offices, sleeping quarters, and the rest. Nothing showed aboveground, except the planes themselves and the little knee-high mounds that were dugout roofs.

One officer, just as he left, tacked on his dugout door a big newspaper map of the latest Russian line, so the Germans could see it when they came.

There were French civilian refugees on our road, but not enough to hinder traffic. Most of them walked, carrying brown suitcases and bundles. I noticed they did not carry much, so they apparently had faith in our coming back. There were few Arabs in the stream. The Arabs usually stayed put. They get along, whoever comes to take charge of their country.

French artillery and infantry also were withdrawing. They did hinder traffic, after we were safely back to Kasserine Pass and the road grew narrow and poor. Across the soft sand French horses and horse-drawn ammunition carts by thousands lined the roads. We well knew the French were the best fighters in the world. But this delaying stream of high-wheeled carts, toiling along so last-century-like, seemed symbolic of France's whole disaster. The big fine French hospital just outside Kasserine was evacuated too, and the French supervisor gave away everything he had to American soldiers.

I chatted with one soldier—Sergeant Donald Schiavone, 666 Fourth Avenue, Brooklyn—who had just been given an alarm clock, a silver letter opener, a basket of eggs, three dozen olives, and a bottle of peach brandy. A truckful of soldiers passed as we were talking. Seeing the bottle, they began yelling at Schiavone, who apparently had no hoarder's blood in his veins. He ran after the truck and gave his bottle to the other soldiers.

That little everyday episode is an example of how unflustered, how unretreatlike our retreat was.

You folks at home must have been disappointed at what happened to our American troops in those Tunisian battles. So were we over here. Our predicament was damned humiliating, as General Joe Stilwell said about our getting kicked out of Burma the year before. We lost a great deal of equipment, many American lives, and valuable time and territory—to say nothing of face. Yet no one over here had the slightest doubt that the Germans would be thrown out of Tunisia. It was simply in the cards.

It was even possible that our defeat would not postpone Rommel's exodus, for actually our troops formed only a small part of the total Allied forces in Tunisia. Estimates among men at the front ran anywhere from two to six months for finishing the Tunisian campaign. (This was late February.)

One thing you folks at home must realize is that the Tunisian business up to then was mainly a British show. Our part in it was small. Consequently, our defeat was not so disastrous to the whole picture as it would have been if we had been bearing the major portion of the task.

We Americans did the North African landings and got all the credit, although the British did help us. The British were doing the Tunisia job and would get the credit, though we were giving them a hand. That was the way it had been planned all the time. That was the way it would be carried out. And it would really be the British who would run Rommel out of Tunisia.

The fundamental cause of our trouble over here lay in two things: we had too little to work with, as usual, and we underestimated Rommel's strength and especially his audacity.

Both military men and correspondents knew we were too thinly spread in our sector to hold if the Germans were really to launch a big-scale attack. Where everybody was wrong was in believing they didn't have the stuff to do it with.

Personally, I feel that some such setback as that—tragic though it was for many Americans, for whom it would always be too late— was not entirely a bad thing for us. It was all right to have a good opinion of ourselves, but we Americans were so smug with our cockiness. We somehow felt that just because we were Americans we could whip our weight in wildcats. And we had got it into our heads that production alone would win the war.

There were two things we had still to learn: we would have to spread ourselves thicker on the front lines and we would have to streamline our commands for quick and positive action in emergencies.

As for our soldiers themselves, you need not have felt any shame or concern about their ability. I saw them in battle and afterward and there was nothing wrong with the American soldier. His fighting spirit was good. His morale was okay. The deeper he got into a fight the more of a fighting man he became.

I saw crews that had had two tanks shot out from under them but whose only thought was to get a third tank and "have another crack at those blankety-blanks."

It is true they were not such seasoned battle veterans as the British and Germans. But they had had some battle experience before that last encounter, and I don't believe their so-called greenness was the cause of our defeat. One good man simply can't whip two good men. That's about the only way I know to put it. Everywhere on every front we needed more stuff before we could start going forward instead of backward.

11. SIDELIGHTS

The central part of Tunisia is a sandy-colored, desertlike country. It is made up of mountain ridges with wide, flat, fertile valleys between them. The ridges have fir trees high up, but the valleys are without vegetation except for the crops and a knee-high growth of bush. Consequently, the valleys were poor places for hiding big motorized troop concentrations. About the only thing that afforded any natural cover was an olive grove or a cactus patch.

Some of the cactus grew wild, and some of it was planted in rows just like any other crop. The plants were shoulder-high, and had big thick leaves of the prickly-pear type, with thorns an inch long, vicious and cruel. The cactus was grown for camel feed, and I actually saw camels eating the leaves off the bush. How they did it I don't know, for the stickers were as hard as steel needles, and they didn't bend. But the camels didn't seem to mind.

The soldiers learned to tread cautiously through a cactus patch, for those stickers could cause grave trouble. They frequently started bad infections. I saw a soldier one day being taken to the rear with his arm swollen so badly he had to carry it on a sort of rack. And I myself had a small experience with them. I'd noticed for several days that my right knee was so sore I could hardly put any weight on it when I got down to tie up my bedroll. But I supposed I'd just bruised it on a rock, and didn't pay much attention. It wasn't until I returned to the city and took off my clothes for the first time in weeks that I saw an angry-looking lump on my knee. So, like a country boy, I squeezed it and out popped a cactus thorn half an inch long.

In a day or two the soreness was gone. Anybody else would probably have lost his leg, but I was leading such a pure life that my blood was clear and strong.

146

The soldiers all laughed when I started out to battle armed only with a shovel. That does seem a ridiculous instrument to carry to the wars, but I'd figured the thing all out ahead of time. My calculations were verified when I got up front where the boys actually knew what the zing of a bullet sounded like. None of them laughed then. Because, brother, when you are up there where the dive bombers play, digging becomes instinctive.

I've heard of dive-bombings so severe that soldiers lying in shallow trenches would try to dig deeper with their fingernails. And I know of many a man who is alive today because he happened to be near an empty foxhole some previous warrior had dug. Long live the shovel!

There are some unusual people in the American Army. For instance, I knew a corporal who could recite the Versailles Treaty by heart, and also could quote from memory every important military treaty since the Franco-Prussian War. That man was Corporal William Nikolin, of 1105 West New York Street, Indianapolis. Nick was twenty-eight and had a gold tooth. He had lived fourteen years in America and fourteen years in Europe, and he could talk the language of almost every country there. Although born in America, he spoke English with quite an accent.

Nick studied journalism at Butler College and Columbia University. Then he went on to Europe, and took an M.A. degree in political history at Belgrade University. For six years he worked on various European newspapers. He knew the Balkans intimately, and his manner of thinking was really more Balkan than American.

In 1939 Nick returned to America, because he saw the war coming and he wanted no part of it. He was disillusioned and sad over the state of things. He resolved he would never return to Europe under any circumstances. He turned his back. And then he was drafted, and there he was headed right back for the old stamping grounds. But by then he was glad to go. He made an excellent soldier, and was outstandingly conscientious. He could be of great value when our armies got onto the Continent. But Nick saw further than that. He wanted to be a part of the peace building. He wanted to get his discharge on this side, and stay on to cover the peace conferences. He felt himself especially equipped for the job.

In addition to his other duties, he was a sort of personal assistant for two officers—Major Charles Miller of Detroit and Captain Tony Lumpkin of Mexico, Missouri. Nick looked after them as if they were babies. They had a tent buried in the ground with a kerosene stove in it, and every night just before bedtime they heated up some beans and made some chocolate and called Nick in, and then they all sat there and ate and drank and discussed the world.

We correspondents have many little memories of the Central Valley in Tunisia. I remember one night, for instance, when four of us were eating supper with Colonel Edson Raff, the famous paratroop leader, and his young adjutant, Lieutenant Jack Pogue. It was my first meeting with Raff, and I felt some awe of him, but he was so attentive that I soon got over that. Raff and Pogue were both dressed in the paratroop uniform and carried their tommy guns with them. Tanks clanked and rumbled by constantly outside the door, shaking the ground and the building itself, and making the candles dance on the table.

Lieutenant Pogue and I got to talking, and it turned out he lived just over the hill from me in New Mexico. He was from Estancia, in the valley behind Albuquerque, only about forty miles away. So there in the Tunisian desert we did a couple of hours' reminiscing about our own special desert back home.

The very first time I ever pitched my pup tent I had to have help, of course, for I didn't even know how to button the thing together. My assistant on that first venture was Sergeant Walter Hickey, of 401 76th Street, Brooklyn. He was a clerk before the war. Sergeant Hickey and I picked out a fairly level spot on a sloping mountainside and put up the tent under a fir tree, after pulling out a few shrubs to make a clear space. When we had the tent finished and staked down, I noticed the ground was crawling with ants. We had unwittingly opened up an enormous ant nest in the loose soil when we pulled up the shrubs. So we had to take the whole tent down and pitch it under another tree.

It wasn't long, however, before I could put up my tent all by myself, in the dark, with a strong wind blowing and both hands tied behind my back.

We had a little incident with road strafing one day. Three soldiers were riding in a jeep when strafers came diving. The soldier in the back seat was riding backwards so he could keep a watch to the rear. The jeep took off across the fields, with the strafers after it. The rear guard kept calling "Right" or "Left" to indicate which way the driver should turn to dodge. But finally it got too hot for the boys up front, and they just bailed out and left the jeep running. That left our hero alone, riding backwards in a driverless jeep, yelling "Right-Left" to nobody, while the bullets splattered around. Finally he looked around to see why the driver wasn't obeying. Then he too hit the dust.

We hardly ever heard Italian soldiers referred to as Italians. It was either "Eyeties" or "Wops" or "Guineas." In one case the reason for abandoning "Italian" was a concrete one. A mountain lookout reported that "Three Italians" were coming up the hill. The officer who heard it thought the man had said "three battalions" and ordered a heavy barrage dropped in that area. When the lookout called back to ask why such heavy shooting, the misunderstanding was straightened out. From then on, all men in that outfit were instructed to refer to Italians as "Guineas."

I saw the tragic remnants of a jeep that got a direct hit from a 500-pound German bomb. Three soldiers were in it, and they were blown to disintegration. Nothing was found of them to bury. But searchers did find scattered coins, knives, and bits of clothing. One soldier had a pocket Bible, and about half of its sheets were found. Another had a large pad of currency—bills just folded over once. Those bills were blown together with such force that it was impossible to get them apart. We couldn't even strip off one bill with a pocketknife. The blast had vulcanized them together, without tearing any holes in them.

Little things come to mean much in wartime. At the front I was the only person I knew who had a can opener, and it was in constant demand. I had to carry it in my coverall pocket to keep it from being stolen. Somebody swiped my comb one day. Stealing ceased to be just stealing when something a man needed badly was taken. I never stole anything, but I wouldn't have put it past me under favorable circumstances.

I had a pair of fingernail scissors with me, and one day I lent it six times to soldiers who were just passing and asked if I had any nail clippers or scissors. Cold water and cold weather were hard on hands, fingers got hard and cracked around the nails.

Our troops did manage to look fairly clean and presentable, even though sanitary facilities were skimpy. The Air Forces allowed their soldiers to grow beards, but the rest of the army didn't. Consequently, the men had to shave regardless of how inconvenient it might be.

A soldier becomes eminently practical in wartime. A chaplain, after he had gone through the pockets of ten Americans killed in battle, said the chief thing he found was toilet paper. Careless soldiers who were caught without such preparedness had to use twenty-franc notes.

Everything was so scarce we always took anything that was offered us whether we needed it or not. I took a proffered cigarette while already smoking one. I drank wine, which I detest, just because somebody was sharing his bottle. I had no shame about accepting candy, cigarettes, clothing or anything else anybody offered. We all learned to live on the policy which Colonel Raff put in these words: "I never refuse anything."

If somebody had offered me a bottle of castor oil I would have accepted it and hidden it away.

Soldiers at the front were good about sharing whatever they had. The average soldier when he had a windfall and got a package of candy from home doled it out to his friends. It was share and share alike for times were tough.

Late one night I was bedding down as a transient visitor in a front-line American hospital. Just before bedtime a soldier came past and introduced himself and asked if I would like some fruitcake. I didn't especially care for any fruitcake but as I have mentioned I never refuse anything so I went along with him and ate three pieces of fruitcake and half a pound of chocolate candy before going to bed.

The soldier was Corporal Lester Gray, of 2443 Farwell Avenue, Chicago. He had been married two years. The fruitcake we ate was made by his wife. It was, incidentally, the first one she ever made. Her success with it apparently went to her head, for Corporal Gray said five more like it were on the way.

Gray was a laboratory technician with the hospital. Before the war he had been a salesman for a wholesale jewelry concern. Ever since he had landed in Africa he had kept a steady flow of letters going back to every one of his old customers. How's that for salesmanship?

One day in an olive grove where some troops were camped, I saw a beautiful German shepherd dog nosing around. It turned out that the soldiers had brought her all the way from America. Our soldiers in Africa picked up literally thousands and thousands of dogs as pets, but that was one of the few I had heard of that came all the way from home.

Originally she had belonged to Sergeant Edward Moody of Minneapolis, who was killed in an accident. After his death the whole battery adopted her as a mascot. She had been on two long convoy trips, had served in Ireland and England, and had been in several battles on the Tunisian front. She had eight pups on the way down from England.

Her name was "Lady." She was only three weeks old when the soldiers got her, so her entire life had been spent with men in uniform. She was suspicious of civilians, and a person in civilian clothes couldn't make up to her. Despite her martial career, Lady was afraid of gunfire. She got the trembles when the big guns began to thunder. The boys hoped she would get over it and go charging right along with them into battle.

I came across another dog that came all the way from America. He was a black-and-white springer spaniel, and he sprang from the dog pound at St. Petersburg, Florida. Two pilots originally had him —Lieutenant Richard East, of East Orange, New Jersey, and Lieutenant Harold Taft, of Jeffersonville, Indiana. They named him Duckworth, after the third member of their original flying-school trio —Lieutenant John Stewart Duckworth of Boston. Duckworth had taken off in seven different kinds of airplanes. He had flown across the Atlantic, and twice across Africa, and once up and once down Africa. He loved to fly.

I heard of one pilot who had a pet cat that burst its eardrums on its first flight and became stone deaf. But the boys stuffed cotton in Duckworth's ears and he was O.K. He had a little ritual of always running around to the left wheel the moment he got out of a plane, and paying a little formal call on Mother Nature.

The dog's namesake, Lieutenant Duckworth, was then at Randolph Field, Texas, fretting because he wasn't overseas in combat. The dog's co-owner, Lieutenant East, was one of those who never came back from a Tunisian mission. So Duckworth finally belonged only to Lieutenant Taft, who humored him and cussed him and was very proud of him.

He said Duckworth was the biggest ladies' man in Africa.

One night I ate dinner with eight Air Force officers in the little hotel at Feriana. At the only other table in the dining room was a bunch of French officers. We ate and made a lot of noise, and they ate and made a lot of noise, and neither table paid any attention to the other.

When we were about through eating some of the Americans started singing. I will have to say they were probably the worst singers I had ever heard. They were so bad they finally just sort of bogged down, and we all laughed at ourselves.

Seeing that, the French raised their glasses to us in toast—a tribute for a good try, I suppose. Then we toasted back, and they stood up, and we stood up, and we toasted each other back and forth till everybody was embarrassed. Finally the French relieved the tension by saying they'd like to sing a song for us. And could they sing! It was like a professional glee club. Three of them were wounded veterans of the last war and covered with medals. One looked like an escapee from Devil's Island. One was a chaplain. He was just a youth but he had a ferocious long beard and a bass voice like Singin' Sam of the radio.

Those Frenchmen sang for an hour. Not ordinary songs, but fighting regimental songs and catchy tunes with an almost jungle-like rhythm. The coal-oil lamp threw shadows on their faces, and it was truly an Old World scene out of a book.

The touching part was just at the last, when the officer who looked like Devil's Island came over and told us the reason for the gathering. Their outfit had gone into the lines two weeks before. That day they had come out. Those who survived were having a reunion, eating and drinking and singing for the ones who did not come back. Twenty-five had gone into the lines. Eleven were at the dinner.

American tent hospitals in the battle area were favorite hangouts for correspondents. The presence of American nurses was alleged to have nothing whatever to do with it. At one hospital three correspondents just moved in and made it their headquarters for a couple of weeks. They roamed the country in their jeeps during the day, then returned to the hospital at night just as if it were a hotel.

There were two favorite hospitals where I dropped in now and then for a meal or a night. The first was the one where the other boys stayed—which was always kept some eighty miles or more back of the fighting. That was the one staffed largely from Roosevelt Hospital in New York. The other was a mobile surgical hospital, which was usually only about an hour's drive back of the fighting. That was the hospital that landed at Arzeu on the day of the North African occupation, and whose nurses were the first ashore in North Africa.

Mary Ann Sullivan, of Boston, of whom I have made mention, was in that outfit. Some of the other girls I knew were Mildred Keelin, of 929 Ellison Avenue, Louisville, Kentucky; Amy Nichols, of Blythe, Georgia; Mary Francis of Waynesville, North Carolina; Eva Sacks, of 1821 North 33rd Street, Philadelphia; Kate Rodgers, of 2932 Wroxton Avenue, Houston, Texas.

Like the soldiers, they thought and talked constantly of home, and would have liked to be there. Yet it was just as Amy Nichols said— she wouldn't have gone home if they had told her she could. All the others felt the same way, practically one hundred per cent.

They were terrifically proud of having been the first nurses to land in Africa, and of being continually the closest ones to the fighting lines, and they intended to stay. They were actually in little danger, except from deliberate or accidental bombing.

Major General Terry Allen was one of my favorite people. Partly because he didn't give a damn for hell or high water; partly because he was more colorful than most; and partly because he was the only general outside the Air Forces I could call by his first name.

If there was one thing in the world Allen lived and breathed for, it was to fight. He had been all shot up in the last war, and he seemed not the least averse to getting shot up again. This was no intellectual war with him. He hated Germans and Italians like vermin, and his pattern for victory was simple: just wade in and murder the hell out of the low-down, good-for-nothing so-and-so's. Allen's speech was picturesque. No writer could fully capture him on paper, because his talk was so wonderfully profane it couldn't be put down in black and white.

Allen was shot through the jaw in the last war. That wound causes him to make an odd hissing noise when he is intense. He breathes by sucking the air in between his teeth, and it sounds like a leak in a tire. That reverse hissing will doubtless confuse the Japs when he gets around to their part of the world.

It was General Allen's outfit that took Oran, in the original landings. Then it was necessary to hold his troops there, and for a couple of months Allen not-so-quietly went nuts sitting back in an Oran olive grove watching the war from a distance. Finally he couldn't stand it any longer, so he went to the high command and said, "Is this a private war, or can anybody get in?" At least that's the way the legend goes, and it sounds like him. At any rate, Allen got in and was forthwith as happy as a lark.

After he went to the front I drove over to visit him. When I finally found him he said, "Don't bother to pitch your tent. You sleep in my tent tonight."

An invitation from a general was an order, so I carried my bedroll up to the general's tent and looked in. There was one bedroll on the ground. That took up half the tent. The other half was occupied by a five-gallon tin of water sitting on some rocks over a gasoline flame on the ground, and by a rough, unpainted folding table.

I couldn't figure out where he expected me to sleep. But it was all solved that evening by the general's orderly, who simply carried out the water can, smothered the fire with sand, moved the table, and unrolled my bedroll on the ground beside the general's.

As far as I know, Terry Allen was the only general in Tunisia who slept on the ground. All the others carried folding cots. General Allen wouldn't allow any of his staff to sleep on a cot. He said if everybody in his headquarters had a cot it would take several extra trucks to carry them and he could use the trucks to better purpose. He liked to fight rough anyway.

Allen is an old cavalryman. He still wears his high-laced cavalry boots when he dresses up. He is known as one of the best polo players in the army. He hadn't any horse to ride in Africa, but he kept in shape by doing a three-mile after-breakfast jog on foot through the hills several times a week. He smoked incessantly. He is married to an El Paso girl, and calls El Paso home. He carried pictures of his wife and fifteen-year-old son in a leather pocket case, and was tremendously proud of them.

I went out on a shooting expedition that night with some of Allen's men, and it was midnight when I got back. He had left the light on for me, and the wind was making the tent heave and groan, but Allen was sleeping like a child.

Dirt blew in and filtered over us. My bedroll was right over where the fire had been, and I slept warmly for the first time in weeks. Toughly trained sentries with itchy fingers stood at the front and rear of our tent. Boy, did I feel protected!

At seven next morning one of the sentries came in and awakened General Allen, who grunted and went back to sleep. Five minutes later another sentry came in, knelt over him and kept saying, "General, sir, general, sir" till Allen responded and started to get up.

I had slept in all my clothes; the general in his long underwear. We were both covered with sifted dirt from the windstorm. It took us about thirty seconds to dress, and then we just walked out of the tent and went to breakfast, without washing or anything.

That's how life was for one general at the front.

12. DESERT SORTIE

UNTIL January of 1943 most of the American fighting in North Africa had been in the mountains, and Americans saw little of the real desert. But they would sooner or later, so I jumped at the chance to go along on a sortie far into the Sahara, just to see what it would be like.

There were fifteen of us in two big ten-wheeled trucks. We took our bedding rolls and enough rations for five days. The purpose of the trip was to salvage the parts from some airplanes that had made crash landings in the desert. Our trip was to take us within twenty miles of German outposts. We weren't much afraid of being captured, but we were afraid of being strafed by German planes.

We started one morning, and made a French desert garrison at lunchtime. We got out tins of corned beef, sweet potatoes, peas, orange marmalade and hardtack. The French soldiers built a nice little fire for us to heat water for tea. They cleared off a table in one of their barracks rooms, and did everything they could do for us.

For months I had been carrying around some cigars I got on the boat coming from England, waiting for a propitious moment to give them away. So when we left I gave some to the French soldiers, and they were delighted. They all lit up right away, and puffed and held the cigars off and looked at them approvingly, as if they were diamonds.

After we left, our soldiers kept talking about how nice the French were to us, and how they didn't have much but whatever they had they'd give us the best. The Americans liked the French, and everywhere we went the French were grand to us.

That French garrison gave us one of its Arab enlisted men as a guide. He was a picturesque figure, rather handsome in his white turban, blue sash and khaki smock. He carried a long knife and a long-barreled rifle. He spoke no English whatever, and no French that we could understand. He said "wah" to everything we asked him.

He knew the way all right, but the communication system between him and us needed some improvement. All we ever got out of him was "wah." We finally nicknamed him Wah, and before the trip was over we were all saying "wah" when we meant "yes."

What we saw of the Sahara didn't look exactly the way it does in the movies, but that's maybe because we didn't go far enough. The Sahara is more than a thousand miles wide, and we weren't in more than two hundred miles.

We saw nothing more spectacular than the country in the more remote parts of our own Southwest. Certainly it was beautiful. At one point it was so utterly flat and bare that we could have landed anywhere and said, "This is an airport."

At other places it had dry river beds, very wide, their bottoms strewn with rocks. That surprised us, for what was a river doing on a desert? Farther along the country was rolling, and covered with a scrublike vegetation. Parts of it were so exactly like the valley around Palm Springs, even down to the delicate smoke-tree bush, that it made me homesick. And one bare, tortured mountain could have been the one behind El Paso. Only once did we see a place with no vegetation at all, where the yellow sand was drifted movielike in great rippled dunes.

At long intervals we came to what was known locally as an oasis. I used to think an oasis was three palm trees with a ragged guy crawling toward them, his parched tongue hanging out. But in that part of the desert an oasis was a village or a city. It didn't have three palm trees; it had tens of thousands of them, forests of them, which made their owners rich from the bounteous crop of dates.

It had big adobe buildings like the Indian pueblos, and narrow streets and irrigation ditches, and hundreds of children running around. It was a big community, and getting to an oasis was like getting to Reno after Death Valley.

During most of our 200-mile journey the soil seemed to be dirt rather than sand, and the trucks swirled up a cloud of dust that was truly suffocating. The trucks were open, and we sat in the back ends on bedding rolls and boxes. We all wore goggles or dust glasses. Most of us hadn't shaved for days. Within half an hour everybody's whiskers were so caked with dust that we looked like a new kind of fur-bearing animal. It took days to get the dust out of our eyes and noses.

During the trip we ate a two-gallon can of hard stick candy, which the army issued. We talked some, but it was too rough and dusty to talk much.

We had our first sight of the famous Sahara mirages. Several times we all saw a long line of trees, straight and regular as though lining an avenue, about three miles away. Unfortunately they were sitting on top of a lake, and since trees don't grow on lakes and since there wasn't any lake anyhow, we figured we must be seeing things.

We met a few small camel trains when we first started, and we thought that was big stuff, seeing real camels on the desert. But before the trip was over we'd seen so many camels we didn't even look. They were as common as cattle are at home. The desert was full of them, grazing in herds. Always there was an Arab, often a child, tending them. The camels twisted their necks and looked at us as we went by. I'd never noticed it in circuses, but up close a camel's head and neck look just like a huge snake. And when a camel turns around and looks at me, it gives me the creeps. I don't think I shall lay plans for running a camel ranch after the war.

Often the Arab shepherds waved at us, and occasionally they gave us the V sign. But they were too far in the desert to have heard of the American "okay."

Once we saw a fox, or what looked like a fox, and one of the soldiers shot at it with his rifle. Again just at dusk we saw another, and there was a mad scramble for all the rifles lying on the floor. The fox got away, and I was thankful I didn't get shot myself, what with rifle barrels whisking past my nose in all directions.

On the first day we went through a large village that was built for camel traffic, and camels only. It was so narrow the truck scraped on both sides. I remarked that I hoped we wouldn't come to a right-angle turn in the street, and no sooner had I spoken than we did come to one. Well, not quite a right angle, or we couldn't have made it, but it was a jog of about twenty feet. It took us a quarter of an hour of backing and filling to get the trucks into position to make the turn.

Hundreds of Arabs came pouring out of the mud buildings, and we had a large and appreciative audience. One black-bearded old Arab with a wooden leg took charge of the free-advice department, and told the drivers in language they didn't understand just how to do it. They paid no attention.

No matter where or when we stopped an Arab would suddenly appear. He would stand around just looking unless we spoke to him, and then he would smile and try to answer. Several times we were stopped far out in the desert by white-gowned Arabs with long rifles slung over their shoulders. Apparently they were soldiers, although they looked and dressed like all the others.

The first night we continued to drive after dark. The moon was brilliant, and it gave the whole vast desert and the hills that dotted it a kind of ghostliness.

Suddenly the truck stopped and there around us were five Arabs out of nowhere, all gowned in white, and riding five beautiful white horses. Over their shoulders were slung the longest rifles I had ever

seen. In the half-light they did indeed seem romantic and like men of
mystery. They sat far back on their horses, and they could ride like
the wind. They spoke in low voices, almost in harmony with the
spookiness of the desert moonlight. I don't know what they said, but
it was obvious they were patrolling throughout the night in that
special part of the world which is their own, and which only they can
ever fully comprehend. If we had been Germans instead of Americans, I doubt that we would have gone any farther that night, or any
other night.

It was late at night when we finally arrived near where the wrecked
American planes were supposed to be. Our Arab friend Wah directed
us over a multitude of tracks, winding around through bare wraith-
like hills, to a little group of sand-colored buildings standing lonesomely in the moonlight. We stopped about five hundred yards
away, yelled, and waited. At last there was a shout from far off. We
shouted back, "Les Américains," and then we could see two figures
start toward us. Two of us went out to meet them. We proceeded
cautiously in the desert at night when we were within half an hour's
drive of the enemy.

The place turned out to be a French garrison, as we had thought.
And they acted just as they had at the other French post—anything
they had was ours. The commandant was a tall, thin fellow with long
hair, who looked like a poet. We didn't know for a long time that he
was the commandant, because he wore a civilian topcoat.

He and the one American officer with us went off to another part
of the garrison to see about our sleeping quarters, and the rest of us
hung around a big mud-walled corral which turned out to be the
stables of the Camel Corps.

The Arab cavalrymen, or whatever they call camelback soldiers,
gathered around in the moonlight and smiled at us and tried to talk.
An old camel hobbled past, and I said, "Look, there's a three-legged
camel. It must have lost a front leg in an accident."

It wasn't until next day that we realized the Arabs had merely
hobbled the camel by bending its leg and lashing one foot up to its
foreleg.

The Arabs had a tiny black burro that was a pet. It wasn't any
bigger than a dog, and it just stood around among us looking sadly
at the ground, waiting to be scratched. The soldiers were astounded
at such a tiny animal, and all of us took turns picking it up in our
arms to see how light it was. The truck driver jumped into his cab
and came out with some cube sugar, and from then on he was the
burro's man.

After a while the French said everything was arranged, and we all
walked to another building. They turned over one big empty room

with a tile floor for the soldiers to sleep on, and then insisted that the one officer and I have supper with them. It was late, but apparently they ate late on the desert.

The American officer was the kind all the mechanics called by his first name, and he would have preferred to eat and sleep with them, and so would I. But we talked it over with the enlisted men and decided it would be a breach of etiquette if we didn't accept the invitation.

There were eight French officers and we two Americans at dinner. The French were dressed in all sorts of half-military getup. Apparently they had had no new supply issues since the fall of France, and they wore whatever they could get their hands on. They apologized for not having any wine with the meal. They hadn't had any for months.

We ate at a long bare wooden table. The room was lighted by a dim bulb hooked to a battery they'd taken off one of the wrecked American planes. Candles were used in the other rooms. One of the officers spoke a few words of English, and that was our only avenue of contact with our hosts.

We had a delicious omelet for an appetizer, and then a stew of vegetables and what was either goat or camel meat. The French can make anything taste good.

Just as we were finishing, one of the Frenchmen said, "Shhhh," and cocked his ear. We all ran outside, and sure enough we could hear German planes high in the sky, bound for a night of bombing.

Some of the French officers slept in beds, some of them on the concrete floor. They made room for our two bedrolls on the floor, and the next thing we knew it was daylight.

Frenchmen don't eat a regular breakfast, so they came out and watched while we cooked our breakfast over small cans of burning gasoline.

One of the soldiers let the French commandant shoot his rifle, and then all the Frenchmen took turns. Their skill amazed the soldiers. Even with a strange rifle they could hit a small rock 150 yards away at every shot.

The commandant had a car—a sort of delivery wagon—and said he'd lead us to the wrecked planes if we could give him some gasoline. No wine, no gasoline. Soldiers at those far outposts fought a lonely and bleak kind of war.

We gave him five gallons and off we went, with several Arabs hanging onto the truck. We had at last reached our pinpoint in the vast desert, and were ready to start our work.

The mechanics started taking off usable parts from the wrecked airplanes, and four others of us appointed ourselves the official ditch-diggers of the day. We were all afraid of being strafed if the Germans came over and saw men working around the planes, and we wanted a nice ditch handy for diving into. The way to have a nice ditch is to dig one. We wasted no time.

Would that all slit trenches could be dug in soil like that. The sand was soft and moist; just the kind children like to play in. The four of us dug a winding ditch forty feet long and three feet deep in about an hour and a half.

The day got hot, and we took off our shirts. One sweating soldier said, "Five years ago you couldn't have got me to dig a ditch for five dollars an hour. Now look at me. You can't stop me digging ditches. I don't even want pay for it; I just dig for love. And I sure do hope this digging today is all wasted effort, I never wanted to do useless work so bad in my life. Any time I get fifty feet from my home ditch you'll find me digging a new ditch and, brother, I ain't joking. I love to dig ditches."

Digging out there in the soft desert sand was paradise compared to the claylike digging back at our base. The ditch went forward like a prairie fire. We measured it with our eyes to see if it would hold everybody. "Throw up some more right here," one of the boys said, indicating a low spot in the bank on either side. "Do you think we've got it deep enough?"

"It doesn't have to be so deep," another said. "A bullet won't go through more than three inches of sand. Sand is the best thing there is for stopping bullets."

A growth of sagebrush hung over the ditch on one side. "Let's leave it right there," one of the boys said. "It's good for the imagination. Makes you think you're covered up even when you're not."

That was the new outlook, the new type of conversation, among thousands of American boys. It's hard for a civilian to realize, but there were certain moments when a plain old ditch could be dearer than any possession on earth. For all bombs, no matter where they may land eventually, do all their falling right straight for a guy's head.

Only those of you who know about that can ever know all about ditches.

While we were digging, one of the boys brought up for the thousandth time the question of that letter in *Time* magazine. What letter, you ask? Why, it was a letter you probably don't remember, but it had become famous around these parts. It was in the November 23, 1942, issue which eventually found its way over here. Somebody read it, spoke to a few friends, and pretty soon thousands of men were commenting on that letter in terms which the fire department won't permit me to set to paper.

It was written by a soldier: "The greatest Christmas present that can be given to us this year is not smoking jackets, ties, pipes or games. If people will only take the money and buy war bonds . . . they will be helping themselves and helping us to be home next Christmas. Being home next Christmas is something which would be appreciated by all of us boys in service!"

The letter was all right with the soldiers over here until they got down to the address of the writer and discovered he was still in camp in the States. For a soldier back home to open his trap about anything concerning the war was like waving a red flag at the troops over here. They said they could do whatever talking was necessary.

"Them poor dogfaces back home," said one of the ditchdiggers with fine soldier sarcasm, "they've really got it rugged. Nothing to eat but them old greasy pork chops and them three-inch steaks all the time. I wouldn't be surprised if they don't have to eat eggs several times a week."

"And they're so lonely," said another. "No entertainment except to rassle them old dames around the dance floor. The USO closes at ten o'clock and the night clubs at three. It's mighty tough on them. No wonder they want to get home."

"And they probably don't get no sleep," said a third, "sleeping on them old cots with springs and everything, and scalding themselves in hot baths all the time."

"And nothing to drink but that nasty old ten-cent beer and that awful Canadian Club whisky," chimed in a philosopher with a shovel.

"And when they put a nickel in the box nothing comes out but Glenn Miller and Artie Shaw and such trash as that. My heart just bleeds for them poor guys."

"And did you see where he was?" asked another. "At the Albuquerque Air Base. And he wants to be home by next Christmas. Hell, if I could just see the Albuquerque Air Base again I'd think I was in heaven."

That was the way it went. The boys felt a soldier wasn't qualified to comment unless he was on the wrong side of the ocean. They were gay and full of their own wit when they got started that way, but just the same they meant it. It was a new form of the age-old soldier pastime of grousing. It helped take their minds off things.

While the rest of the men were working on the planes, I spent the day wandering around the desert talking to nomadic Arab shepherds. I walked up to one, said "Bonjour," and shook hands. The French and the Arabs are great handshakers. The first one I hit was a young fellow, handsome in a way but badly pock-marked.

I was looking for a long-bladed Arabian knife for one of the officers back at our airdrome. So after shaking hands and giving my new friend a cigarette, I started asking him if he had a knife with a long blade, sharp on both edges, and with a wire-wrapped handle. I might as well have saved the description, for he never even got it through his head I was asking for a knife.

He didn't speak French, which left us no common ground, particularly since I don't speak it either. But I got out my own pocket-knife, and then went through all the motions which, in almost any other country, would have conveyed to him that I was engaged in some sort of general discussion about a cutting implement. But not that baby.

Arabs aren't dumb, but somehow they didn't seem to understand our brand of sign language. That Arab boy and I talked our heads off, neither of us understanding a word the other said, and then he chortled and shook his head as if to say, "This is silly but it's fun, isn't it?" The Arabs were all very friendly and they smiled easily. It made us feel kindly toward them, even if we couldn't talk with them.

My friend was herding about fifty camels grazing just like cattle, on little clumps of sagebrush. I made signs that I wanted to see his camels close up, so we walked over. On the way over I did learn that the Arab word for camel is something like "zu-mel."

He had his eye on a certain one he wanted to show me. It was very old and shaggy, and was hobbled by having its right legs tied together with rags. I asked why, and the best I could make out was that it was a bad camel. As we came near, the camel rolled its tongue out one side of its mouth and gave forth a series of the most repulsive belching noises I had ever heard. At this the Arab looked at me and laughed and then started imitating the camel.

This went on and on. Every time the camel belched the Arab mimicked him and laughed derisively at the rowdy old camel. Finally he had to go round up some of the herd that was getting too far away, so we shook hands and off he went across the desert.

Late that afternoon I was sitting on the sand near one of the planes when an Arab boy, and a little girl on a donkey, came past. A white dog was running ahead of them, and we called to the pup. One of the soldiers had the dog coaxed up almost to him when the Arab boy got there and started throwing rocks at the dog to drive it away. We all frowned and said, "No, no, no," and indicated to the boy that we wanted him to call the dog back so we could pet it. He nodded his understanding, then picked up another rock and threw it at the dog. Arabs just don't understand sign language.

The boy himself was perfectly friendly. He sat down beside me and I gave him a cigarette. From the way he choked I guess he wasn't a smoker, and was smoking just to be polite. He sat around about fifteen minutes watching us and smiling. After a while I tried the dog business again, pointing at the dog and making motions for him to call it over. He smiled and nodded, then got up and threw another rock at the dog, before bidding us good-bye.

The Arabs, incidentally, had beautiful dogs as well as horses. Some of the dogs looked like small collies, but most of them, strangely, seemed to have a strain of the Arctic husky in them. Usually they were white with just a touch of cream.

The goat and sheep flocks were large. Once we saw a flock of sheep that were all black. Of course we made wisecracks about there being enough black sheep to furnish one for every family back home. It wasn't unusual to see a sheep spotted black and white like a dog.

The desert was literally alive with shepherds. We could see their tents in the distance—dark brown with wide dark stripes. The average Arab had camels, goats, sheep, horses, burros and dogs. And it seemed a little incongruous somehow, but we also saw lots of plain old Missouri mules.

We finished the salvage work on the wrecked planes and cooked our supper on the ground. As we ate, the soldier-mechanics got to talking about the trip, and our presence so close to enemy territory. "Back in the States," one of the truck drivers said, "the commanding officer made us a speech one day. He told us we were lucky to be driving trucks. Almost made us feel like slackers. Said we'd go through the whole war and never be within five hundred miles of the enemy. I'd like to get hold of that guy now. He's still back there."

"And here we are within thirty miles of the Germans," one boy said.

"Thirty miles?" the officer said. "It's only twenty miles."

"I'm going to make it ten miles in my dispatch," I chimed in. "We've got to be heroes, haven't we?"

That set the boys off. They told me how to write the story about our trip. "Write about digging the ditch," they said. "Tell them how we dug our heads off and got finished just as a German plane came over. You don't have to say it was thirty thousand feet high and couldn't have seen us with bifocals."

That's the way they joked about it, but they were only half-joking all the time. The boys were really afraid of strafing. They held a consultation about going home. One soldier and I wanted to spend the night there, and then make the long journey home next day. But the mechanics and truck drivers didn't relish driving in daytime so near the enemy lines. They voted to leave that night. And leave we did. We finished our supper, gave what rations there were left to the French, rounded up our Arab guide, and pulled out just at dusk.

We drove all night, without lights. It was easy to follow the tracks. Yet we had to cross rocky river beds with steep banks, and dodge countless holes, and thread our way over drifted sand dunes, and pick the right trail where tracks branched out in all directions.

It was a truly beautiful night. The sky was cloudless and the moon so bright that it dimmed out all but a few of the most lustrous stars. And it was warm when we started. We all felt relieved, somehow, and in high spirits. But we had forgotten the chill that comes with night on the desert. By eight o'clock we were getting cold. By nine we were scrunched on the floor and wrapped in blankets. From ten o'clock on we were in agony. Nothing could keep out the cold. Finally it became an intense pain, and we suffered all night.

The slow dusty miles dribbled away behind us in the moonlight. Far off little red fires dotted the desert where the shepherds camped. Dark forms of grazing camels passed in the weird light. Once we stopped and turned off the motors, and heard a German plane very high in the night sky. And once Wah, apparently unaccustomed to motoring, got carsick and we had to stop and let him out for a while.

We went through little towns, and awakened the dogs. At two o'clock we came back past our first French garrison, where guards stood watch on the high walls day and night. Their grapevine signal system was uncanny. For when we pulled up the commandant was out of bed, with an overcoat over his pajamas, waiting for us.

I've heard tales of the Arab grapevine. They tell of one case where it carried the news of a crashed German plane 150 miles, and faster than the French Army's wireless system.

We said good-bye to Wah and shook hands with the commandant and barged on into the night. The miles and hours grew longer as we neared home. The last twenty miles seemed to take weeks. Once the driver stopped for our routine stretch, and the rigidly cold soldiers growled at him to keep going.

Finally we got home, an hour before daylight, and just as the moon played out on us. We hadn't seen any war, but we had seen the Sahara by day and by night. "I'll be telling my grandchildren someday about the time I crossed the Sahara Desert," one of the soldiers said.

"You didn't cross it," another one said.

"Oh, well, what the hell, I crossed part of it. Let's get to bed and stay there all day."

And that's what we did.

13. THE FRENCH FOREIGN
LEGION

At Sidi-bel-Abbes, in Algeria, I visited the home of the renowned French Foreign Legion. Probably, over the years, the most famous fighting unit in the world.

The Legion comprises the only true mercenaries left in existence. They'll fight whomever their leaders tell them to; on either side, with the same emotions.

A Legionnaire lives with but one high goal—death on the battlefield. On the walls of one of the barracks is inscribed this message from a former commander: "You, Legionnaires, are soldiers made to die. I send you where you die." The message is looked upon with reverence, almost as holy.

Like a good many things in this world, the Legion isn't as romantic close to as it is from a distance. It has a fine fighting history, no question of that, but life in the Legion is much more modern than most of us have thought. And yet it is an empty life, by most standards. It is a bleak life. Men with fine minds, who for reasons of their own go into the ranks of the Legion, find that after a few years their minds have dwindled to a common denominator of mere existence.

They say that most Americans who have joined the Legion can't stick out their five-year enlistments. Before the war Americans and British could get out of the Legion with a little diplomatic pressure. When a German enlisted he was stuck for the five years, no matter how he hated it. But Germans don't hate it the way Americans and Englishmen do.

The Legion consists of about ten thousand men. In this war it fought the Germans in France and in Norway. Its record, as usual, was superb. After the fall of France it withdrew to Algeria, its life-long home. In 1942 it fought against the British in Syria—it doesn't make any difference to the Legion whom it fights.

When I visited its headquarters, the Legion was scattered. Some of its units were bottled up by the Japanese in French Indo-China. A few were fighting the Germans in Tunisia. The rest were spotted over North Africa, preparing for future battles. Fewer than two thousand men were at Sidi-bel-Abbes.

The morning the Americans landed in North Africa, the Legion started north on the 50-mile run to Oran to join the fighting. But they never arrived. Allied airplanes bombed and machine-gunned them along the highways, and they had to turn back. I saw their burned-out trucks still lying along the roadside. Fortunately, there were almost no casualties. The Legionnaires felt badly that they didn't get to Oran in time. Not because they disliked Americans, but simply because they missed a fight.

After our arrival the Legion was hand in glove with the Americans, and started readying itself to join in the great fight on our side. The soldiers were impatient and itching to get going.

The headquarters of the Legion was a great and pleasant surprise to me. I expected it to be a slovenly tent-camp out in an almost unbelievable desert, with dirty cutthroat troops and brutal-looking officers.

Everything was just the opposite. The headquarters was in a city of sixty thousand people with fine sidewalk cafés and paved streets and modern apartment houses. It was not in the desert at all, but in rich farming country.

The Legion buildings formed a sort of academy, right in the heart of the city. There were four-storied permanent barracks, and fine parks inside the walls, with many flowers and extraordinarily clean grounds and buildings. There were museums, and beautiful statues and monuments about the grounds. There were nice homes for officers and noncoms and their families.

Officers were uniformed as though by Bond Street, and most of them might have been American businessmen or professors as far as their looks were concerned. At Saint-Cyr, the West Point of France, the top man in each class used to have the privilege of choosing where he would serve. And it was a tradition that he always chose the Foreign Legion. So the Legion is led by career men.

Legionnaires told me that many of the officers, though strict, were almost fatherly in their attitude toward the soldiers. And certainly the ones I met were, without exception, gentlemen in anybody's country.

The Legion had changed greatly from the dregs-of-humanity catchall that it once was. But it was still wholly a fighting outfit, and anything that exists solely to fight is bound to be tough. As a result, the Legionnaire lived in a mental environment that was deadly. There was little reason or inclination for high thinking.

The Legionnaires were lonely. There was little outside their military life for them. They could sit in the cafés and drink, and that was about all. Many of them carried on regular correspondence with women all over the world whom they had never seen, even with Americans. They said it wasn't unusual to see among the want ads in the Paris papers a plea from a Foreign Legionnaire for a pen-pal.

The loneliness and longing for other days was proved, it seemed to me, by one little vital statistic. Every year around Christmas five or six Legionnaires committed suicide.

The Legion was full of "characters." There was one Russian, a carpenter, who had been indulging in a peculiar routine as long as Legionnaires could remember.

Every payday, which was twice a month, he bought himself a large bucket of wine. He put it on the floor beside his cot, got plenty of cigarettes, then lay down and started drinking and smoking. He drank himself into a stupor, slept a few hours, then woke up and started drinking again. He never got out of bed, made any noise, or caused any trouble. His jag lasted two days. It had been going on so long that the officers just accepted it.

But let a Legionnaire get out of control on the street or on duty, and the penalties were severe. For extreme drunkenness a Legionnaire could get nine months in the Disciplinary Regiment—which meant nine months far away on the desert, working from dawn till dusk, with poor food, no cigarettes, no wine, no mail.

Discipline in the Legion is probably the strictest in the world. It isn't just a brutal discipline; it is what professional soldiers point to admiringly as the absolute ideal in military precision of conduct. There was no sloppiness of dress, no relaxing of respect. Soldiers saluted an officer clear across the street. They saluted officers sitting at tables fifty yards away. Neglect to salute cost a Legionnaire eight days in jail. Even for slight infractions he got eight days in jail, with his head shaved. They said any man who got through a five-year enlistment without getting his head shaved was either an angel or extremely lucky.

At the end of a five-year enlistment the Legion gives a Good Conduct Certificate. The Legionnaires were so tough that only half of them got the certificate. Those who didn't get it had only two choices: re-enlistment for another five years or lifetime expulsion from the entire French Empire. The bad ones signed up again.

There were still rough, murderous men in the Legion, but many of them were high-type persons who left their home countries for political reasons. Fifty-five nationalities were represented. There were only three Americans. (They were not at headquarters when I was there.)

A large percentage of the Legion was Spanish and German. Once we took over in Africa, the question arose what to do with the German Legionnaires. That was solved by sending them far to the south, with a detachment that would never come into contact with Axis troops and would fight no World War battles.

The Germans made excellent Legionnaires, but they had become so numerous there was some resentment against them among the French. In one kitchen I noticed a sign in French saying "French is spoken here." I asked the cook the significance of it. He said it got so that German was the predominant language around the kitchen. He put up the sign to show there were some Frenchmen left.

The Legion did many things for its men. At Sidi-bel-Abbes there was a huge modern theater, where movies were shown and band concerts given. The men even put on their own theatricals, and the Legion had a 350-piece band.

Near by was a new concrete swimming pool, the largest in North Africa. I've never seen anything in Hollywood to beat it. It was surrounded by tiled terraces, with tables and chairs and cabanas, and with green trees and a riot of flowers.

Officers and noncoms were provided with houses, and might have their families with them. A sergeant got only $10 a month, but his pay was increased if he had a family. A sergeant in the Legion rated salutes the same as a commissioned officer.

The Legion had shops where its men could study trades during spare hours after supper. After the Americans arrived they put in a voluntary English course.

The Legionnaires at home base slept in concrete-floored barracks much like our own. They had iron cots and their stuff was packed to move at a moment's notice.

Every barracks and recreation hall had cartoons drawn all over the walls—well-done cartoons making jokes about Legion life. That was another Legion tradition. Whenever a new company moved in, it had the right to erase all cartoons and draw its own.

Since the French Foreign Legion was created in 1831, it has more than a century of tradition behind it. The Legion was extremely proud of the two museums which depicted its history. On the museum's tiled floors there were beautiful brown-and-white Algerian rugs, somewhat similar to our own Navajo Indian rugs. Around the walls stood case after case of Legion mementos—old swords, flags, pieces of uniform, guns, bullets, decorations.

The walls were hung with hundreds of pictures of Legion members who had died gloriously. Life-sized wax figures standing around the walls of one room showed the dozen or so types of uniform worn by the Legion over the years.

The museum wasn't wild or exotic as you might think. It was almost like a little section of the Smithsonian. A Belgian corporal acted as guide and gave a little Cook's-tour explanation of everything. Souvenir postcards and booklets were for sale.

The Legion's most prized memento was, of all things, a wooden hand. In 1854 the Legion fought in the Russian Crimea, and in that campaign a Captain Danjou had one hand shot off. He had a wooden hand made to replace it. The hand was of fine workmanship, the fingers were all jointed, and the thing looked almost lifelike.

The Legion went to Mexico during Maximilian's reign, and there fought the most memorable battle in its history. A tiny party of 115 Legionnaires barricaded themselves in a hacienda at the town of Camerone, and battled a force of four thousand Mexicans. All but three of the Legionnaires were killed. It was much like our own Alamo. Captain Danjou with the wooden hand was killed in that battle. Later his hand was found, and sent back to Sidi-bel-Abbes.

The battle was fought on April 30, 1863. Each year the Legion observes April 30th with great parades and reviews. Captain Danjou's hand is brought out in its glass case and is displayed as a symbol of what the Legion means.

It all seemed a little gruesome, but the Legion felt deeply about it.

The Legion, though hard, is just as sentimental as any other organization. I saw it especially among the cavalrymen. The Legion was abandoning its cavalry. All its beautiful horses were being sold to farmers, and the cavalry was being motorized. And you know how cavalrymen feel about their horses. As I came unexpectedly into the stables, so neat and clean they hardly resembled stables at all, I caught a glimpse of one young soldier kissing his horse's forehead as he finished currying it. He was a tough-looking boy who didn't seem capable of tenderness or sentiment. Something would be lost when the Legion's cavalrymen started riding iron horses.

Sidi-bel-Abbes has become practically a shrine for Americans over here. More than four hundred American officers went through the Legion's home quarters every week. The Legion put on parades for visiting American generals. American doughboys and Foreign Legion privates walked the streets together and sat in cafés, trying their best to talk to each other.

My visit was made particularly pleasant by a Legionnaire who was an Englishman—Sergeant John Whiteway. Whiteway was not an adventurer at all; he was a normal kind of businessman.

Just after the last war he went to Paris to live. For twenty years he was the Paris representative for American refrigerator and radio companies. He married a French girl, and they had three handsome children, the youngest of whom he had never seen although the child was then nearly three.

When war seemed imminent in 1939, Whiteway felt he should fight for the country that had supported him for twenty years. He couldn't join the regular French Army, so he joined the Foreign Legion. They fought through the fall of France, and then were shipped to Algeria. And there Whiteway had been ever since.

It was tough going, the first few months, for a man of his maturity and intellect. But his business ability and office experience made him invaluable to the Legion, and he was soon put into administrative work at headquarters. Thus he escaped most of the rigors and the deadly barracks life.

When the Americans came, Whiteway was one of the few English-speaking men in the Legion. So he was immediately attached to American headquarters as a liaison man. He wore civilian clothes when I met him and it was he who took me to Sidi-bel-Abbes.

Although Whiteway had been away only a month, his return was like a royal homecoming. Everywhere we went both soldiers and officers of the Legion saluted and stopped and shook hands and jabbered as though he'd been gone for years. Little French girls, whom he had been teaching English, came running down the street to kiss him. He seemed to be one Englishman who had made the French like him.

We were a gay party who visted the Legion. In addition to Sergeant Whiteway and myself, there were five American army officers—Lieutenant Colonel Egbert W. Cowan, who had served all over the world in the Regular Army and whose daughter Shirley was about to become a ferry pilot at home; Captain Art Nillen, a boisterous dentist from Dallas, whose motto was "See your dentist every day and brush your teeth twice a year"; Lieutenant Albert Deschenes, a young Boston doctor who spoke French, and well he might with a name like that; Lieutenant Max Kuehnert of Chicago, who was America's best brick salesman before the war and still carried around his sales booklets of model homes; and Lieutenant Leonard Bessman, a likable Milwaukee lawyer who didn't speak French but had the virtue of continually trying to speak it.

Lennie and Max were enthusiasts. Everything they saw was wonderful. Lennie had been a Foreign Legion fan ever since his childhood, and we almost had to hold him to keep him from signing up right on the spot.

It was Lennie's efforts at French that endeared him to a Rumanian cavalry sergeant named Paul Baron Ecsedy de Csapo, who hung around with us all day and wound up by almost tearfully pinning his most prized medal on Lennie's blouse, as a token of his esteem.

Max hit his stride when we dropped in at a little bar patronized almost exclusively by the Legion. It was run by a man named Lucett Paume, a Swiss who had spent twenty years in the Legion and was then retired. His wife and two children helped him run the bar.

Max spoke German, and this was how it wound up: Max and the Swiss in one huddle talking German; Lieutenant Deschenes and the proprietor's daughters in another huddle speaking real French; Colonel Cowan with a little group around him telling about hunting elephants in Indo-China; Art Nillen standing in the doorway shouting, "Zid, yalla, you little——" at all the passing Arab kids; Lennie and the sergeant in another huddle speaking pidgin and making motions, and me sitting all alone in a corner ordering my breakfast in Spanish, over and over to myself.

Breakfast words happened to be the only Spanish I knew, and damned if I wasn't going to talk some kind of foreign language amidst all that international sewing circle, even if I had to keep ordering hypothetical breakfasts all afternoon. Vive la Légion étrangère!

*　　　*　　　*

It was a marvelous experience to visit, after all these years and in that remote part of the world, the men about whom *Beau Geste* was written. I couldn't help admiring the Legion's pride in itself, its fastidious discipline, its cleanliness, its whole tradition.

But beyond that, life in the Foreign Legion seemed horrible to me. Living to fight merely for the fight's sake is something I cannot understand.

14. ROVING REPORTERS

THERE were more than seventy-five American and British correspondents and photographers in North Africa. Since Allied Headquarters was in a big city to the rear, that was where most of the correspondents stayed. The number actually in Tunisia at any one time fluctuated between half a dozen and two dozen. Each of the three big press associations had a five-man staff—usually three men back at headquarters and two at the front. They rotated every few weeks.

The correspondents in the city lived a life that was pretty close to normal. They lived in hotels or apartments, ate at restaurants or officers' messes, worked regular hours, got laundry done, dressed in regulation uniforms, kept themselves clean, and got their news from communiqués and by talking to staff officers at headquarters.

But some of us spent as much as two months in Tunisia without ever returning to the city. When we did it was a great thrill to come back to civilization—for the first day.

But then a reaction set in, and almost invariably we got the heebie-jeebies and found ourselves nervous and impatient with all the confusion and regimentation of city life, and wished ourselves at the front again.

The outstanding thing about life at the front was its magnificent simplicity. It was a life consisting only of the essentials—food, sleep, transportation, and what little warmth and safety a man could manage to wangle out of it by personal ingenuity. Ordinarily, when life is stripped to the bare necessities it is an empty life and a boring one. But not at the front. Time for me had never passed so rapidly. I was never aware of the day of the week, and a whole month would be gone before I knew it.

At the front the usual responsibilities and obligations were gone.

There were no appointments to keep, nobody cared how anybody looked, red tape was at a minimum. There were no desks, no designated hours, no washing of hands before eating, or afterward either. It would have been a heaven for small boys with dirty ears.

And it was a healthy life. During the winter months I was constantly miserable from the cold, yet paradoxically I never felt better in my life. The cold wind burned my face to a deep tan, and my whole system became toughened. I ate twice as much as usual. I hadn't been hungry for nigh onto forty years, but in Tunisia I ate like a horse and was so constantly hungry it got to be a joke.

It was a life that gave a new sense of accomplishment. In normal life, all the little things were done for us. I made my money by writing, and then used that money to hire people to wash my clothes, shine my shoes, make my bed, clean the bathtub, fill my gas tank, serve my meals, carry my bags, build my fires.

But not in Africa. We did everything ourselves. We were suddenly conscious again that we could do things. The fact that another guy could write a better story than I could was counter-balanced by the fact that I could roll a better bedroll than he could.

Last, and probably most important of all, was the feeling of vitality, of being in the heart of everything, of being a part of it—no mere onlooker, but a member of the team. I got into the race, and I resented dropping out even long enough to do what I was there to do—which was write. I would rather have just kept going all day, every day.

I've written that war is not romantic when a person is in the midst of it. Nothing happened to change my feeling about that. But I will have to admit there was an exhilaration in it; an inner excitement that built up into a buoyant tenseness seldom achieved in peacetime.

The army accepted us correspondents as a part of the family. We knew and were friends with hundreds of individual soldiers. And we knew, and were known by, every American general in Tunisia. There was no hedging at the front. I've never known an instance where correspondents were not told, with complete frankness, what was going on.

In the beginning no restrictions were put on us; we could go anywhere we pleased at any time. But things gradually changed, as the established machinery of war caught up with us. Then there was a rule that correspondents couldn't go into the front lines unless accompanied by an officer. Maybe that was a good rule, I don't know. But there were about two dozen of us who felt ourselves in an odd position, as if we were being conducted through our own house. The rule died in a few weeks and we were again free to wander alone at random.

When correspondents first went to the Tunisian front in the fall of 1942 there were no special facilities for them and every man was on his own. Some of us got around by hitchhiking on army vehicles. Some of us bought French sedans. We wrote wherever we could; sitting in our cars or in some bleak country hotel. We got our copy back to the city by many methods, including the one of walking up to anybody about to get on a plane and saying, "Hey, Joe, would you mind taking this in for me?"

By spring things were different. The Army Public Relations Office had set up an advanced post well back of the lines. They looked after a regular aerial courier service back to headquarters and sent out our mail to us. They had a few jeeps to dole out to correspondents, and for a while they had a house where meals were served and correspondents could throw their bedrolls on cots when they came back from the lines. The PRO hoped eventually to acquire tents and tables and a regular kitchen crew, so that it could move right along with the advancing troops, just like a circus. That would be covering the war in style.

At first I traveled by hanging around some headquarters until I hit somebody who was going my way by truck or jeep, then threw on my stuff and set out. A little later I was lucky enough to get a jeep. The man responsible for that was Captain Ed Atkins, of Ford City, Pennsylvania, who controlled a certain motor pool. He and Lieutenant Max Kuehnert did so much for me in the way of little things all through the campaign that it will take me ten years to repay them.

Only two or three of us had jeeps at first, so we always tried to double up. I shared mine for some time with Don Coe of the

United Press. Will Lang of *Time-Life* and I made a couple of trips together. And some of the time I wandered around alone, although that wasn't particularly wise, for one man was needed to watch the rear for strafing planes.

On the jeep we carried everything we had—bedroll, typewriter, musette bag, tent. Also we carried extra cans of gasoline, a camouflage net, and a box of canned rations, in case we got stuck somewhere away from an army kitchen.

We knew where all the gasoline dumps were throughout the hundred miles or so of American front. We'd simply drive up to one, tell the soldier in charge we needed some gas, get out our pliers, tap a couple of five-gallon cans, and pour it in. He'd say, "Who's this to be charged to?" And we'd tell him any outfit number that popped into our heads, or even some mythical unit such as "The Sahara Task Force." He'd seldom put it down anyway, for obviously it was army gas going into an army vehicle.

I remember once a stalled British truck flagged us down, and the kid driver said he was out of gas. Much to his astonishment we said we'd give him five gallons. And when he asked if we had a form for him to sign and we said hell no, just pour it in, his amazement was complete. Those crazy Americans, they make things so simple.

Correspondents on the prowl slept wherever they stopped. Usually we found a bare tile floor in some old farmhouse being used as a headquarters. We'd discovered that after a few nights on the floor or on the ground it didn't seem hard. I believe I was about the only correspondent who frequently pitched his pup tent. Some correspondents carried folding camp cots, but I didn't because I hadn't one; besides, it was much warmer sleeping right on the ground.

Our main difficulty was in keeping warm. I used to put my bedroll cover and two blankets under me, then three blankets over me, plus a mackinaw and sometimes the canvas top to the jeep. We always slept with our clothes on, taking off only our mackinaws and shoes.

The greatest mistake I made in the campaign was in not bringing a sleeping bag and rubber mattress from home. They were just as light to carry as a bedroll, twice as comfortable, and three times as warm. I think about half our line officers did bring sleeping bags. But when spring came it wasn't so important.

Oddly enough, we didn't get up terribly early at the front. Breakfast at a field headquarters usually ran till 8:30, so we could sleep till around eight.

When we correspondents were moving about, we ate wherever we happened to be at mealtime. Right smack at the front officers and men stood in the same line and ate together, but back a few miles they ate separately. At those posts the correspondents usually ate at the officers' mess, where chow was served in trays from the back end of a kitchen truck. We found a rock or sat on the ground.

Still farther back, the messes were in tents. Sometimes we sat at a table and had plates and waiters served us.

Correspondents were always welcome. We spent so much time traveling that we knew some of the officers in every unit in Tunisia and popping in for a meal once in a while became a small reunion. But whether we knew the officers or not, we invariably knew the mess sergeant—the old law of self-preservation.

I personally had two favorite kitchen friends. Both happened to be Pittsburghers. One was Sergeant Pat Donadeo, from Allison Park, a suburb of Pittsburgh. The other was Private First Class Joe Fox, of 4513 Filmore, the Oak Hill section of Pittsburgh. Pat worked ten years at the Wildwood Golf Club. He hoped the job would still be there after the war. He was mess sergeant of an armored outfit and he set a mighty fine tray. We had a special link because just a couple of hours before I showed up at the mess for the first time Pat had received a letter from his wife commenting on one of my stories (favorably, I might add).

Pat was of Italian extraction and spoke Italian fluently, which he figured would be handy when he got to Italy.

Joe Fox was not a mess sergeant. He was a table waiter at the headquarters to which I retired occasionally to hole up and write. But there was nothing wrong with being a waiter, I can assure you, especially one like Joe. He could fry two or three eggs when we showed up hungry in midafternoon, or fix a hot cup of tea late at night. Joe was quite a guy. All the officers chuckled and said, "That Fox, he's something." His nickname was Double Exx. He had had it ever since he struck out in a high school game with the bases loaded. He was a sport fan, and used to usher at a ball park, but incongruously developed into a salesman of ladies' shoes. Joe thought Westbrook Pegler and I were both wonderful. We in turn thought Joe was wonderful. Of course Peg never heard of Joe, so I cast an affirmative vote for him. Since Joe was four thousand miles away, I guessed Peg could afford to break his standing rule and like him just a little bit, by proxy.

Most officers managed to wash once a day, but I personally went more on the enlisted man's psychology and just skipped it. After a few weeks of front-line living a man's whole perspective on the niceties and necessities of life changed.

My perspective changed radically, and as a correspondent I had only the barest taste of the rough going. For a lifetime I had bathed with becoming regularity, and I thought the world would come to an end unless I changed my socks every day. But in Africa I sometimes

went without a bath for two months, and I went two weeks at a time
without even taking off my socks. Oddly enough, it didn't seem to
make much difference.

My ideas of sleeping accommodations also underwent considerable
change. I used to be sore if I drew a lumpy bed in some hotel. Over
here I struck gold when I found a spot where I could lie down out
of the wind. One evening another correspondent and I arrived at a
new front-line headquarters. It was centered around a Tunisian farmhouse, as practically all command posts were. Soldiers and officers

alike were sleeping just anywhere they could—in trucks, under trees,
in the barn and chicken houses. It was cold and damp, as usual.

Nobody told a correspondent where to sleep or what to do when
he was gypsying around the front. He shifted for himself. So I nosed
around and found a place to sleep. It was under a big French grain
wagon sitting in the barnlot. Some soldiers had found several strips
of corrugated tin roofing and set them around three sides of the
wagon, making walls. The wagon bed formed a room overhead. They
had brought straw from a near-by stack and put it on the ground
under the wagon. There we threw our bedding rolls.

It was the coziest place I'd slept in for a week. It had two magnificent features—the ground was dry, and the wind was cut off. I
was so pleased at finding such a wonderful place that I could feel my
general spirits go up like an elevator. When the detachment got
orders to move the next day I felt a genuine regret at leaving this
little haven. And to think after all it was only some pitiful straw on
the hard ground under a wagon.

As we were bedding down on that straw, Hal Boyle of the Associated Press, who was bunking next to me, said, "I believe that in
wartime physical discomfort becomes a more dominant thing in
life than danger itself."

And I believe that's true. The danger came in spurts; discomfort
was perpetual. Dirt and cold were almost constant. Outside of food

and cigarettes there were none of the little things that made life normal back home. There were no chairs, lights, floors, or tables. There wasn't any place to set anything, or any store to buy things. There were no newspapers, milk, beds, sheets, radiators, beer, ice cream or hot water. A man just sort of existed, either standing up working or lying down sleeping. There was no pleasant in-between. The velvet was all gone from living.

Another time Don Coe and I stayed all night at a forward command post a few miles back from a pass where fighting was going on.

We were in a big farmyard. Trucks and jeeps were parked around the edge of the lot under trees. We picked out a vacant spot and threw our bedrolls on the ground. We rolled our jeep in front of us to keep trucks from running over us in the blackout while we slept.

There is something good about sleeping outdoors. For a long time we lay back rolled tight in our blankets, looking straight up into the sky. There were millions of stars, and every few seconds one of them fell. A couple of times stars went shooting horizontally across the heavens. The sky at night is a majestic and inspiring thing, yet we had to come to far-off Africa and sleep on the ground in order to see and feel it.

After a while we went to sleep. The next thing I knew a gruff voice was saying, "What the hell is this jeep doing out here in the open like this?"

I opened one eye. It was just daylight, and the voice was no less than that of the general, out on an early-morning inspection prowl. Whereupon I shut my eye and let Don handle the situation.

The general made a few more choice remarks before Don got his sleepy head out of the blankets. Then all of a sudden the general said, "Oh, I'm sorry. I didn't realize it was you. Forget it. Everything's all right."

I lay very still, pretending to be asleep, and chuckling to myself. Later in the day the general apologized to me too, but I was sorry he did and told him so, for we had done something very thoughtless which endangered other people as well as ourselves. And the fact that we were correspondents instead of soldiers didn't excuse us.

But at least we learned our lesson. We didn't leave jeeps showing after daylight again.

We American war correspondents in Tunisia worked hard and conscientiously; we became frightened and exhilarated; and frequently we were depressed by the tragedies around us. We were doing a job which most of us found extremely interesting, but we all wished it was over.

The most picturesque of the correspondents was Jack Thompson of the Chicago *Tribune*. He was a husky fellow, and had grown a terrific black beard. He looked ferocious, but he was gentle-mannered and considerate, and always willing to help a newcomer get onto the ropes. He had been in Tunisia from the beginning, and spent more time there than any other correspondent.

The only other bewhiskered member of the corps was Eliot Elisofon, photographer for *Life*. He had grown a Continental goatee which made him look like a magician. Elisofon was afraid, like the rest of us, yet he made himself go right up into the teeth of danger. I never knew a more intense and enthusiastic worker.

I liked practically all the correspondents, but one of my favorites was Graham Hovey of International News Service. I liked him because he was quiet and undemanding, and because he was sensitive to the beauties as well as the horrors of war.

Hovey had an unusual baptism. He had been in the headquarters office for some time, pestering his boss to get to the front. Finally he went, and on the first day almost got killed.

The very first bomb he ever saw fall, the very first one he ever heard explode, was a 500-pounder that hit within fifty feet of him and killed three men. He and Boots Norgaard of the Associated Press, a veteran at such things, escaped only by the freakish luck of finding a ready-made slit trench just where they stopped. Hovey was shaken by the experience, yet after a few weeks he felt that same fascination for the front that I did.

Most of the correspondents kept themselves pretty presentable at the front. I think it is not going too far to say that I was the worst-looking one of the lot. Correspondents had officer status and wore regular officers' uniform without insignia. But in order to keep warm I dressed like a cross between Coxey's Army and the Ski Patrol. I wore army coveralls, enlisted man's mackinaw, knit cap, goggles and overshoes. The only way a person could tell me from a private was that I was too old.

The two oldest correspondents over here at first were Gault Macgowan, of the New York *Sun*, and myself. Gault was in his late forties and had been wounded in the last war. He always had his pad and pencil out, and was a fiend for writing down names and addresses of New York soldiers. One day we saw him right up among the men who were firing, writing down names. It was almost like a cartoon. He told one soldier, "I do on the battlefield what Winchell does at home."

Bill White of the New York *Herald Tribune* was in Tunisia for two months before returning to the city. When he came back he was tanned completely black, was so pure and healthy from rough living that he wouldn't even smoke a cigarette. The first night he insisted on sleeping on the hotel-room floor in his bedroll.

Bill Stoneman of the Chicago *Daily News* was the first correspondent to be wounded in Tunisia. He was furious about it too. In the first place, he got shot in his behind; secondly, when the surgeons dug out the bullet it turned out to be only .22 caliber. Bill felt that the whole thing was ignominious.

Stoneman was one of the few professional foreign correspondents. He had been in Europe for fifteen years, knew all the capitals intimately, had a colossal diplomatic acquaintance throughout Europe, and spoke many languages, including some Russian. While convalescing from his wound he decided to learn Arabic. So he called up an agency and told them to send him an instructor, preferably a luscious Arab girl. But just as Bill expected, the teacher turned out to be a bedraggled male pedagogue who worked him to death. In no time at all he was rapidly packing his bags for the front again.

Down in Central Tunisia, in the village of Feriana, there was a little country hotel where four or five of us correspondents used to drop in now and then for a day or two to sleep under a roof and eat some of Papa's meals.

The hotel was run by a French family. Papa was big and mustached, always wore a cap and a dirty apron and always had a burned-up cigarette in his mouth. He took an instant like or dislike to newcomers, and the ones he didn't like got short shrift.

Mamma was plain and gray and sweet, and although she couldn't speak a word of English she could understand it. She never did a bit of the cooking; that was Papa's job and privilege. She sat at the kitchen table and sewed and knitted.

There were three sons in the vicinity of fifteen, all handsome and superior boys. Roget was our favorite, because he had studied English in his school and we could converse with him. The three boys served the meals. They also acted as chambermaids.

Once when I was trying to write in the hotel, Roget came in to clean up. Immediately he called his two brothers, and for half an hour they all stood in a circle looking over my shoulder admiringly —not at the magic of my wonderful words, but at how fast my fingers worked the keyboard.

The hotel had one very dirty toilet, and in the rooms were merely washbowls and kerosene lamps. French soldiers slept on straw in the little lobby. There were always at least ten people in the kitchen, including a few neighbors, some stray French privates helping to wash the dishes, and a French officer or two trying to learn English from Roget.

Jack Thompson found this place soon after we arrived in November. As far as I know, it was the only operating hotel in all of Central Tunisia. Jack kept two rooms there all winter, and they were like a headquarters. Jack himself might not be there one night a week, but if any other correspondents blew in we'd just walk in and settle down as if the rooms belonged to us.

Jack could do no wrong in Papa's eyes. Papa was so prejudiced in Jack's favor that he would never serve breakfast to anybody else until Jack came down for his.

Frank Kluckhohn of the New York *Times* used to get up early, hoping to get breakfast and get started out; and after a while he'd come back upstairs alter lately cussing and laughing at the incongruity of being refused breakfast until Monsieur Thompson also was ready to eat.

Papa just sort of tolerated me. He didn't detest me as he did some of the others; it was just that I hardly existed in his eyes. But I was one of Mamma's favorites. She always got out her private homemade confiture, in this case marvelous peach jam, for me when I ate alone with the family in the kitchen.

I remember one morning when four of us correspondents were eating breakfast in the kitchen, and Mamma got out the jam and made it quite plain it was for me alone. But Frank Kluckhohn didn't follow her reasoning, and helped himself to some of MY jam. Fortunately he didn't see the daggers Mamma was looking at him. Poor Frank, he had a tough time eating in that place.

The little hotel was a peaceful place for many weeks. Not much of the American Army knew about it. We correspondents and a few fliers from a near-by airdrome, who came in once a week for dinner, were the only Americans around.

And then all of a sudden everything changed. The battle lines drew near. Within an hour one day the village was deluged with American troops. Trucks with Negro drivers filled the olive grove across the street. The grove on the other side was pitted deep with sudden slit trenches and great holes where tanks and half-tracks were nearly hidden in the ground.

Soldiers flowed in and out of the hotel like water. The Germans were coming nearer. A couple of us correspondents sped in from another front, packed a few things into our jeep, and Papa and Mamma and the boys stood waving at us as we dashed off again.

The next thing we knew Feriana was gone. The end came suddenly, and Papa and Mamma and the boys had to get out in the middle of the night. Some of us saw them next day—nearly thirty miles away—trudging uphill behind a mule cart with a few of their things on it.

The German tide that washed over Feriana was brief. Maybe Papa and Mamma and the boys have things fixed up again by now. No doubt the Germans cleaned out Papa's meager wine cellar. I don't care about that, but I hope they didn't find Mamma's peach jam.

15. THE END IN SIGHT

W E FINALLY left Central Tunisia behind us and pushed north, Americans as well as British. The end of the long Tunisian trail was in sight. The kill could not be long delayed.

The British had more troops, and more experienced troops, in Tunisia than we had. In some measure we had divided the load earlier, but with the arrival of the Eighth Army the affair had become predominantly British.

It would be wrong to try to make anything sinister out of that, for it was the way it should have been. Since Montgomery had chased Rommel all the way from Egypt in one of the great military achievements of history, it was only right that the British should make the kill.

The Eighth Army was a magnificent organization. We correspondents were dazzled by its perfection. So were our troops. It must surely be one of the outstanding armies of all time. We trailed it several days up the Tunisian coast, and we came to look upon it almost with awe.

Its organization for continuous movement was so perfect that it seemed more like a big business firm than a destructive army. The men of the Eighth were brown-skinned and white-eye-browed from the desert sun. Most of them were in shorts, and they were a healthy-looking lot. Their spirit was like a tonic. The spirit of our own troops was good, but those boys from the burning sands were throbbing with the vitality of conquerors.

They were friendly, cocky, confident. They had been three years in the desert, and they wore the expression of victory on their faces. We envied them, and were proud of them.

The north country was entirely different from the semidesert

182

where we Americans had spent the winter. In the north the land
was fertile and everything was violently green.

Northern Tunisia was all hills and valleys. There were no trees at
all, but there in the spring the earth was solidly covered with deep
green—pastures and freshly growing fields of grain. Small wildflowers
spattered the countryside. I never saw lovelier or more gentle country. It gave a sense of peacefulness, it seemed to speak its richness. It
was a full, ripe country, and there in the springtime living seemed
sweet and worth-while.

There were winding gravel roads everywhere, with many roads of
fine macadam. Villages were perched on the hillsides, and some of

them looked like picture postcards. It was all so different from the
Tunisia we had known that all of us, driving up suddenly one sunny
afternoon into that clean cool greenness, felt like holding out our
arms to such verdant beauty.

Yet that peaceful green gradually turned red with blood. The
roads were packed with brown-painted convoys, and the trailers
sprouted long rifle barrels. The incredibly blue sky with its big white
clouds was streaked with war planes in great throbbing formations.
And before long the whole northeastern corner of Tunisia roared and
raged with a violence utterly out of character with a landscape so rich
in nature's kindness.

The only thing we could say in behalf of ourselves was that the human race even in the process of defiling beauty still has the capacity to appreciate it.

Thousands of soldiers want someday to bring their wives and children back to Tunisia, in time of peace, and take them over the battlefields we came to know so well. But except for the cities they will not find much to remind them of the ferocity that existed there.

I traveled over the Tunisian battle area—both the part we knew so intimately because it was on our side and the part we didn't know at all because the Germans lived there at the time.

I didn't see the sort of desolated countryside I remembered from pictures of France in the last war. That was because the fighting had been mobile, because neither side used permanent huge guns, and because the country was mostly treeless and empty. But there were some marks left.

East of El Guettar, down a broad valley through which ran a nice macadam road, I saw dark objects sitting far off on the plain. They were the burned-out tanks of both sides. A certain two sat close together like twins, about a mile off the road. The immense caterpillar track was off one of them and it lay trailed out behind for fifty feet. The insides were a shambles. Seared and jumbled personal and mechanical debris was scattered around outside. Our soldiers had already retrieved almost everything worthwhile from the German debris, but there were still big wrenches, oil-soaked gloves, and twisted shell cases lying about.

There were many of those tanks scattered miles apart through the valley. And in the shade of one tank, not five feet from the great metal skeleton, was the fresh grave of a German tanker, marked by a rough wooden cross without a name.

On the hillsides white splotches were still visible—powder marks from our exploding artillery shells. Gnarled lengths of Signal Corps telephone wire, too mauled to retrieve, strung for yards along the roadsides.

There were frequent filled-in holes in the macadam where artillery or dive bombers had taken their toll. Now and then a little graveyard with wooden crosses stood lonesomely at the roadside. Some of the telephone poles had been chopped down. There were clumps of empty ammunition boxes. But for all these things a person had to look closely. There had been a holocaust but it left only a slight permanent mark. It is difficult to disfigure acres of marigolds and billions of blades of fresh desert grass.

Sidi bou Zid was the little white village I saw destroyed by shellfire back in February. It was weeks later before I could get close enough to see the details, because the village remained German territory for some time. It was one of the little towns I had known so well, but when I went back it was a pitiful sight. The village almost didn't exist. Its dozens of low stone adobe buildings, stuccoed a snowy white, were nothing but rock piles. The village had died. The reason for the destruction was that German and American tank columns, advancing toward each other, met there. Artillery from both sides poured its long-distance fury into the town for hours. There will have to be a new Sidi bou Zid.

Faid Pass is the last pass in the Grand Dorsal before the drive eastward onto the long flat plain that leads to the Mediterranean at Sfax. For months we looked with longing eyes at Faid. A number of times we tried to take it and failed. But when the Germans' big retreat came they left Faid Pass voluntarily. And they left it so thoroughly and maliciously mined that we never dared drive off onto the shoulder of the road for fear of getting blown to kingdom come.

Our engineers went through those mine fields with electrical instruments, located the mines, and surrounded them with warning notices until they could be dug up or exploded. Those notices were of two types—either a white ribbon strung around the mine area on knee-high sticks or else stakes with oppositely pointing arrows on top. The white arrow pointing to the left meaning that side was safe, the red arrow pointing to the right meaning that side was mined.

And believe me, after seeing a few mine-wrecked trucks and jeeps, we feared mines so dreadfully that we found ourselves actually leaning away from the side of the road where the signs were, as we drove past.

I hate to think of poor little Sfax. I believe it was one of the prettiest of all the Tunisian cities we saw. Somehow it had something of Miami's Biscayne Boulevard in it, and a little of San Diego too. But it was demolished—at least the downtown business part was, for it lay right on the water front and our Allied bombers played havoc with it. The whole business section, however, was evacuated before the bombing started, so probably there was only a slight loss of life.

After the bombing, parts of Sfax looked like London during the blitz. A locomotive sprawled on its side across a sidewalk. Royal palms, uprooted, lay pitifully in the street. Little parks were no-man's-lands of craters. The macadam streets had great cracks across them. There was no square inch left unwrecked in the downtown area.

The French felt that we shouldn't have bombed Sfax, because it was French. But it was one of Germany's big supply ports, and not to have bombed it would have been cutting our own throats as well as the throats of all Frenchmen.

Kairouan was a holy city, one of the minor Meccas, but it wasn't holy to the Germans. They used it all winter as a big rail and highway supply point.

We got to Kairouan shortly after the Germans had fled before the Eighth Army. That was the first time I had been close on the heels of a reoccupation. Three of us correspondents rode into the town in jeeps, and to our astonishment found the streets lined with crowds waving and cheering and applauding each passing vehicle.

Not knowing the difference, they gave us correspondents as big a hand as the rest. And we beamed and waved back just as if we'd run the Germans out ourselves.

Kairouan had been under Axis domination for nearly three years but it was not damaged much by bombing. Therein lay a slight mix-up somewhere, for it had been reported that one of our fliers destroyed the Splendide Hotel, which housed a German headquarters. Yet the Splendide was still standing, quite unharmed.

In Kairouan we saw the first white woman most of us had seen in a long time. Three French girls stood on a street corner for hours waving and smiling at the Allied tanks and trucks as they passed through the town. One of the girls had on a blue skirt and a white blouse, which made her stand out from the others. After that episode countless soldiers told me about the wonderful girl they had seen in Kairouan. Eventually they described how she was dressed, and it always turned out to be Miss Blue-Skirt-and-White-Blouse.

That one girl, merely by standing in the street and waving, had given to scores of women-hungry men an illusion of Broadway and Main Street that they'd not known in months.

Gafsa was the southern town we took back after it had been in German hands for a couple of months. Gafsa was not much damaged by shot and shell, but it was gutted by the cruel hands of ruthless men. Whether those were the hands of Germans or Arabs I wasn't able to find out.

One French officer estimated that the Arabs of Gafsa were 85 per cent for the Germans, 5 per cent for the French, and 10 per cent indifferent. That was a testimonial to the power of German propaganda, for the Arabs are lovers of might.

At any rate, when we returned to Gafsa the streets were littered, and the homes of all the Jews and better-off French and Arabs were wrecked. Windows had been broken, rugs and all other valuables stolen, furniture smashed and thrown out into the streets for desert Arabs to steal. Marauders went into a nice little hotel, apparently with hammers, and smashed every lavatory, every mirror and every window. They smashed the mechanism of every refrigerator in town.

Their crippling of the city power plant was legitimate. But their senseless smashings and their uprooting of private gardens was barbarism, solely for barbarity's sake.

The Germans, by stripping the country of provisions, probably caused more grief than either side did by actual battle. The tank-tracked fields would grow over. The blowing sands would fill the hundreds of thousands of expedient slit trenches. Ammunition boxes and gas cans and abandoned tanks would rust themselves into oblivion. Desiccated little towns would be rebuilt. And the Arab, as he has done for centuries, would go on about his slow business in the old way that suits him best.

Africa is a strange country, and this war is very little like the last war in France. Yet in Africa too many Americans sleep beneath fields of poppies—poppies so red and vivid that their beauty is strangely saddening.

The desert battlefields and the northern battle ground too were alive with flowers. They grew wild, in patches as thick as grass, blanketing solid acres. They grew together in vast stretches of red, yellow and orange, all of it framed by the lush green of new grass. Even the dullest spirits among us couldn't help being touched by their ironical loveliness.

I stopped now and then to see some of the battle graveyards. The Germans buried their dead on small cemeteries along the roadside, but we concentrated in fewer and bigger graveyards, usually on the edge of some town. Arabs were hired to dig the graves.

At Gafsa there was an American cemetery with more than six

hundred graves. It was in desertlike country, and the graves were aligned in precise rows in the naked gray earth. Each was marked with a waist-high wooden cross. In a near-by tent was a great pile of ready-made crosses, and a stack of newly carpentered wooden markers in the form of the Star of David for the Jewish dead.

The little German cemeteries were always bordered with rows of white rocks, and in some there were phrases neatly spelled out in white rocks with a border. One that I remember said, in rough translation: "These dead gave their spirits for the glory of Greater Germany."

In one German cemetery of about a hundred graves we found eleven Americans. They lay among the Germans, not segregated in any way. Their graves were identical with those of the Germans except that beneath the names on the wooden crosses was printed "Amerikaner," and below that the army serial number. Presumably their "dog tags" were buried with them.

On one of the graves, beneath the soldier's serial number, was also printed: "T-40." The Germans apparently thought that was part of his number. Actually it only showed that the man had had his first antitetanus shot in 1940.

My friend Sergeant Pat Donadeo was with me when we looked at this graveyard, and as we left he said, "They respect our dead the same as we do theirs. It's comforting to know that."

We also came upon a number of Italian graveyards set out in fields. Those graves too were well marked, and each had a bouquet of wilted marigolds. At the side of one little Italian cemetery, which was beautifully bordered and decorated, were half a dozen additional graves apparently dug at the last minute before the retreat. They were just rough mounds, unmarked except for an empty quart wine bottle stuck upside down at the head of each. Inside the bottles we could see scraps of paper, apparently with the dead Italians' names and numbers on them. Naturally we wouldn't violate the graves by pulling out the bottles, but even if our inclination had been rowdy we would have been afraid to. There were rumors, which I was not able to verify, that such grave-marking bottles were sometimes booby traps.

The Germans left clean country behind them. Their salvage organization was one of the best in the world—probably because of desperate necessity. We went all over the Tunisian country from which they had fled, and evidences that they had been there were slight. We saw burned-out tanks in the fields and some wrecked scout cars and Italian trucks lying in roadside ditches, and that was about all. Nothing was left behind that was repairable. Wrecked cars were stripped of their tires, instruments and lights. They left no tin cans, boxes or other junk as we did.

We saw little evidence of German earth-scorching, probably because the retreat northward was too fast. Some bridges were blown up. Mountain passes and the paths around wrecked bridges were heavily mined. But the most noticeable thing was the destruction of all telephone lines. They cut down about every other pole along the highways, and snipped most of the wires. The poles weren't chopped down. They were sawed off about two feet above the ground, and very neatly sawed off too.

When we moved north the heavens seemed bent on bounteous amends for all the misery they scourged us with during the winter. It was one time when nobody wanted to do anything about the weather. It was perfect. The rains were over. The cold was gone. Everything was green, and flowers sparkled over the countryside. The sun was up early and bright, and it was a blessing after all the dreary months of wet and wind. It was like June in Virginia.

I don't know how it affected the fighting troops, but in my own case I got spring fever so badly my conscience hurt. All I wanted to do was lie in the sun.

For a while we correspondents camped in an apricot grove, on ankle-high bluegrass. The sun beamed down between the trees, and occasional bees buzzed around with that midwestern summer drone that to me is synonymous with lazy days. That apricot grove was one of the most peaceful places I had ever known, and I found myself lying for hours outside my tent, flat on my back in the grass, reveling in the evil knowledge that I was shirking my work, the war, and everything else.

We were so close to the front lines we could base permanently in our own camp and still get to the firing line in half an hour. German raiders came over daily, but our air superiority was so great then that oftentimes we didn't even look up. All night the artillery rumbled, and the ground quivered. When I first arrived I couldn't sleep because of it, but I got used to it.

Unaccustomed as I was to air superiority, I must say that after an even brief association with that notorious stranger I found him one of the pleasantest companions.

With air superiority on his side a man could sit down in his tent and just keep on sitting, without running out for a cautious check-up every time he heard a plane. With air superiority a man could drive along in his jeep and not hit the ditch every time he saw a bird soaring in the distance. With air superiority a man could hear great droning formations approaching and know automatically that they were his, not theirs. We got so we didn't even fuss if we saw a German plane, because we knew the skies were so full of our patrolling Hawks that they would get him before he could do much damage.

We had air superiority in Tunisia those days, and how! Shortly before we were supposed to have a five-to-one advantage, and the odds were growing every day as the Germans withdrew some planes and others bit the eternal dust.

Our ground troops at last knew the exalting experience of fighting all day without a single Stuka diving on them. As our air strength grew and the enemy's dwindled we almost began to feel sorry for the poor troops on the other side who were then tasting the bitter brew from the skies.

For a time there I lived again with some of our American fighter pilots, and I found that the shift in balance had done as much for them as for our ground troops. They flew themselves punch-drunk in that big push, yet they flew with a dash they had never known before. For at last they were on the upper end of things.

We made great hay while the sun shone. The ground crews worked like fiends keeping the planes flyable. Pilots were going at a pace they couldn't possibly have stood very long. Some fighter pilots flew as many as five missions a day; formerly one was tops. The fighters did all kinds of work—escorting, ground sweeping, dogfighting, and even light bombing.

Let me tell you how that air superiority worked. In the old days we had sent a cover of fighters along with the bombers, but there were hardly ever enough of them. When we came into our own, we not only sent an enormous cover but we sent a second layer to cover the cover. A sort of double insulation. We didn't even stop there. We sent out groups of fighters known as "free lances," far out of sight of our bombers, just to intercept anything that might be wandering around. And to wind it all up we sent out fresh planes to meet the bombers just after they left the target, in case the regular cover of fighters might have trouble or run low on gas. They were called "delousing missions," and they scraped off any pests that got tenacious.

Both sides had kept constant airdrome patrols in the air all winter —from two to half a dozen planes circling each airdrome constantly from dawn to dusk, to be already in the air if enemy planes ap-

peared. After we got the upper hand, we still patrolled, but we also took on a little extra work, and this I think is the ultimate in air superiority: we patrolled the German airdromes too!

Our fighters actually patrolled one whole afternoon over a big German drome, just flying back and forth and around, and prevented every single German plane from even taking off. Of course that was an isolated case, and I'm not trying to make you believe we patrolled all the German dromes all the time, but the fact that it could happen at all was practically phenomenal.

Yes, air superiority was a wonderful thing. It was one of life's small luxuries to which I was eager to become more accustomed.

Our army in North Africa was still full of rumors. Most of them had to do with when we would go home. There was a rumor that

President Roosevelt had made a radio address saying that the mothers, wives, and sweethearts of the men in North Africa were due for a big surprise as soon as the Tunisian campaign was over. The rumored remark spread and was immediately interpreted by the men as meaning that everybody was going home the minute the last German was out of Africa. Some of our troops sincerely believed that would happen.

The orange and tangerine season was over. Those richly juicy North African tangerines were one of the pleasantest things of our war over here. For months we ate them by the daily dozen. When they were all gone we went back to occasional canned fruit juice from America. And on British mess tables we found a little can of pills called ascorbic tablets, which we took daily to make up for the lack of fruits in our diet.

A new type of American ration showed up in answer to the British compo, which small groups of traveling soldiers had found so superior to anything of ours. The new stuff was called "U ration." It was wonderful. It had everything that was needed by four or five men who had to fix their own meals out on a trip.

It came in a pasteboard box inside a wooden box. Everything was done up in small cans or packets just big enough to be used up at one meal. With it came two printed menus, guides in eating the rations. I lost No. 1 but No. 2 was: Breakfast—tomato juice, whole-wheat cereal, sliced bacon, biscuits, coffee; dinner—bean soup, roast beef, quick-cooking rice, biscuits, lemonade, hard candy; supper—meat and vegetable stew, dried prunes, coffee, apricot spread.

The ration also included root beer, gumdrops, canned butter, tomato juice in powdered form, and two big envelopes of toilet paper. The tomato juice was fairly lousy, but the canned bacon was superb. God bless the U ration!

As was bound to happen in wartime, close friends sometimes disappeared. And as soon as they were gone we sat of an evening and recounted stories about them, just as we did in the old aviation days after a mail pilot didn't come back from his run.

One of my closest friends was Lieutenant Leonard Bessman, a lawyer from Milwaukee. We had almost definite proof that Bessman was captured, and not killed, so we all hoped to see him again before too long if things turned out right. I've mentioned Lennie Bessman before. Of all the soldiers I have ever known he was the most sensitive to the little beauties of war and to the big tragedy of life. Maybe that was because he was a Jew, or maybe it wasn't. I don't know.

His bravery was a byword among us long before he was captured. It was a bravery based on pure idealism—the invulnerable kind of bravery—and it was inevitable that sooner or later he would either die or fall prisoner. I never heard of anyone who didn't love and admire him.

We sat around on our cots at night and laughed about things we had heard Lennie say, because they sounded so melodramatic, yet, knowing him as we did, we knew they weren't melodramatic at all and that Lennie had meant what he said.

A good example is the day he was trapped, overwhelmed and captured. He was far up forward of our advance troops, for that was his job, and suddenly he found himself cut off, with a German tank in front of him and a machine-gun nest on his side. Lennie jumped out of his jeep, pulled his .45 and yelled at the heavily armed enemy, "Come on out and I won't shoot." In other people that would have been artificial bravado; but Lennie really meant it.

Most of us found our emotions becoming jaded as month after month of war piled up on us, but Lennie was never jaded. He had a facility for mirroring in his fertile mind every hman thing that crossed his path. We had a certain type of antiaircraft gun, mounted on a half-track, which required two men to fire. The gunners sat in two metal bucket seats just back of the guns. Lennie was lying near this ack-ack outfit during a terrific dive-bombing and strafing, and he kept his eyes on those two special gunners as the Stukas came down right upon them.

The two never wavered. They sat there firing until suddenly and in unison they toppled sideways out of their seats—dead. And all within the same instant two more Americans rose like twins from the bed of the half-track, took the seats just vacated by death, and went right on with the firing. Lennie was terribly moved by that little drama of duty automatically performed, and he almost choked up when he told the story.

The incident that most tickled his admiration happened at the time we had a big concentration of artillery that was giving the Germans plenty of trouble. They couldn't locate it, so at night they sent planes over hunting for it. Of course it was then our cue to lay low and silent, so as not to give away our position by firing at them.

They came night after night, and never did find us. But each night after they had circled and were finally leaving, one lone contemptuous gunner fired one lone contemptuous shot at them, just as if to say, "Here we are, you silly fools!"

Night after night that one gunner fired his one slapstick shot just as they were leaving. His sauciness exalted Lennie's soul. I heard him say, "I'd rather shake hands with that man than anybody in the American Army. I'm going to try to find him, and even if he's a private I'm going to salute him."

We had heard that the Germans took the few Americans captured at El Guettar and marched them up the main street of Tunis, then loaded them in trucks and paraded them back again, then unloaded them and marched them through town once more—to make it look as if there were lots of prisoners. One of Lennie's friends said he could just see Lennie, on his third compulsory trip down the main street of Tunis, screwing up his nose in the special mask of comic disgust which was one of his little habits, and observing, "Seems as if I've seen this before somewhere."

Another friend, whom I've already mentioned, was also among the missing. He too, we knew almost definitely, was a prisoner. He was Captain Tony Lumpkin, of Mexico, Missouri. Tony was headquarters commandant of a certain outfit—a headquarters commandant being a sort of militarized hotel manager.

Just before he disappeared Tony got to going by the nickname of "Noah" Lumpkin, because he always seemed to pick out such a miserably wet place for a command post. On their last move before he was captured, the commanding general—a swell guy with a sense of humor—called Captain Lumpkin over, stood with him outside a tent looking out over the watery landscape, and congratulated him on locating them in the center of such a beautiful lake.

Tony Lumpkin needn't have been captured at all if he had been content to stick to his comparatively safe "hotel managing." But he wanted to get a crack at the Jerries himself. He was an expert gunner, and he finally talked the commander into letting him take five men and a small gun on wheels and go out to see what he could pick off.

The first day they got one German truck plus something that turned out later to be a camel, although it looked like a truck at the distance they were firing from. The second day they moved farther into the mountains to get into a better shooting position, but bagged nothing. On the third day they went even farther into the hills, hunting a perfect spot for firing.

Captain Lumpkin used to share a tent with Major Chuck Miller of Detroit, and with their assistant, Corporal William Nikolin of Indianapolis, both of whom I've mentioned, they formed an intimate little family.

That third night Major Miller came in late. He was astonished, and a little bit concerned, to see Tony's cot empty. When he woke up next morning there was still no Tony. Major Miller went to the general and got permission to start out with a squad of his own military police and hunt for his lost companion.

They covered all the ground Tony had covered, and finally, by studying the terrain and talking with others who had been near by, and interviewing German prisoners, they pieced together what had happened. The hill that Captain Lumpkin had been trying to get to had been simply lousy with German machine gunners. The Germans saw him all the time. They sent out a party that worked behind and surrounded him. A German who was captured later said that a captain with a tommy gun killed one German and wounded another before being taken.

There wasn't grief in the little Lumpkin-Miller-Nikolin family, but there was a terrible vacancy. "We were a perfect team," Major Miller said. "Tony was slow and easygoing, and I'm big and lose my temper too quickly. We balanced each other. I'd keep him pepped up and he'd calm me down. We sure miss him, don't we, Nicky?"

That spring I was away from the front lines for a while, living with other troops, and considerable fighting took place while I was gone. When I got ready to return to my old friends at the front I wondered if I would sense any change in them. I did, and definitely.

The most vivid change was the casual and workshop manner in which they talked about killing. They had made the psychological transition from their normal belief that taking human life was sinful, over to a new professional outlook where killing was a craft. No longer was there anything morally wrong about killing. In fact, it was an admirable thing.

I think I was so impressed by that new attitude because it hadn't been necessary for me to make that change along with them. As a noncombatant, my own life was in danger only by occasional chance or circumstance. Consequently I didn't need to think of killing in personal terms, and killing to me was still murder.

Even after a winter of living with wholesale death and vile destruction, it was only spasmodically that I seemed capable of realizing how real and how awful the war was. My emotions seemed dead and crusty when presented with the tangibles of war. I found I could look on rows of fresh graves without a lump in my throat. Somehow I could look on mutilated bodies without flinching or feeling deeply.

It was only when I sat alone away from it all or lay at night in my bedroll re-creating what I had seen, thinking and thinking and thinking, that at last the enormity of all those newly dead struck like a living nightmare. Then there were times when I felt I couldn't stand it and would have to leave.

But to the fighting soldier that phase of the war was behind. It was left behind after his first battle. His blood was up. He was fighting for his life, and killing then for him was as much a profession as writing was for me.

He wanted to kill individually or in vast numbers. He wanted to see the Germans overrun, mangled, butchered in the Tunisian trap. He spoke excitedly of seeing great heaps of dead, of our bombers sinking whole shiploads of fleeing men, of Germans by the thousands dying miserably in a final Tunisian holocaust of their own creation.

In that one respect the front-line soldier differed from all the rest of us. All the rest of us—you and me and even the thousands of soldiers behind the lines in Africa—we wanted terribly yet only academically for the war to be over. The front-line soldier wanted it to be terminated by the physical process of his destroying enough Germans to end it. He was truly at war. The rest of us, no matter how hard we worked, were not. Say what you will, nothing can make a complete soldier except battle experience.

In the semifinals—the cleaning out of Central Tunisia—we had large units in battle for the first time. Frankly, they didn't all excel. Their own commanders admitted it, and admirably they didn't try to alibi. The British had to help us out a few times, but neither American nor British commanders were worried about that, for there was no lack of bravery. There was only lack of experience. They all knew we would do better the next time.

The First Infantry Division was an example of what our American units could do after they had gone through the mill of experience. Those boys did themselves proud in the semifinals. Everybody spoke about it. Our casualties included few taken prisoners. All the other casualties were wounded or died fighting. "They never gave an inch," a general said. "They died right in their foxholes."

I heard of a high British officer who went over the battlefield just after the action was over. American boys were still lying dead in their foxholes, their rifles still grasped in firing position in their dead hands. And the veteran English soldier remarked time and again, in a sort of hushed eulogy spoken only to himself, "Brave men. Brave men!"

We moved one afternoon to a new position just a few miles behind the invisible line of armor that separated us from the Germans in Northern Tunisia. Nothing happened that first night that was spectacular, yet somehow the whole night became obsessed with a spookiness that leaves it standing like a landmark in my memory.

We had been at the new camp about an hour and were still setting up our tents when German planes appeared overhead. We stopped work to watch them. It was the usual display of darting planes, with the conglomerate sounds of ack-ack on the ground and in the sky. Suddenly we realized that one plane was diving straight at us, and we made a mad scramble for foxholes. Two officer friends of mine had dug a three-foot hole and set their tent over it. They made for their tent, and I was tramping on their heels. The tent flap wouldn't come open, and we wound up in a silly heap. Finally it did open, and we all dived through the narrow opening at once.

We lay there in the hole, face down, as the plane came smack overhead with a terrible roar. We were all drawn up inside, waiting for the blow. Explosions around us were shatteringly loud, and yet when it was all over we couldn't find any bomb holes or anybody hurt. But we could have found a lot of nervous people.

Dusk came on, and with dusk began the steady boom of big guns in the mountains ahead of us. They weren't near enough for the sound to be crashing. Rather it was like the lonely roll of an approaching thunderstorm—a sound which since childhood has always made me sad with a kind of portent of inevitable doom.

We went to bed in our tents. A near-by farmyard was full of dogs and they began a howling that lasted all night. The roll of artillery was constant. It never stopped for twenty-four hours. Once in a while there were nearer shots which might have been German patrols, or might not. We lay uneasily in our cots. Sleep wouldn't come. We turned and turned. I snapped on a flashlight.

"What time is it?" asked Chris Cunningham from the next cot.

"Quarter to one," I answered. "Haven't you been asleep?"

He hadn't.

A plane droned faintly in the distance and came nearer and nearer until it was overhead. "Is that a Jerry or a Beaufighter?" Chris asked out of the darkness.

"It hasn't got that throb-throb to it," I said, "so it must be a Beaufighter. But hell, I never can tell really. Don't know what it is."

The plane passed on, out of hearing. The artillery rolled and rolled. A nearer shot went off uncannily somewhere in the darkness. Some guinea hens set up a terrific cackling. I remembered that just before dusk a soldier had shot at a snake in our new camp, and they had thought it was a cobra. And we'd just heard our first stories of scorpions. I began to feel creepy and wondered if our tent flaps were tight.

Another plane throbbed in the sky, and we lay listening with an awful anticipation. One of the dogs suddenly broke into a frenzied barking and went tearing through our little camp as if chasing a demon. My mind seemed to lose all sense of proportion, and I got jumpy and mad at myself.

Concussion ghosts, traveling in waves, touched our tent walls and made them quiver. Ghosts were shaking the ground ever so lightly.

Ghosts were stirring the dogs to hysteria. Ghosts were wandering in the sky peering for us cringing in our hide-outs. Ghosts were everywhere, and their hordes were multiplying as every hour added its production of new battlefield dead.

We lay and thought of the graveyards and the dirty men and the shocking blast of the big guns, and we couldn't sleep.

"What time is it?" came out of darkness from the next cot. I snapped on the flashlight.

"Half past four, and for God's sake go to sleep!"

Finally just before dawn we did sleep, in spite of everything.

Next morning we spoke around among ourselves and found that all of us had tossed away all night. It was an unexplainable thing. For all of us had been through greater danger. On another night the roll of the guns would have lulled us to sleep.

It was just that on some nights the air became sick and there was an unspoken contagion of spiritual dread, and we were little boys again, lost in the dark.

16. THE FINAL PUSH

Dᴜʀɪɴɢ the final push I attached myself to the First Infantry Division in the front lines before Mateur. That northern warfare was in the mountains. We didn't do much riding then. It was walking and climbing and crawling country. The mountains weren't big, but they were constant. They were largely treeless, easy to defend and bitter to take. But we took them.

The Germans lay on the back slope of every ridge, deeply dug into foxholes. In front of them the fields and pastures were hideous with thousands of hidden mines. The forward slopes were left open, untenanted, and if the Americans had tried to scale those slopes they would have been murdered wholesale in an inferno of machine-gun crossfire, plus mortars and grenades.

Consequently, we didn't do it that way. We fell back to the old warfare of first pulverizing the enemy with artillery, then sweeping around the ends of the hill with infantry and taking them from the sides and rear.

The big guns cracked and roared almost constantly throughout the day and night. They laid a screen ahead of our troops. By magnificent shooting they dropped shells on the back slopes. By means of shells timed to burst in the air a few feet from the ground, they got the Germans even in their foxholes. Our troops found that the Germans dug foxholes down and then under, in an effort to get cover from the shell bursts that showered death from above. Our artillery was really sensational. For once we had enough of something and at the right time. Officers told me they actually had more guns than they knew what to do with.

All the guns in any one sector could be centered to shoot at one spot, and when we laid the whole business on a German hill the entire slope seemed to erupt. It became an unbelievable caldron of fire and smoke and dirt. Afterward, veteran German soldiers said they had never been through anything like it.

A salute to the infantry—the God-damned infantry, as they like to call themselves. I loved the infantry because they were the under-dogs. They were the mud-rain-frost-and-wind boys. They had no com-forts, and they even learned to live without the necessities. And in the end they were the guys without whom the Battle of Africa could not have been won.

I wish you could have seen just one of the unforgettable sights I saw. I was sitting among clumps of sword grass on a steep and rocky hillside that we had just taken, looking out over a vast rolling country to the rear. A narrow path wound like a ribbon over a hill miles away, down a long slope, across a creek, up a slope and over another hill. All along the length of that ribbon there was a thin line of men. For four days and nights they had fought hard, eaten little, washed none, and slept hardly at all. Their nights had been violent with attack, fright, butchery, their days sleepless and miser-able with the crash of artillery.

The men were walking. They were fifty feet apart for dispersal. Their walk was slow, for they were dead weary, as a person could tell even when looking at them from behind. Every line and sag of their bodies spoke their inhuman exhaustion. On their shoulders and backs they carried heavy steel tripods, machine-gun barrels, leaden boxes of ammunition. Their feet seemed to sink into the ground from the overload they were bearing.

They didn't slouch. It was the terrible deliberation of each step that spelled out their appalling tiredness. Their faces were black and unshaved. They were young men, but the grime and whiskers and ex-haustion made them look middle-aged. In their eyes as they passed was no hatred, no excitement, no despair, no tonic of their victory— there was just the simple expression of being there as if they had been there doing that forever, and nothing else.

The line moved on, seemingly endless. All afternoon men kept coming round the hill and vanishing eventually over the horizon. It was one long tired line of antlike men. There was an agony in your heart and you felt almost ashamed to look at them.

They were just guys from Broadway and Main Street, but maybe you wouldn't remember them. They were too far away now. They were too tired. Their world can never be known to you, but if you could have seen them just once, just for an instant, you would know that no matter how hard people were working back home they never kept pace with those infantrymen in Tunisia.

After four days in battle, my division sat on its newly won hill and took two days' rest, while companion units on each side of it leapfrogged ahead.

The men dug in on the back slope of the hill before any rest began. Everybody dug in. It was an inviolate rule of the commanding officers and nobody wanted to disobey it. Every time there was a pause, even if a man thought he was dying of weariness, he dug himself a hole before he sat down.

The startling thing to me about those rest periods was how quickly the human body could recuperate from critical exhaustion, how rapidly the human mind snapped back to the normal state of laughing, grousing, yarn-spinning, and yearning for home.

Outposts were placed, phone wires were strung on the ground, some patrol work went on as usual. Then the men lay down and slept till the blistering heat of the sun woke them up.

After that they sat around in bunches recounting things. They didn't do much of anything. The day just easily killed itself. That evening was when life began to seem like Christmas Eve. The mail came up in jeeps just before dark. Then came the men's blanket rolls. At dark, hot food arrived—the first hot food in four days. This food was cooked in rolling kitchens several miles back and brought up by jeep, in big thermos containers, to the foot of the hill. Men carried the containers, slung on poles over their shoulders, up goat paths in the darkness to all parts of the mountain.

Hot food and hot coffee put life into the men, and then in a pathetic kind of contentment they lay down and slept. The all-night crash of the artillery behind them was completely unheard through their weariness. There were no mosquitoes in the mountains, and very few fleas, but we discovered that our ridge was inhabited by a frightening menagerie of snakes, two-legged lizards, scorpions, centipedes, overgrown chiggers and man-eating ants.

Hot food arrived again in the morning before daylight. Breakfast was at four. Then began a day of reassembling. Word was passed that mail would be collected that evening, so the boys sat on the ground and wrote letters. But writing was hard, for they couldn't tell in their letters what they had just been through.

The men put water in their steel helmets and washed and shaved for the first time in days. A few men at a time were sent to a creek in the valley to take baths. The remainder sat in groups on the ground talking, or individually in foxholes cleaning their guns, reading, or just relaxing. A two-month-old batch of copies of the magazine *Yank* arrived, and a two-week-old bunch of *Stars and Stripes*. Some of the men read detective magazines and comic books that had come up with their bedrolls. At noon everybody opened cans of cold C ration. Cold coffee in five-gallon water cans was put in the sun to warm.

Soldiers cut each other's hair. It didn't matter how it looked, for they weren't going anywhere fancy anyhow. Some of them stripped nearly naked and lay on their blankets for a sunbath. Their bodies

were tanned as if they had been wintering at Miami Beach. They wore the inner part of their helmets, for the noonday sun was dangerous.

Their knees were skinned from crawling over rocks. They found little unimportant injuries that they didn't know they had. Some took off their shoes and socks and looked over their feet, which were violently purple with athlete's foot ointment.

I sat around with them, and they got to telling stories, both funny and serious, about their battle. "We always get it the toughest," they said. "This is our third big battle now since coming to Africa. The Jerry is really afraid of us now. He knows what outfit we are, and he doesn't like us."

Thus they talked and boasted and laughed and spoke of fear. Evening came down and the chill set in once more. Hot chow arrived just after dusk. And then the word was passed around. Orders came by telephone. There was no excitement, no grouching, no eagerness either. They had expected it. Quietly men rolled their packs, strapped them on, lifted their rifles and fell into line.

There was not a sound as they moved like wraiths in single file down tortuous goat paths, walking slowly, feeling the ground with their toes, stumbling, and hushfully cussing. They moved like ghosts. They couldn't have been heard or seen three feet away. Now and then a light flashed lividly from a blast by our big guns, and for just an instant a long slow line of dark-helmeted forms was silhouetted in the flash. Then darkness and silence consumed them again, and somehow you were terribly moved.

Our battalion marched in two sections. The first left early, with orders to attack a certain forward hill at 3:00 A.M. The other section was to start after midnight, reach a certain protected wadi before dawn, dig itself in, and stand by for use whenever needed. I went with the second batch.

The men weren't upset about going into the line again so soon. They just accepted it. They felt they had already done more than their share of the war's fighting, but there was in their manner a touchingly simple compliance with whatever was asked of them.

At one o'clock we were ready to go. Blanket rolls and personal gear were left behind. I carried only my mackinaw and small hand shovel. In two columns we plowed down a half-mile slope waist-high in wild grass. The slope was full of big bomb craters. We had to feel for them with our feet and walk around them. There were big rocks hidden in the grass, and soldiers stumbled and fell down awkwardly in their heavy gear, and got up cussing.

Finally we hit a sort of path and fell into a single line of march. It was very slow at first, for we were crowding the last stragglers of the first section. For long periods we stopped for some unexplained reason and just sat on the ground.

The man ahead of me, Private Lee Hawkins of Everett, Pennsylvania, had a 50-pound radio strapped onto his back, plus two boxes of ammunition. How he kept on his feet in that rough sightless march, I don't know.

After a couple of hours the route ahead seemed to clear up. We walked briskly in single file. We had to keep our eyes on the ground and watch every step. The moon came up, but it was behind a great black cloud and gave only a little light. We talked some, but not much. We made a few more brief unexplained stops, and then suddenly word came down the column: "No more talking. Pass it back."

From then on we marched in silence except for the splitting crash of German artillery ahead, and of ours behind. The artillery of both sides was firing almost continuously. We could hear the heavy blast of the guns, then the eerie rustle from each shell as it sped unseen across the sky far above our heads. It gave the night a strange sense of greatness. I couldn't help but feel a sort of exaltation from the tense, stumbling march through foreign darkness up into the unknown.

It did have its lighter touch, if a man had been inclined to hunt for a laugh. Another soldier with a portable radio had been trying since early evening to make contact with our leading column. He was having static trouble, and all night long he kept walking around trying various locations. Wherever we turned, wherever we stopped, we could always hear that same voice, gradually growing pitiful in its vain quest, calling softly: "Lippman to Howell. Come in, Howell."

As the night wore on and that voice kept up its persistent wandering and fruitless calling for its mate, it got to be like a scene out of a Saroyan play.

Shells from both sides kept going far over our heads. They were landing miles away. Then all of a sudden they weren't. With the quickness of an automobile accident a German shell screamed toward us. Instinct tells a man, from the timbre of the tone, how near a shell is coming to him. Our whole column fell flat automatically and in unison.

The shell landed with a frightening blast two hundred yards to our right. We got up and started, and it happened again, this time to our left. I felt weak all over, and all the others had the creeps too.

Then off to the left we heard German machine-gun fire. We could always tell it from American machine-gunning, because it was so much faster. Word was passed down the line for us to squat down. We sat silent on our haunches for a minute. On another order we all crept over into some grass and lay hidden there for about five minutes. Then we started on.

We got to where we were going half an hour before dawn. It was an outcropping of big white rocks, covering several acres, just back of the rise where the earlier half of our unit was already fighting.

The commanding officer told us to find good places among the rocks, get well scattered, and dig in immediately. He didn't have to do any urging. Machine guns were crashing a few hundred yards off. Now and then a bullet ricocheted down among us.

The order went around to dig only with shovels, for the sound of picks hitting rocks might give us away to the Germans. We talked in whispers. The white rocks were like ghosts and gave an illusion of moving when we looked at them. I picked out an L-shaped niche formed by two knee-high rocks, and began shoveling out a hole in front of them. At dawn we were all dug in, and the artillery had increased to a frenzy that seemed to consume the sky.

We had then been without sleep for twenty-four hours, and we lay in our holes and slept wearily, oblivious of the bedlam around us and the heat of the bright early sun. As I fell off to sleep I heard a low voice just behind my rock, pleading, it seemed to me then, a little hoarsely, but still determinedly: "Come in, Howell. Come in, Howell."

Much of our Northern Tunisian mountain fighting was done at night, and in the dark of the moon too. It had always been a mystery to me how troops could move on foot in total darkness over rough, pathless country that was completely strange to them.

The going was just as difficult as I had thought it would be. The pace was slow—one mile an hour in moving up into the lines was a good speed. The soldiers usually went single file. They didn't march, they just walked. Each man had to pick and feel for his own footholds. Sure, he fell down. He stepped into a hole or tripped on a telephone wire, or stubbed his toe on a rock, and down he went, but he got right up again and went on. He tried to keep close enough to the man in front so that he could see his form dimly and follow him. Keeping his course at night was as difficult as navigating during a stormy night at sea, for it was total darkness and he had no landmarks to go by.

Captain E. D. Driscoll, of New York, said, "We have gremlins in the infantry too. And the meanest gremlin is the one who moves mountains. We start for a certain hill in the dark, we check everything carefully as we go along, and then when we get there some gremlin has moved the damned mountain and we can't find it anywhere."

At the head of the column were guides who had reconnoitered the route in daytime patrols and memorized the main paths, hills and gullies. In addition, an officer with a compass was at the head of the column, and in case of doubt he got down and threw a blanket over himself for blackout, and looked at the compass by flashlight.

Other guides were posted along the line to keep the rear elements from straying off on side paths. Furthermore, the leaders marked the trail as they went along. They usually did this by leaving strips of white mine-marking tape lying on the ground every hundred yards or so. On our march they had run out of white tape so they used surgeon's gauze. Sometimes they marked the trail by wrapping toilet paper around rocks which they left lying on the path.

In spite of all that, two or three dim-witted guys out of every company got lost and spent the next couple of days wandering around the hills asking everybody they met where their company was.

A column advancing into new country strings its own telephone wire. You probably know that army telephone wire is simply strung along the ground. We used very light wire, and even a bantam weight like myself could carry a half-mile reel of it under his arm. On our first night march we carried two miles of phone wire with us. At the end of a half-mile reel we made contact with a field telephone and called back to battalion headquarters to tell them how far we'd got, what we had seen and heard, and whether there was any opposition. As soon as another half mile was strung, the phone was advanced.

The Germans were adept at one thing. That was in digging and camouflaging their gun positions. Once we captured a dug-in 88-millimeter gun while driving the Germans off a hill, and after the battle was over and we came back to get the big gun we couldn't find the damned thing, though obviously it was still right there.

Also they dug in machine-gun snipers on the hillsides and left them there. When the rest af the Germans withdrew those guys stayed hidden in the rocky hillsides right among our own troops. After we had occupied the hill they fired on our troops to the rear, and generally made pests of themselves. We had an awful time finding them.

There were two machine gunners who stayed in their little dugouts and kept firing for three days after we had occupied their hill, despite the fact that our troops were bivouacked all over the hillside, living within a few feet of them, walking past or over their gun positions scores of times a day.

The Germans had a trick of digging a good-sized hole and covering it with the rocks that abounded on those hillsides, leaving a little hole just big enough to fire through. They kept a few days' rations, and just stayed there until captured. The place looked like any other of thousands of places on the hillside. We could walk past it or stand on it and not know what was beneath us. Once we did know, we found we couldn't get the gunners out without practically tearing the rocks out by hand.

On one unforgettable Tunisian day between three and four thousand shells passed over our heads. True, most of them were in transit, en route to somewhere else, but enough of them were intended for us to make a fellow very somber before the day was over. And just as a sideline, a battle was going on a couple of hundreds yards to our left, mines were blowing up jeeps on our right, and German machine-gun bullets were zinging past with annoying persistency.

My outfit was in what was laughingly called "reserve" for the day. But when I heard soldiers who had been through four big battles say with dead seriousness, "Brother, this is getting rugged!" I felt I would rather be in complete retirement than in reserve.

All day we were a sort of crossroads for shells and bullets. All day guns roared in a complete circle around us. About three-eighths of that circle was German, and five-eighths of it American. Our guns were blasting the Huns' hill positions ahead of us, and the Germans were blasting our gun positions behind us. Shells roared over us from every point of the compass. I don't believe there was a whole minute in fourteen hours of daylight when the air above us was silent.

The guns themselves were close enough to be brutal in their noise, and between shots the air above us was filled with the intermixed rustle and whine of traveling shells. A man can't see a shell, unless he's standing near the gun when it is fired, but its rush through the air makes such a loud sound that it seems impossible it can't be seen. Some shells whine loudly throughout their flight. Others make only a toneless rustle. It's an indescribable sound. The nearest I can come to it is the sound of jerking a stick through water.

Some apparently defective shells got out of shape and made queer noises. I remember one that sounded like a locomotive puffing hard at about forty miles an hour. Another one made a rhythmic knocking sound as if turning end over end. We all had to laugh when it went over.

They say a man never hears the shell that hits him. Fortunately I don't know about that, but I do know that the closer they hit the less time there is to hear them. Those landing within a hundred yards are heard only about a second before they hit. The sound produces a special kind of horror that is something more than mere fright. It is a confused form of acute desperation.

Each time it seemed certain that was the one. Ducking was instinctive. Whether I shut my eyes or not I don't know, but I do know I became so weak that my joints felt all gone. It took about ten minutes to get back to normal.

Shells that came too close made veterans jump just the same as neophytes. Once we heard three shells in the air at the same time, all headed for us. It wasn't possible for me to get three times as weak as usual, but after they had all crashed safely a hundred yards away I knew I would have had to grunt and strain mightily to lift a soda cracker.

Sometimes the enemy fire quieted down and we thought the Germans were pulling back, until suddenly we were rudely awakened by a heinous bedlam of screaming shells, mortar bursts, and even machine-gun bullets.

Things had died down late one afternoon, and the enemy was said to be several hills back. I was wandering around among some soldiers who were sitting and standing outside their foxholes during the lull. Somebody told me about a new man who had had a miraculous escape, so I walked around till I found him.

He was Private Malcolm Harblin, of Peru, New York, a 24-year-old farmer who had been in the army only since June of '42. Harblin was a small, pale fellow, quiet as a mouse. He wore silver-rimmed glasses, his steel helmet was too big for him, and he looked incongruous on a battlefield. But he was all right in his very first battle, back at El Guettar—an 88-millimeter shell hit right beside him, and a big fragment went between his left arm and his chest, tearing his jacket, shirt and undershirt all to pieces. He wasn't even scratched.

He still wore that ragged uniform, for it was all he had. He showed me the holes, and we were talking along nice and peaceful-like when all of a sudden there came that noise and, boy, it had all the tags on it.

Harblin dived into his foxhole and I was right on top of him. Sometimes a man didn't hear a shell soon enough, and in that case we would have been too late, except that it was a dud. It hit the ground about thirty feet ahead of us, bounced past us so close we could almost have grabbed it, and finally wound up less than a hundred yards behind us.

Harblin looked at me, and I looked at Harblin. I just had strength enough to whisper bitterly at him, "You and your narrow escapes!"

I lived, of course, just as the men did. Our home was on the ground. We sat, ate, and slept on the ground. We were in a different place almost every night, for we were constantly moving forward from hill to hill. Establishing a new bivouac consisted of nothing more than digging new foxholes. We seldom took off our clothes, not even our shoes. Nobody had more than one blanket, and many men had none at all. For three nights I slept on the ground with nothing under or over me. Finally I got one blanket and my shelter-halves sent up.

We had no warm food for days. Each man kept his own rations and ate whenever he pleased. Oddly enough I was never conscious of the lack of warm food. Water was brought to us in cans, but very little washing was done.

Sometimes we were up all night on the march and then we slept in the daytime till the hot sun made sleep impossible. Some of the men slept right in their foxholes, others on the ground alongside. Since rocks were so abundant, most of us buttressed our foxholes with little rock walls around them.

We were shot at by 88s, 47s, machine guns, tanks. Despite our own air superiority we were dive-bombed numerous times, but the Germans were always in such a hurry to get it over and get home that usually their aim was bad and the bombs fell harmlessly in open spaces. We could always count on being awakened at dawn by a dive-bombing.

After being both shelled and bombed, I decided an artillery barrage was the worse of the two. A prolonged artillery barrage came very close to being unbearable, and we saw many pitiful cases of "anxiety neurosis."

The nights were sometimes fantastic. The skies flashed all night from the muzzle blasts of big guns. Parachute flares shot from the ground and dropped from planes hung in the sky. Armored vehicles rumbled across country all night. German planes thrummed through the skies seeking some flash of light on the ground.

At dusk groups of litter-bearers set out to carry the wounded from forward companies. Just after dawn each morning the stretchers and the walking wounded came slowly downhill from the night's fighting. Ammunition carriers in long lines toiled up to us, carrying triple clusters of heavy mortar shells on their shoulders.

A couple of miles behind us the engineers worked day and night without cease, digging and blasting and bulldozing passes through the hills so that our wheeled vehicles could follow the advance.

Sometimes we didn't sleep at all for thirty hours or more. At first the activity and excitement kept me awake. I didn't want to go to sleep for fear of missing something. Also, at first the noise of the artillery was terrific. But on my last two nights in the lines I slept eight hours solid and never heard a thing.

During all the time we were under fire I felt fine. The catch-as-catch-can sleep didn't seem to bother me. I never felt physically tired even after the marches. The days were so diverse and so unregimented that a week sped by before I knew it. I never felt that I was excited or tense except during certain fast-moving periods of shelling or bombing, and those were quickly over. When I finally left the line just after daylight one morning I had never felt better in my life.

And yet, once I was safe back in camp an intense weariness came over me. I slept almost every minute of two days and nights. I just didn't have the will to get up, except to eat. My mind was as blank as my body was lifeless. I felt as if every cell in my make-up had been consumed. It was utter exhaustion such as I had never known. Apparently it was the letdown from being uncommonly tense without realizing I was tense. It was not until the fourth day that I began to feel really normal again, and even then I was afraid I thought too much about the wounded men.

Moral—German 88-mm. shells are evil companions and their company should be avoided.

Early in the campaign I said that the part the Americans would play in the final phase of the Tunisian war would be comparatively small. That was true, if looked at from the big angle. But after the worm's-eye view I got in the front lines during a big portion of the fight, it was hard to see anything from the big angle, and I felt constrained to eat my words.

Our part did seem mighty large to me at times. For our American troops had a brutal fight in the mountain phase of the campaign. It was war of such intensity as Americans on this side of the ocean had never known. It was a battle without letup. It was a war of drenching artillery and hidden mines and walls of machine-gun fire and even of the barbaric bayonet. It was an exhausting, cruel, last-ditch kind of war, and those who went through it would seriously doubt that war could be any worse than those two weeks of mountain fighting.

The Germans battled savagely and desperately from hill to hill until the big break came. There were times when we had to throw battalion after battalion onto an already pulverized hill before we could finally take it. Our casualties must surely have run high.

Nobody will care to underrate the American contribution to the end of Rommel in North Africa.

Apparently there were some intimations in print back home that the First Division did not fight well in its earlier battles. The men of that division were wrathful and bitter about that. They went through four big battles in North Africa, made a good name for themselves in every one, and paid dearly for their victories. If such a criticism was printed it was somebody's unfortunate mistake. The First Division always fought well.

It is natural to be loyal to your friends, and I feel a loyalty to the First Division, for I lived with it off and on for six months. But it is a sad thing to become loyal to the men of a division in wartime. It is sad because the men go, and new ones come and they go, and other new ones come until at last only the number of the division is left. Finally, it is only a numbered mechanism through which men pass. As long as we have an army, the First Division will exist, but my friends in it may not.

For you at home who think the African campaign was small stuff, let me tell you just this one thing—the First Division did more fighting then than it did throughout all of World War I.

When they were about to go into battle, some men were very introspective and thoughtful. Other men carried on as if everything were normal. I remember one night when chow had come up just after dusk and a dozen or so of us were opening tin cans to the tune of constant shellfire. Somebody started singing a parody of some song. Others joined in, and for five minutes there in the night they sang funny songs. A silly feature of that episode is that now I can't remember what we sang.

Another time we were sitting in the darkness on a rocky ledge waiting to start a night march that would culminate in an attack in which some of the men were to die before dawn. As we sat there, the officers who were to lead the attack got into a long discussion comparing the London and New York subways. The sum total of the discussion was that the London subways were better than ours. After that the conversation drifted off onto the merits and demerits of the Long Island Railroad. The only "warlike" thing about the discussion was that somebody expressed a hearty desire to be riding on the Long Island Railroad that very minute.

War sometimes gets to be almost like Hollywood. We had a fantastic example one day. A company of our troops worked far ahead of us and got pinned down on the far side of a hill. That back slope was almost a cliff. It was practically straight up and down. Our men were trapped there, just hiding behind rocks and on little ledges. The Germans had worked their way up onto a long slope in front of them, and around each and behind them.

The first Hollywood effect was that, although the enemy completely surrounded our men, we still had telephone communication with them. So their company commander asked us to start shooting mortars over onto the Germans on the face of the hill.

We set up a battery of mortars and let fly a practice round at the Germans a mile or so away. As the mortars roared, our battery commander said over the phone, "They're on the way, Mac."

Then we waited about thirty seconds and Mac's voice came back: "They went clear over our heads. Bring her down a little."

Thus with him directing us to right and left, up and down, we kept shooting until our mortar shells were landing smack on the Germans.

Of course that is the way all artillery is directed. But usually there is an observer on some other hill a mile or so away, watching through binoculars. In this case our observer was beyond our own falling shells and so close he had to duck down behind his cliff every time they came over. Even veterans had to laugh at the situation. And just as in Hollywood, it had a happy ending. Our shells ran off the Germans and our men were rescued.

One afternoon Captain Russell Wight and I were lying in the sun against a bank alongside a dirt road, waiting for some tanks to come past so he could show them where to attack. While we lay there, machine-gun bullets sang over our heads. Once a dozen Messerschmitts dived and bombed hell out of an empty field a quarter of a mile away. Just behind us a German tank was whamming 75-mm. shells into a hillside with such rhythmic fury that we felt the gunner must be shooting from personal outrage. But we were quite safe from it all in our ditch behind the hill, and we lay drowsily in the sun as if on a picnic back home.

Captain Wight was the kind of person I felt at home with. The enlisted men loved him more than any officer I had ever heard them speak about. His home was in Cambridge, Massachusetts, and before the war he was an executive of a big soap company. His business experience with personnel really fitted him for some safer work, but he wound up in the fightingest job in the army—as an infantry company commander. He had no kicks. He was already living on borrowed time, for three times 88-mm. shells had landed within ten feet of him and freakishly left him untouched. He had no bad effects at all other than being deaf for about twenty-four hours. He said he heard no explosions, the only sensation was that of an enormous bear giving him a sudden hug.

As we were talking, the tanks came by and the leader got out and chinned for a few minutes before going into battle. The young tank commander's boss drove up in a jeep and gave him some instructions, winding up with, "If it gets too hot, button up and pray for darkness."

The young tank commander laughed and said that's what he would do. A half hour later he was dead. Captain Wight and I sat on our hillside and saw it happen.

That was the way it went. After a while a man didn't feel too deeply about it. He didn't dare.

At dawn, after a particularly tough battle, I was watching the wounded being brought back when I noticed that a man on one of the stretchers coming toward us wore a British officer's cap. I had a hunch, and ran over to look closely. Sure enough, it was my tentmate of the previous three nights—a British captain. When I got there, the litter-bearers put down the stretcher, and I knelt beside it. As I did so the captain opened his eyes. He smiled and said, "Oh, hello, hello. I was worrying about you. Are you all right?"

How's that for British breeding?

I started to say something about being sorry, but before I could get a word out he said, "Oh, it's nothing at all, absolutely nothing. Just a little flesh wound. It isn't as if I'd been hit in the spine or anything."

But the captain had a big hole in his back, and his left arm was all shot up. They had given him morphine and he wasn't in much pain. His shirt was off, but he still wore his pistol and his cap. There was blood all over his undershirt and his tanned face had a pale look, but his expression was the same as usual.

Our first-aid station was too much under fire for ambulances or any vehicles to be brought up, so four litter-bearers still had to carry the captain a mile and a half back to the rear. When he heard that he said, "That's perfectly ridiculous, carrying me that far. They'll do no such thing. I can walk back."

The doctor said no, it would start him bleeding again if he got up. But the captain got halfway off the litter and I had to give him a push and a few cusswords before he would consent to being carried.

The captain was a young fellow, sort of pugilistic-looking but with a gentle manner and an Oxford accent. He had been in the British Eighth Army two years without getting hurt. He had just joined us as liaison officer, and was shot in the first half hour of his first battle.

We'd had nice talks about England and the war and everything. It seemed impossible that someone I'd known and liked and who had been so whole and hearty such a few hours before could then be torn and helpless. But there he was.

A few minutes later two German prisoners came down the hill, with a doughboy behind them making dangerous motions with his bayonet at their behinds. The captor was a straight American of the drawling hillbilly type, who talked through his nose. I'm sorry I didn't get his name. When he walked the Germans back to his sergeant he said, in his tobacco-patch twang, "Hey, sarge, here's two uv Hitler's supermen fer yuh."

The two prisoners were young and looked very well fed. Their uniforms were loose-fitting khaki, sort of like men's beach suits at home. With their guns and all their other soldier gear taken away, they had the appearance of being only half dressed. The expression on their faces was one of wondering what came next.

They were turned over to another soldier, who marched them across the fields to the rear. I couldn't help grinning as I watched, for the new guardian stayed well behind them and walked as if he were treading on ice.

Our aid station was merely a formation of outcropping rocks on the hillside. The wounded all stopped there to await new litter-bearers to carry them farther.

The battalion surgeon, Captain Robert Peterman of Hicksville, Long Island, had told me how our wounded never groaned or made a fuss when they came in, so I paid special attention. And it was true; they just lay on their stretchers, docile and patient, waiting for the medics to do whatever they could. Some of them had been given morphine and were dopey. Some of them smoked and talked as if nothing much had happened. A good many had been hit in the behind by flying fragments from shells. The medics there on the battlefield would either cut the seat out of their trousers or else slide their pants down, to treat the wounds, and they were put on stretchers that way, lying face down. It was almost funny to see so many men coming down the hill with the white skin of their backsides gleaming against the dark background of brown uniforms and green grass.

Some of the boys who were not too badly wounded seemed to have an expression of relief on their faces. I knew how they felt, and I didn't blame them. I remembered from the last war the famous English phrase of "going back to Blighty"—meaning being evacuated to England because of wounds. In Africa we had a different expression for the same thing. It was "catching the white boat," meaning the white hospital ship that took wounded men back across the Atlantic.

I hope somebody in this war writes a book about the medics who served on the African front. I don't mean the hospitals so much as the units that were actually attached to troops and worked on the battlefields under fire. They were a noble breed. They and the telephone linemen deserve more praise than I have words for. Their job was deadly, and without respite. Just in one battalion several of the battlefield medics were killed, and a number were decorated.

But noble as it was, it seemed to me—and to the doctors themselves—that our battlefield medical system wasn't all it should have been. There weren't enough stretcher-bearers in an emergency, and in a battle at which I was present some of our wounded lay out as long as twenty hours before being brought in. The work of the medics came in peaks. If they had had enough stretcher-bearers for all emergencies there would have been thousands of men sitting around most of the time with nothing to do. Yet when an emergency did come and there were not enough, it was an awful thing.

Wounded men had a rough time of it in that rocky, hilly country of Northern Tunisia. It was hard enough to walk when a man wasn't carrying anything, but when two or four men were lugging two hundred pounds on a stretcher it was almost impossible to keep on their feet. I saw litter-bearers struggling down a rocky hillside with their heavy burden when one of them would slip or stumble on a rock and fall down, and the whole litter would go down, giving the wounded man a bad shaking up.

Litter-bearers sometimes had to carry wounded men five miles or more over that rugged country. A bearer was just about done in by the time he did that, yet in battle he had to start right back again. And somehow, even though it got to be just a miserably tough job, I noticed that they managed to keep their sympathetic feeling for the wounded.

We heard stories about the Germans shooting up ambulances and bombing hospitals, and I personally knew of instances where those stories were true. But there were also stories of just the opposite nature. Many of our officers told me the Germans fought a pretty clean war in Tunisia. They did have scores of crafty, brutal little tricks that we didn't have, but as for their observance of the broader ethics of war, our side had no complaint.

One battalion surgeon told me of running his ambulance out onto a battlefield under heavy artillery fire—whereupon the Germans stopped shelling and stayed stopped while he evacuated the dead and wounded for eight hours.

I heard other stories about our ambulances going past German machine-gun nests without knowing it until the Germans came out and stopped them and, seeing they had wounded, waved them on. And so far as our doctors knew, the German doctors gave our captured wounded good medical care—as we did theirs.

In the last war nerve cases were called "shell shock." In this war they're called "anxiety neurosis." About fifty per cent of our neurosis cases were recoverable, and even returned to fighting units. A large proportion of those cases were brought about by complete fatigue, by fighting day and night on end with little sleep and little to eat.

Surgeons sometimes spotted neurosis cases that they suspected of being faked in order to get out of the front lines. Their system was to put those men on stretcher-bearer duty—a hard, thankless, dangerous task. If they were faking they got well quickly and asked to be returned to their regular outfits.

In the front lines we got so used to the constant boom of artillery that we stopped jumping every time a big gun went off. If we hadn't we would have looked like victims of St. Vitus's dance. However, there was another reaction—we became irritated. We became irritated in the same way a person loses patience with a baby that cries all day or a dog that barks all night. The damned noise just went on and on. There was hardly a second of the day when the guns weren't rolling or those ghostly shells rustling through the air. Finally we got so bored with the everlasting clamor that we felt like jumping up in a huff and yelling, "Oh, for God's sake, stop it!"

This particular story has three heroes, if you want to call them that. I do. They were the three men who commanded, one after the other, the same infantry company—all within five hours of battle. For lack of a better name we'll simply call it Company K.

It was daytime. The whole company was pinned down on a green wheatfield that led up onto the slope of a hill. We were trying to take the Germans on the back slope of the hill, but if our men stirred the enemy could butcher them with their machine guns up on the ridge.

Lieutenant Richard Cole, of Worcester, Massachusetts, was commander of Company K. In midafternoon a German shell found him as he lay in hiding with his men in the wheat. One leg got only a slight wound, but the other was shattered. Lieutenant Cole saved his life by using his head. He made a tourniquet of his handkerchief, and using a fountain pen for a lever he twisted the tourniquet and held it, and at the same time began slowly crawling to the rear. For he knew the medics didn't dare to venture onto the shell-raked field looking for possible wounded.

After about an hour he loosened the tourniquet, to prevent gangrene. Darkness came on and he continued to crawl slowly, attending to the tourniquet at intervals. Sometime during the night he felt a telephone wire under him. That was what he had been hunting for. He got out his knife and cut the wire, knowing that eventually linemen would come looking for the break. Then he lay down on the wire and waited. And finally they did come, just as he had anticipated. It was long after daylight, and Lieutenant Cole had by then been wounded twenty hours. But they got him to a hospital and he didn't even lose a leg.

As soon as Lieutenant Cole was wounded, Lieutenant Theodore Antonelli, of New Britain, Connecticut, automatically took command of Company K. They waited in the wheatfield till dusk, then began slowly working around the left end of the hill that was facing them. They took the Germans from the rear, completely by surprise. They rushed up the hill and attacked with bayonets.

Lieutenant Antonelli, instead of staying behind his company, pulled out his .45 and led the company up the hill. Usually a company commander doesn't do that, but at the time it was the thing to do. Antonelli paid for his bravery. A hand-thrown German grenade scattered fragments over his chest, and he fell. His wounds were not serious, but they put him out of action. He had had command of Company K just four hours.

Next in line of command was Sergeant Arthur Godwin. He instantly assumed the command expected of him, and he carried it so well that after the battle his praises were sung throughout the whole division. Sergeant Godwin led his men in one of the few bayonet charges Americans made in the Tunisian war. They didn't kill or capture the enemy. He just fled in terror, yelling, "Madmen! Madmen!" The hill was taken.

Sergeant Godwin was from Enterprise, Alabama, the cotton town that is famous for its statue to the boll weevil. Back home he used to drive a truck, and in season he roved the Florida orchards as a fruit picker. He had been in the army more than three years. Godwin was a tall, nice-looking fellow of twenty-six. He swore in good soldier fashion, but his manner was quiet and considerate. There was something calmly forceful about him, a good man to have faith in.

Everybody in the regiment, including its commanding officer, wished that Godwin could have kept Company K, he had served it so well. But it was impossible. Other officers in the battalion deserved a company command, so Sergeant Godwin was replaced the next day.

But wait—the story hasn't a bitter end or a sad one. Godwin had had a commission in the offing ever since he landed in Africa six months before. It was one of those army things. Months had passed and nothing happened. Like a good soldier, he kept on plugging as a sergeant. But the division commander put a stop to that nonsense. He exercised his right to promote a man on the battlefield, and within a few hours after the last German was marched off the hill Sergeant Godwin was Lieutenant Godwin. A company command was bound to follow.

Everybody was delighted. That's the way good men rise to their rightful niche in battle, where true character shows and red tape is a hated phrase.

It had been one of those days when I sat down on a rock about once an hour, put my chin in my hand, and thought to myself, "What the hell am I doing here, anyway?"

During a lull, I decided I had to catch up with my work and, not having a typewriter with me, I was writing with a pencil, sitting on the ground. The midday sun was so bright and hot I couldn't sit out in it and write. Where we were was the only spot of shade in miles. That was a tiny patch, made by a big rock behind which our battalion staff lay directing the battle. So I picked out that spot of shade for my writing room.

It would have been all right at that, except my special spot of the rock was the front side and consequently afflicted with bullets. I wrote for ten or fifteen minutes, when suddenly machine-gun slugs came singing down from the hilltop and buzzed past overhead. They came from a dugout sniper on our own hill. Apparently my paper made a target for him. I stayed put until three or four bullets went past, then I went around to the other side of the rock and told the battalion staff, "That guy is shooting at me."

After a while I went back to try to recapture the muse. Four times in one day that fellow chased me out of my shady place. The fourth time three bullets went past so close they had fuzz on them, and the fourth went into the ground with a squish just ten feet away. At that

I went around the rock so fast I made a groove in the ground. From then on I stayed on the correct side. Finally, late that afternoon, one of our soldiers dug out that sniper and captured him.

I don't know which was the greater mental hazard—my writing, the bullets, or snakes. That rocky hill country was a reptilian paradise. After the machine gunner had made me flee in shame, I sat down in a foxhole and tried to write. If I had just kept my eyes on the paper it would have been all right, but for some perverse reason I happened to look down on the ground. There, alongside my leg in the bottom of the hole was one of our dear little slithery friends. A movie of me leaving that foxhole would look like a shell leaving a rifle.

When I finally crept back to peer into the hole, my new roommate turned out to be one of those mistakes of nature with which Africa abounds—something or other that is two thirds snake and one third lizard. It was a snake, except that it had two legs, side by side, about halfway down its body. Before we could exterminate this monstrosity, he wiggled back under a sunken rock which formed one end of my foxhole.

Corporal Richard Redman of Struthers, Ohio, occupied a shallow foxhole adjoining. An hour or so after my episode, Corporal Redman was catching some daytime sleep in his trench when I happened to walk by. There, within a foot of his head, was a real snake. That time I let out my special snake-fright whoop, which can be heard for miles. The battalion surgeon grabbed a shovel and killed the thing. He said it was an adder, very poisonous. Later they killed another at the same spot.

When Corporal Redman woke up I told him how I had practically saved his life. He was very grateful. Indeed, it turned out that he also was cursed with snake horrors. If circumstances had been a little different I think Corporal Redman and I would just have left those snakes to the Arabs, and come on home.

Corporal William Otter of Hazleton, Pennsylvania, had the next foxhole. So he joined in our snake discussion. He said he, too, had had a complex about snakes all his life, but since being in Tunisia he had seen so much horror of battle that a snake seemed minor stuff to him and his unreasonable fear had gone.

Maybe I felt a little like that myself. I thought I couldn't possibly lie down in my foxhole that night, with that lizard still there and snakes all around. Yet, when the time came, there was nothing else to do. So I made myself crawl in, and I slept soundly all night.

Sergeant Eugene Box, of Babylon, Long Island, was an infantryman, one of those lighthearted blonds. He was always grinning, and he had a tooth out in front. He had been through four big battles, had his bookful of close shaves, and killed his share of Germans.

Sergeant Box was an expert with the dice and the cards. When I met him he had already sent $1,200 home to be banked, in addition to a $25-a-month allotment. Furthermore, he had another $700 ready to send.

Whenever he went into battle he gave his wallet to a friend back of the lines to keep for him, just in case. He wore a diamond ring, and before every battle he took it off his third finger, where it fitted, and forced it onto his middle finger, where it was terribly tight. In case he was captured or wounded the Germans couldn't steal the ring without cutting off his finger, which he apparently thought they wouldn't do.

Private First Class William Smith, of Decota, West Virginia, was an infantryman who sometimes doubled as a stretcher-bearer. One day he and a fellow stretcher-bearer found a badly wounded German soldier, so they put him on a litter and started back to an aid station with him. But he was almost gone, and he died after they had walked only a few minutes. They kept on with him anyhow. Then suddenly the German batteries started dropping 88s right around them, so Private Smith finished the episode by this means—to use his words: "I just dumped that s.o.b. in a crick and took off from there."

Another time he and another soldier were carrying a wounded American back from a battle area. They had got about halfway back when those familiar 88s started falling. But they didn't dump this guy in any crick. No, sir, the wounded man took off from that stretcher all alone and lit out on a dead run. He beat the two panting litter-bearers back to the aid station.

On one night march we stopped about midnight and were told to find ourselves places among the rocks on a near-by hillside. This hillside was practically a cliff. We could barely stand on it. And it was covered with big rocks and an especially vicious brand of thistle that grew between the rocks. It was pitch-dark, and we had to find our little places to lie down—several hundred of us—largely by feel.

I climbed almost to the top of the cliff, and luckily found a sloping place without bumps, just long enough for my body. I tromped down the thistles, thought a few trembling thoughts about snakes and lizards, then lay down and put one shelter-half on the ground, wrapped my one blanket around me, and drew the other shelter-half over me. The thistles had such a strong and repugnant odor that I thought I couldn't go to sleep, but I was dead to the world in two seconds. In fact, I never slept better in my life.

The next thing I knew the entire universe seemed to be exploding. Guns were going off everywhere, and planes screaming right down on top of us. It was a dawn dive-bombing. I thought to myself, "Oh, my God, they've got us this time!" I didn't even look out from under the shelter-half. I just reached out one arm to where I knew my steel helmet was lying, and put it on my head under the covers. And I remember lying on my side and getting my knees up around my chin so there wouldn't be so much of me to hit.

The planes had bombed some vehicles in the valley below us, and were pulling out of their dives right over our hill. They just barely cleared the crest as they went over. They couldn't have been more than a hundred feet above us. We were all lying there in the open, perfect targets for machine-gunning.

They never did shoot, but it was my worst dive-bombing scare of the war, and I felt mighty glad that the whole Tunisian business was about over.

17. VICTORY

THE thing that Americans in Africa had fought and worked six months to get was finally achieved. When it did come, it was an avalanche almost impossible to describe. The flood of prisoners choked the roads. There were acres of captured material.

It was a holiday, though everybody kept on working. We all felt suddenly free inside, as if personal worry had been lifted. It was the way we used to feel as children on the farm, when our parents surprised us by saying work was finished and we were going to the state fair for a day. And when we had looked all day goggle-eyed at more Germans than we had ever expected to see in our lives, we really did feel as if we had been to a fair.

We saw Germans walking alone along highways. We saw them riding, stacked up in our jeeps, with one lone American driver. We saw them by hundreds, crammed as in a subway in their own trucks, with their own drivers. And in the forward areas our fairgrounds of mile after mile contained more Germans than Americans. Germans were everywhere. It made me a little light-headed to stand in the center of a crowd, the only American among scores of German soldiers, and not have to feel afraid of them. Their 88s stood abandoned. In the fields dead Germans still lay on the grass. By the roadside scores of tanks and trucks still burned. Dumps flamed, and German command posts lay littered where they had tried to wreck as much as possible before surrendering.

But all those were sideshows—the big show was the mass of men in strange uniform, lining roads, swamping farmyards, blackening fields, waiting for us to tell them where to go. High German officers were obviously down in the mouth over the tragic end of their campaign. We saw some tears. Officers wept over the ghastly death toll taken of their men during the last few days. Officers were meticulously correct in their military behavior, but otherwise standoffish and silent.

Not so the common soldiers. I mingled with them all day and sensed no sadness among them. Theirs was not the delight of the Italians, but rather an acceptance of defeat in a war well fought— why be surly about it? They were friendly, very friendly. Being prisoners, it obviously paid them to be friendly; yet their friendliness seemed genuine. Just as when the French and Americans first met, the Germans started learning English words and teaching us German words.

But circumstances didn't permit much communion between them and our troops. Those Americans who came in direct contact with them gave necessary orders and herded them into trucks. All other Americans just stared curiously as they passed. I saw very little fraternizing with prisoners. I saw no acts of belligerence and heard neither boos nor cheers. But I did hear a hundred times: "This is the way it should be. Now we can go on from here."

German boys were as curious about us as we were about them. Every time I stopped a crowd would form quickly. In almost every group was someone who spoke English. In all honesty I can't say their bearing or personality was a bit different from that of a similar bunch of American prisoners. They gave us their cigarettes and accepted ours, both for curiosity's sake. They examined the jeep, and asked questions about our uniforms. If I passed one walking alone, usually he would smile and speak.

One high American officer told me he found himself feeling sorry for them—until he remembered how they had killed so many of his men with their sneaking mines, how they had had him pinned down a few days before with bullets flying; then he hated them.

I am always a sucker for the guy who loses, but somehow it never occurred to me to feel sorry for those prisoners. They didn't give the impression of needing any sorrowing over. They were loyal to their country and sorry they lost but, now it was over for them, they seemed glad to be out of it.

Before that first day of the great surrender on the Bizerte-Tunis front was over, I believe half the Americans in the area had German souvenirs of some sort. But there was very little of what one would call looting of German supply dumps. The Germans gave away helmets, goggles and map cases, which they would not be needing any more. The spoils of war which the average doughboy took were legitimate, and little enough recompense for his fighting.

Practically every American truck had a German or Italian helmet fastened to its radiator. Our motorcycles were decorated like a carnival, with French flags and the colorful little black-and-yellow death's-head pennants the Germans used for marking their own mine fields.

Many soldiers had new Lugers in their holsters. Lots of our men were clowning around in German field caps. German goggles were frequently seen on American heads. I got in on the souvenirs too. I got one memento that was a little gem. It was an automobile—yep, a real automobile that ran. I drove back to camp that first evening in my German "Volkswagen," the bantam car the Nazis used as we used our jeep. It was a topless two-seater with a rear motor, camouflaged a dirty brown. Mine was given me by our First Armored Division for—as they said—"sweating it out with us at Faid Pass all winter." As I drove back from the lines, Americans in the rear stared, startled-like and belligerent; then, seeing an American at the wheel they laughed and waved. I have owned half a dozen automobiles in my life, but I was never so proud of one as of my clattering little Volkswagen.

The Germans sat in groups of hundreds in the fields, just waiting. They lay on their overcoats, resting. They took off their shirts to sun themselves. They took off their shoes to rest their feet.

They were a tired army but not a nondescript one. All were extremely well equipped. Their uniforms were good. They had plenty in the way of little personal things, money, cigarettes, and food. Their equipment was of the best materials. One English-appearing soldier had a Gem nail-clipper. He said he paid twenty-five cents for it in New York in 1939.

Some were clean-shaven, some had three- or four-day beards, just like our soldiers. Lots of them had red-rimmed eyes from lack of sleep. As a whole, they seemed younger than our men, and I was surprised that on the average they didn't seem as big. But they did appear well fed and in excellent health.

They thought Americans were fine fighters. They expressed only good-natured contempt for their allies, the Italians. As one of them said, "It isn't just that Italians don't fight well. It's simply that Germans don't like Italians very much in the first place."

Wherever any American correspondents stopped, prisoners immediately gathered around. They all seemed in good spirits. Even those who couldn't speak a word of English tried hard to tell us something.

One little scene on that day of the surrender made me homesick. Hundreds of Germans were standing and sitting around a farmyard. There was a sprinkling of Italian prisoners too, and a scattering of American, British, and French soldiers on various errands. It was indeed an international assembly. In that foreign farmyard there was a windmill. The printing on the windmill's big fan seemed so incongruous that I had to jot it down: "Flint & Walling Manufacturing

Co., Kendallville, Ind." You just can't get foreign enough to lose us Hoosiers.

One of the English-speaking German soldiers asked me why I was copying that down, and when I told him it was because the windmill came from my home state he smiled and said, oh yes, he'd been in Indiana several times himself!

The main impression I got, seeing German prisoners, was that they were human like anybody else, fundamentally friendly, a little vain. Certainly they were not supermen. Whenever a group of them formed, some American soldier popped up with a camera to get a souvenir picture. And every time all the prisoners in the vicinity crowded into the picture like kids.

One German boy had found a broken armchair leaning against a barn, and was sitting in it. When I passed he grinned, pointed to his feet and then to the chair arms, and put back his head in the international sign language for "Boy, does this chair feel good!"

That night they still lounged by thousands in fields along the roads. Our trucks, and theirs too, were not sufficient to haul them away. They just had to wait their turn to be taken off to prison camps. No guards were necessary to keep them from running off into the darkness. They had already done their running and they awaited our pleasure, rather humbly and with a curious eagerness to see what came next.

That colossal German surrender did more for American morale than anything that could possibly have happened. Winning in battle is like winning at poker or catching lots of fish—it's damned pleasant and it sets a man up. As a result, the hundreds of thousands of Americans in North Africa were happy men, laughing and working with new spirits that bubbled.

The finish of the campaign had a definite reaction on everybody. At first there was terrific enthusiasm. Then after a few days a letdown occurred. Each man realized, once he relaxed, how terribly tired he was. He was like a rubber band that had been stretched too tight. A feeling of anticlimax settled over him. Dozens of times I heard such expressions as "I'm all jumpy" and "I feel at loose ends" and "I want to get moving, I don't care where, but somewhere."

Staying in Tunisia was like sitting on in the tent after the circus had finished its performance. Everybody wondered what we were going to do next, and when, and where. Of course the Germans would have liked to know that too. And I can assure you that if they didn't know any more about our plans than the correspondents and the bulk of the army did, they were completely in the dark. We in the common herd had no inkling of what the next act would be. We could only hope it would be soon, for that feeling of intermission was getting us down.

The Germans didn't quite hew to the ethical line in one thing— they continued trying to destroy their own stuff after the surrender. Vehicles were set afire, and soldiers broke their rifles over bridge abutments as they walked along. Sometimes their destructive frenzy was almost laughable. I saw one bivouac where they had left all their big guns, their ten-wheelers, all their heavy gear intact, yet they had smashed such things as personal radios, toilet kits, chairs, and even an accordion. However, what they put out of action was trivial. The collapse was so huge that most of their stuff was taken intact. We saw long convoys of German trucks on the Tunisian highways, but they had American drivers, and the yellow star of the U.S. Army was painted on their sides. Our Military Police acted quickly to throw guards around all captured supply dumps and preserved them until the army could collect, sort, and put to use all the captured material.

Most of the German prisoners were worked out of the forward Tunisian area. Where they went we didn't know; they just left for the west. Handling them and feeding them must have been a tremendous job. It took a lot of transportation to move those thousands of men back across Africa, and if we had kept them in Africa we would have had to use valuable shipping space to bring them food. That colossal batch of human beings was, indeed, a white elephant on our hands. And yet, as somebody said, what we wanted was about fifty more white elephants just like that one.

Although they were usually friendly and pleasant, we seldom found a prisoner who had any doubt that Germany would win the war. They said they lost because we finally got more stuff into Tunisia than they had. But they laughed at the idea of our invading the Continent. On the whole, they couldn't understand why America was in the war at all, figuring it wasn't our business.

Whether from deliberate Nazi propaganda or mere natural rumor I didn't know, but the prisoners had a lot of false news in their heads. For instance, some of them had heard that Japan had been at war with Russia for six months and had practically cleaned the Russians out of Siberia. One of them had heard that the Luftwaffe had bombed New York. When told that this was ridiculous, he said he didn't see himself how it could be possible.

Private Bill Connell, of 183 Menahan Street, Brooklyn, had a talk with an English-speaking prisoner, and the conversation finally unearthed the information that, as Private Connell said, "We know different people together"—meaning, I'm sure, that they had once actually lived in adjoining houses in Brooklyn—Connell at 251 Grove Street and the German at 253 Grove. But that coincidence didn't cause any old-palship to spring up between them, for the prisoner was one of those bullheaded Nazis and Connell got so disgusted he didn't even ask his name.

The first contacts of our troops with prisoners were extremely pleasant. So pleasant in fact that American officers got to worrying because the men found the Germans so likable. But if the Americans talked to them long enough they found in them the very thing we were fighting this war about—their superior-race complex, their smug belief in their divine right to run this part of the world. A little association with a German prisoner, like a little knowledge, was a bad thing, but I think those of our troops who had an opportunity to talk at length with the Germans, came out of it madder than ever at their enemy.

Captured supplies showed that the Germans used excellent materials in all their stuff. However, it seemed to us that there was some room for improvement in their vaunted efficiency. They had more of a hodgepodge and more overlapping designs than we did. They had big ten-wheeler troop carriers with seats running crosswise, but it was far too much vehicle for the service it performed. It couldn't possibly have been used for any other work than troop carrying, and even for that it was an easy target, with men sitting up there in the open. And it was slow.

They also had a gadget that resembled a motorcycle except that the back end ran on two small caterpillar tracks instead of wheels. It was a novel idea but, as somebody said, it could carry only three men and there was enough material wasted to make a young tank.

In rummaging around one supply dump I came upon a stack of copies of a booklet entitled *Tausend Worte Italienisch*. I picked up a handful, thinking to glean a little back-yard Italian. It didn't occur to me at the time that the booklets would be translating Italian into German. The Germans did things thoroughly, we had to admit. My handful of booklets turned out to be not several copies of the same thing but a whole series of different booklets comprising a set of lessons for troops complete enough to give a college course in Italian.

It seemed a prodigal way to use money, yet I suppose it did make things better if the Germans were able to insult their allies in their own language.

I have described the winter's battleground in Tunisia, and told how there wasn't much evidence over the countryside of the fighting that had gone on. That was the Central Tunisian battlefield—the one we had fought over all winter. But after the surrender we had a new battlefield to look over, the Northern one, and it looked vastly more warlike than the Southern. There were two reasons for that—the fighting was more concentrated and on a much greater scale, and the Germans collapsed so quickly they had no time to retrieve vehicles and clean up the battlefields as they had in the South.

After Mateur there were roads in Northern Tunisia that were littered for miles at a stretch with wrecked and burned-out vehicles. Sometimes a skeleton of a tank or a big truck sat right in the middle of a road and we had to drive around it. In spots we saw two or three dozen wrecked tanks scattered across a mile-wide valley. In many places the roads were rough from filled-in shell holes.

In the first day or two after the finish we still saw an occasional blanket-covered body lying at the roadside. Frequently we saw one or two German graves, where victims of vehicle strafing were buried. And as we drove along our noses told us now and then of one that the burial parties had missed.

I was constantly amazed and touched at the number of dogs and mules killed on the highways by artillery and strafing planes. Practically all the bridges in Northern Tunisia had been blown up. We detoured around the smaller ones. Over the larger streams American and British engineers had thrown sudden and magnificent steel bridges, or laid pontoon bridges.

Only a few of the towns in Central Tunisia were really wrecked by shellfire, but in Northern Tunisia all the towns along the line of battle had been truly destroyed. Bizerte was the most completely wrecked place I had ever seen. It was a large city, and a beautiful one. It is impossible to picture in words what it looked like after its destruction. If you remember World War I pictures of such places as Verdun, that was the way it was. Nothing could possibly have lived through the months-long bombing that Bizerte took. Those who say a city can't be destroyed by bombing should go and see Bizerte.

As soon as the Tunisian war was over the Arabs began flocking back to their homes. They had been cleaned out of the battle area by both sides, for two reasons—to keep them from getting hurt and because neither side trusted them. Most of them were simply evacuated to safe hills in the rear, but those under suspicion were arrested and put in outdoor prison camps while the fighting was going on.

They came back across country in long caravans. Scores of Arabs were in each group, with their sheep and their cattle, their burros and their kids. They were a dirty and disheartening lot. Their junklike belongings were piled high on two-wheeled carts. I saw one cart with fourteen oxen hitched to it. The women usually had large bundles on their backs. Now and then one Arab gave the Victory sign and said, "Bonjour," but most of them passed in silence. For the Tunisian Arab had been well sold by German propaganda.

Ferryville and Tunis were the two places where fantastic demonstrations were put on as the Americans and British entered and released the cities from their captivity.

Chris Cunningham of the United Press and I shared a tent and traveled together quite a bit in the Northern campaign. Chris is a stocky fellow, with black whiskers. He looks pretty tough, although he is actually rather bashful. When he drove into Ferryville in his jeep he was immediately surrounded and overpowered by jubilant men, women and children, throwing flowers and shouting, "Vive la France!" and "Vive l'Amérique!"

In the midst of this hubbub a pompous-looking gentleman, a gruffly dignified Frenchman of the old school, arrived on the scene. He stood for a moment at the curb, surveying the outburst with what appeared to be disapproval. Then he took a deep breath, brushed the common herd aside with both hands as if he were swimming, reached over into the jeep and kissed Chris first on one cheek and then on the other. That accomplished, he turned and strode pompously away.

Chris hasn't heard the last of it yet.

Many things had happened since I left my gang of Flying Fortress friends. Often I had watched them plow through the Tunisian skies, miles above, and wondered what they were up to and what they were thinking and how things were with them. When the shooting was over I visited them again briefly.

A few of them were gone forever, but not so many. Practically everybody had gone up one notch in the promotion scale. Some of them had been sent home to help train new groups. And a lot of them had completed their allotted number of missions and were through with combat flying for a while, and assigned to ground duties.

Nearly all of them wore medals. There were Distinguished Flying Crosses and Purple Hearts galore. Some of the boys seemed pretty tired, and those of the old original crews who hadn't got in their full number of missions were anxious to get it done and rest.

Some of my enlisted friends had acquired commissions. Most of the January beards had been shaved off, and shirtless sun tans had replaced the heavy mackinaws the mechanics used to wear. Pet puppies had grown into big dogs.

There were many new faces. Replacements arrived to fill the gaps left by those who didn't return and those who had finished their required missions and gone on ground duty. Everybody knew more about his job than he used to. It had become routine, both on the ground and in the air, and I sensed a confidence that comes from doing a thing a long time.

Shortly after the Tunisian campaign ended, the flying men were given a three-day holiday, the first of its kind since they arrived in North Africa. Some of them went to the nearest cities by jeep or truck for a little fling. Others took planes and went to big cities farther back. Many went to beaches to swim and laze. And a great many went to Tunisia—to see with their own eyes the havoc they had so carefully and perilously wrought all winter.

They found it an odd thing to be there on the ground looking at a place they'd never seen except from miles above and with the sky around them riddled with flak and swarming with fighters. They visited Bizerte, which they had wrecked, and Ferryville and Tunis, whose docks they had demolished in their numberless raids. They were pleased at what they saw. They found that in their precise works of destruction they had done a good job.

"The House of Jackson"—the Fortress crew I had followed since before it left England—didn't exist any more as a "family." The passage of time had scattered and consumed it. Two of the original members were dead. Some had been promoted. Others had completed their goal in missions and were on ground duty. The remaining few had been assigned to other crews.

They were all veterans of veterans by now, and their old Fortress itself was no more. The old "Devils from Hell" that they brought all the way from America nearly a year before had gone down over Palermo one bitter day, but only one of the original House of Jackson was still on her then.

The faithful old ship was on her forty-second mission when she died. She had been on so many raids they had almost run out of room to paint the little white bombs on her nose, each of which denoted a mission. Her list of enemy victims ran high too.

I supposed the boys would feel sentimental about her going, but they didn't seem to.

There was a day when I knew every group of fliers on combat duty in North Africa. But that day had gone. They had multiplied and grown so fantastically that there were more than one man could possibly know, even if he devoted all his time to it.

When I went about the airfields, I felt old in Africa. Those few who carried the torch at first, and still remained, were a sort of grandfather generation among all the hordes that speckled the hard-won skies. And that was well, for that was what we had been waiting for.

The head man of the photographic section at one of our Flying Fortress airdromes was Sergeant Robert Thompson, of Lansing, Michigan. Thompson had four men in the section with him. They were well organized for future conquests, as one of them spoke Italian and one spoke German.

I am mentioning these boys because they built themselves a photographic darkroom that was unique in Africa. It was an underground dugout ten feet deep. Most of it was dug through solid rock, and without any blasting equipment whatever. It took the five boys ten days to do it.

Down some steps, a turn right along a deep, narrow ditch, and then right again, brought them completely underground with a three-foot roof of earth and rock over them for bomb protection. They never had a raid at that field, but where they had previously been stationed raids were frequent.

Everything in the darkroom was homemade. Running water came through some curved piping taken from the hydraulic system of a B-17. On the end of the pipe was a spigot from a wine barrel. All their photographic chemicals were kept in old champagne bottles. Their developing trays were gasoline tins cut in half the long way. Their film-printing box was made from fragmentation bomb cases. Their red safety light was the reflector off a jeep. An electric switch from a bombardier's control-box lid was cushioned with rubber from the pilot's seat of a Fortress.

Besides Thompson, the men in the section were Corporal Bennett Tucker, St. Louis, Private Harold Harrington, Carteret, New Jersey (he was the Irishman), Private First Class Otto Zinkgraff, Plymouth, Wisconsin (he was the German), and Private First Class John Martini, New York (he was the Italian).

They all lived in the same tent, and for such an international hodgepodge you never saw five men prouder of their joint accomplishments.

Another man of especial distinction was Captain A. D. Howell of Maryville, Tennessee, a suburb of Knoxville. Over here he was known as Dixie Howell, but he was never called that before he got in the army. We had met away back in January, and every time I ran onto him after that something new had happened to him. In amazing succession he was slightly wounded and got a Purple Heart, invented a new way to clean up mine fields, was decorated for bravery, promoted to captain, and was wounded in the thumb by a fragment from a dive-bombing.

Captain Howell worked for the Aluminum Company of America before the war. His father-in-law was the regional manager at Alcoa. Young Howell didn't have to live on grits and sowbelly by any means, but regardless of his nice status in life he volunteered in the Canadian Army long before Pearl Harbor, and went to England more than two years ago. He transferred to the American Army in the fall of 1942.

He had been constantly at the front. He was the mine and booby-trap expert with a regiment of fighting Engineers. He probably knew as much about the more fiendish types of German explosives as anyone in North Africa. Howell had a truckful of defanged mines, booby traps, flares, rockets, grenades, scare whistles, and other devices which he used in teaching how to deal with them. Once I saw him demonstrating his sideshow to General Eisenhower, on one of the general's visits to the front.

Captain Howell hadn't seen his little daughter or his beautiful wife for two and a half years. He said he would give anything in the world to see them, but he didn't want to go home till after the next show was over, whatever that would be.

He had more than his share of narrow escapes. He won his Silver Star by working for an hour, under constant fire, setting his charge on a bridge and blowing up the bridge when the advancing Germans were only four hundred yards away.

He was just one of the thousands over here who did things you people at home can hardly conceive of, and who grew very tired but still were willing to go on and on.

One of my favorite anecdotes was about a soldier on guard duty in the front lines one night, for the first time. He heard a strange noise, fired at it, and then called out, "Who went there?"

During the Tunisian campaign I had a chance to visit the Ninth Division only once. I didn't know a soul in that division, and I drove into their shrub-hidden command post with the same feeling of lonely uneasiness a person gets in approaching a strange big city for the first time. But as I piled out of my jeep an M.P. came over and pulled one of my columns out of his pocket—one about the Military Police. He laughed and said he'd been waiting a long time for me to show up. He said he knew the Military Police were good, but he didn't think they were quite as good as I made them out.

That particular soldier was Private Walter Wolfson, of 714 West 181st Street, New York. He was a coffee merchant by profession, a radio actor by avocation, and a soldier by the trend of events. Wolfson's family owned a coffee-importing business in New York City. He had some newspaper pictures of crowds queueing up at their door to buy coffee after rationing started. His mother and brother ran the business after he left. Wolfson's sergeant said of him, "If he can sell coffee like he can stop autos, he must have had a good business."

Before he went into the army, Wolfson was on the "Rainbow House" program. He knew a lot of poetry and opera by heart and was always reciting and singing around camp.

Wolfson's sergeant was Charles Harrington, a former mill-worker from Gary, Indiana. He was the only soldier I ever saw who dug round foxholes instead of rectangular ones. He said that literally it was so it would be harder for strafing bullets to get at him, but figuratively so the devil couldn't get him cornered. He said he was convinced the adage was true that "there are no atheists in foxholes."

Running onto those two was a pretty good start in breaking into new territory. After I left them I went up to the tent where correspondents always checked in and learned what was going on, and who should be there but Major Bob Robb, a good friend of mine whom I had met at the San Francisco Exposition when he was publicizing the big fair. The last time I had seen him was at the Golden Gate a year and a half before. He was a lieutenant then, in army public relations at the Presidio—and rapidly going nuts, I might add, from the chaos. To escape that treadmill he asked for overseas duty—and, boy, did he get it! He was right in the thick of things in the latter phase of the Tunisian campaign, and having the time of his life.

Private Wolfson, Sergeant Harrington, and Major Robb had one thing in common with every soldier in the army—they thought their division was the best extant. Since I was a man without a division, I just agreed with them all.

Private First Class Joseph Lorenze was one of my infantry friends out of the First Division. His home was at 963 Holly Street, Inglewood, California. He was a nice, quiet, friendly fellow who worked in a furniture factory before the war. We were together during that unforgettable period when our infantry was fighting day and night for the hills west of Mateur. I wanted to put Lorenze's name in one of my dispatches, but I told him I didn't like to use names without having some little anecdote to go with them that would be interesting to everybody. So while the shells commuted incessantly back and forth overhead, Private Lorenze and I sat in our foxholes and thought and thought, and damned if we could think of a thing to say about him, even though he had been through four big battles. Finally I said, "Well, I'll put it in anyhow. You live only half a mile from my friend Cavanaugh, so I'll hook it up with him some way."

You may remember my friend Cavanaugh. He was in France in the last war when he was sixteen years old. In this war he was serving his country by writing me funny letters about the home front, to keep up my morale. In one of them he said: "This is just getting around to being a fit country to live in. No gas, no tires, no salesmen, no gadgets, and plenty of whisky to last the duration. Money ain't worth a damn and I'm glad I've lived to see the day. Everybody you talk to has a military secret. I have completed my plans for the postwar world, and I find no place in it for you. Good luck with your frail body, my friend, and try to bring it back to Inglewood sometime. And a can of salmon would be nice too."

So someday Private Lorenze and I will take off our shoes and lie in the grass in Cavanaugh's back yard and tell him all about our narrow escapes on Hill 428, and not even listen when he tries to get in a word about how it was around Verdun and Vimy Ridge.

Men and machines both passed their shakedown period in this war —at least in North Africa. Men who weren't up to their jobs were largely culled out and given different work. There were still some inept ones in office jobs, but among the line troops the mill of experience had pretty well ground out the weaklings, the freaks, and the misfits.

And it was the same with machinery and weapons. Some things

proved themselves almost useless. Other things turned out so perfectly that the engineers would have to scratch their heads to think of any change·in design.

In the mechanical end of our African war three American vehicles stood out above all the others. They were the jeep, the GMC two-and-a-half-ton truck, and the Douglas DC-3 cargo plane.

The DC-3, known in the army as the C-47, is the workingest airplane in existence, I suppose. It lifted incredible loads, and took terrific beatings from rough fields, hard handling, and overuse. Almost any pilot would tell you it was the best airplane ever built.

The GMC truck did the same thing in its field. It hauled big loads, it was easy to ·drive and easy-riding, and the truck drivers could do practically anything with it up to an outside loop. It seldom got stuck, and if it did it could winch itself out. The punishment it took was staggering.

And the jeep—good Lord, I don't think we could have won the campaign without the jeep. It did everything, went everywhere, was as faithful as a dog, as strong as a mule, and as agile as a goat. It consistently carried twice what it was designed for, and still kept

going. I didn't think it even rode so badly after I got used to it. I drove jeeps thousands of miles, and if I had been called upon to suggest changes for a new model I could have thought of only one or two little things. One was the handbrake. It was perfectly useless —it wouldn't hold at all. They should have designed one that worked or else saved metal by having none at all.

And in the field of acoustics, I wish they could somehow have fixed the jeep so that at certain speeds the singing of those heavy tires hadn't sounded exactly like an approaching airplane. That little sound effect caused me to jump out of my skin more than once. But except for those two trivial items the jeep was a divine instrument of wartime locomotion.

Only once in my long and distinguished jeep career did I have anything go wrong. That time the gears got all mixed up and the thing wouldn't come out of low gear. It was while we were still fighting around Mateur. Our road was under heavy German shellfire, so the only thing we could do was to take off across country and make a wide circle around the shell-infested area. We drove through shoulder-high barleyfields, along foot-wide goat trails, up over hills, down steep banks, across creeks, and over huge rockbeds. Then just as we hit the main road and were out in the free again, the gear thing happened.

We still had twenty miles ahead of us, and there was nothing to do but keep on going in low gear. Luckily we hadn't gone more than a mile when we saw a little sign denoting an Armored Force repair depot. We drove in just on a chance, and sure enough they said they could fix the jeep. They not only fixed it but gave us supper while we waited, and were extremely pleasant about the whole thing.

The boss man of that outfit was Lieutenant George P. Carter, of Louisa, Kentucky. He had intended to be a doctor, and had even finished his premedical course, but instead he became a doctor of heavy machinery. His gang retrieved tanks and repaired them, and kept all the mighty rolling equipment of an armored division in order. To them, fixing a jeep was like a boilermaker fixing a watch, but they could do it.

The mechanic who fixed our gears was Sergeant Walter Harrold, of Wadena, Minnesota. Already that day his outfit had been forced to move twice. German artillery had got their range once, and they were dive-bombed another time. Sergeant Harrold had been working and moving and dodging all day and had more jobs to do that night, yet he worked on our jeep with as much interest as if it had been his own. You can tell a mechanic at heart even on a battlefield. Or maybe I should say especially on a battlefield.

The major portion of my time during the Tunisian campaign was spent with the First Infantry Division and the First Armored Division. That was because they were the earliest ones on the scene and I was best acquainted with them. But there were other divisions in Tunisia too, and in the final phase all contributed their part to the cracking of the Hun.

The First Armored Division was the one that made the kill and got the mass of prisoners. Yet their fighting was no better and no greater than that of the First Infantry Division, which lost so heavily cleaning out the mountains, or of the Thirty-fourth Division, which took the key Hill 609 and made the victory possible, or of the Ninth Division, which swept the Heinies out of the rough coastal country in the north, or of the Artillery that softened up the enemy, or of the fighting Engineers who kept streams bridged and highways passable. Or of any other of the countless units that contributed to the whole, and without a single one of which all the others would have been lost.

Our front-line troops became pretty well saturated with little personal things they got from the Germans. Nearly everybody had a souvenir of some kind, running all the way from machine guns to writing paper.

A good many soldiers made new pistol grips for themselves out of the windshields of shot-down German planes. The main advantage over the regulation handle was that the composition was transparent; a man could put his girl's picture under the grip and she showed through.

Sergeant Gibson Fryer, of Troy, Alabama, had a picture of his wife on each side of the handle of his .45. Sergeant Fryer found that the Germans were very neat in some ways. They had little toilet kits in their pockets. Among his souvenirs was a pair of manicure scissors he got from a prisoner long before the big surrender came.

Sergeant Fryer had an experience on one of the last few days of the campaign that will be worth telling to his grandchildren. He was in a foxhole on a steep hillside. An 88-mm. shell landed three feet away and blew him out of his hole. He rolled, out of control, fifty yards down the rocky hillside. He didn't seem to be wounded, but all his breath was gone. He couldn't move. He couldn't make a sound. His chest hurt. His legs wouldn't work.

A medic came past and poked him. Sergeant Fryer couldn't say anything, so the medic went on. Pretty soon two of Fryer's best friends walked past and he heard one of them say, "There's Sergeant Fryer. I guess he's dead." And they went right on too. It was more than an hour before Fryer could move, but within a few hours he was perfectly normal again. He said if his wife saw the story in print she would think for sure he was a hero.

One day out on a Tunisian hillside I sat on a box and got a shave and haircut from a soldier-barber. While I was getting clipped, Carol Johnson, who has been over here doing pen-and-ink battle sketches for NEA service, came along and snapped my picture. The last time I had a barbershop picture taken was over six years before, up on the coast of the Bering Sea, when I got shaved by the only woman barber in Alaska. I was sitting on a box that time too. I don't seem to make any progress in the world.

The soldier who cut my hair was Private Patrick Fitzgibbons, of 315 West 97th Street, New York. He had been barbering for seventeen years—on ocean liners, in Hollywood, on Broadway. Private Fitzgibbons called it cutting hair. He said, "I've been cutting hair ever since I was fifteen. You get used to cutting hair, and you miss it if you can't do it every day."

When I told Private Fitzgibbons I probably would put his name in my dispatch, he fussed around and spent an extra half hour on me, putting on after-shaving creams, washing my neck, and going over and over the remnants of my hair with his scissors. I think he would probably have given me a bath if I hadn't kept an eye on him.

Speaking of baths, I had my first one in six weeks a few days after the Tunisian campaign was finished. That broke my five weeks' record of the winter. I discovered I was a guy who could take baths or leave them alone. Certainly my unsanitary condition didn't undermine my health, for I had never felt better than during those long dirty periods.

We found out one thing about baths at the front—if we didn't bathe for a long time the fleas didn't bother us. Apparently we either built up a protective coating that they couldn't get through or else we became too revolting even for fleas. Whatever the reason, I knew of rash people who took an occasional bath and were immediately set upon by fleas, while we filthy characters sailed along blissful and unbitten.

Some of the boys did find the cleanup process quite a thrilling experience. Will Lang, of *Life* and *Time* magazines, got a haircut and shampoo one afternoon and then went right back next morning to the same shop and got another shampoo. When I expressed astonishment at this unusual procedure he said, why, that was nothing, he'd seen Bob Capa, the *Collier's* photographer, sit in a chair and get three shampoos, one right after another, each one with a different flavor of soap.

Will and I came back from the front in a jeep, because the army up and took my little German Volkswagen away from me. The High Command put out a general order that all captured vehicles were to be turned in, so in she went, even though she had been given to me officially.

Upon hearing of the order my first impulse was to take off the tires and bury them, remove the engine, and put a hand grenade under the front seat, just to show the army they couldn't do that to me. But after seeing my lawyer I decided the army probably could do anything to me it wished, so I bowed gracefully and left the Volkswagen sitting in a plowed field for the army to collect. I didn't really care. The damned thing would hardly run anyway.

Our jeep was stolen on the way back, but the M.P.'s picked it up after twelve hours. That was a stroke of luck, for stolen jeeps were usually gone forever. Since they all looked alike, it was very hard for the M.P.'s to identify a particular one. Ours was easy, however, because the glass was gone from the windshield on the right-hand side, and we knew the thieves couldn't do anything about that, for we had tried to get it fixed ourselves and there was no glass in that whole area.

Jeep thievery was practiced on such a scale that it became practically legitimate. I never heard of a jeep being stolen right out from under the driver, leaving him riding along in mid-air, but I heard of cases almost as bad. Some friends of mine were standing on a sidewalk and actually saw their jeep driven away by thieves. In one city, soldiers stole a jeep with "Military Police" painted all over it. And to top it off, an unthinking private stole Major General Jimmy Doolittle's car.

In the final phase of the Tunisian campaign I never heard a word of criticism of our men. They fought like veterans. They were well handled. They had enough of what they needed. Everything meshed perfectly, and the end was inevitable. We need never be ashamed of our American fighters. Even though they didn't do too well in the beginning, there was never at any time any question about the Americans' bravery. It was a matter of being hardened and practiced by going through the flames.

Tunisia was a good warm-up field for our armies. We would take an increasingly big part in the battles ahead.

The greatest disservice the folks at home did our men over here was to believe we were at last over the hump. For actually—and over here we all knew it—the worst was yet to come.

18. AFTERMATH

THE Tunisian campaign was ended. Our air forces moved on farther into Tunisia, to the very edge of the chasm of sea that separated them only so little from Sicily and Sardinia and then from Europe itself. We and the British leaped upon the demolished ports we had captured, cleared out enough wreckage for a foothold for ships, and as the ports grew and grew in usefulness they swarmed with thousands of men, and ships, and trucks. Our combat troops moved back—out of range of enemy strafers—to be cheered and acclaimed momentarily by the cities in the rear, to take a few days of wild and hell-roaring rest, and then to go into an invasion practice that was in every respect, except the one of actually getting shot, as rigorous as a real invasion.

Surely before autumn we of Tunisia would be deep into something new. Most of us realized and admitted to ourselves that horrible days lay ahead. The holocaust that at times seemed so big to us in Tunisia would pale in our memories beside the things we would see and do before another year ran out.

Tunisia for us was not only an end in itself, but without the War of Tunisia we would have been ill-prepared to go on into the bigger wars ahead. Tunisia has been called a warm-up ground. That is a proper word for it, I suppose. We found through actual test which of our weapons and planes and vehicles were good, and which were bad, and which could be made good with a little changing. We seasoned our men in battle, and we found the defects that needed to be found in our communications systems, our supply lines, our methods of organization.

It is hard for you at home to realize what an immense, complicated, sprawling institution a theater of war actually is. As it appears to you in the newspapers, war is a clear-cut matter of landing so many men overseas, moving them from the port to the battlefield, advancing them against the enemy with guns firing, and they win or lose.

To look at war that way is like seeing a trailer of a movie, and saying you've seen the whole picture. I actually don't know what percentage of our troops in Africa were in the battle lines, but I believe it safe to say that only comparatively few ever saw the enemy, ever shot at him, or were shot at by him. All the rest of those hundreds of thousands of men were churning the highways for two thousand miles behind the lines with their endless supply trucks, they were unloading the ships, cooking the meals, pounding the typewriters, fixing the roads, making the maps, repairing the engines, decoding the messages, training the reserves, pondering the plans.

To get all that colossal writhing chaos shaped into something that intermeshed and moved forward with efficiency was a task closely akin to weaving a cloth out of a tubful of spaghetti. It was all right to have wonderful plans ahead of time, but we really learn such things only by doing. Now, after our forces have had more than six months' experience in North Africa, I for one feel that we have washed out the bulk of our miscomprehensions, have abandoned most of our fallacies, and have hardened down into a work-weary and battle-dirtied machine of great effect, capable of assimilating and directing aright those greener men who are to follow by the hundreds of thousands and maybe millions.

What I have seen in North Africa has altered my own feelings in one respect. There were days when I sat in my tent alone and gloomed with the desperate belief that it was actually possible for us to lose this war. I don't feel that way any more. Despite our strikes and bickering and confusion back home, America is producing and no one can deny that. Even here at the far end of just one line the trickle has grown into an impressive stream. We are producing at home and we are hardening overseas. Apparently it takes a country like America about two years to become wholly at war. We had to go through that transition period of letting loose of life as it was, and then live the new war life so long that it finally became the normal life to us. It was a form of growth, and we couldn't press it. Only time can produce that change. We have survived that long passage of time, and if I am at all correct we have about changed our character and become a war nation. I can't yet see when we shall win, or over what route geographically, or by which of the many means of warfare. But no longer do I have any doubts at all that we shall win.

The men over here have changed too. They are too close to themselves to sense the change, perhaps. And I am too close to them to grasp it fully. But since I am older and a little apart, I have been able to notice it more.

For a year, everywhere I went, soldiers inevitably asked me two questions: "When do you think we'll get to go home?" and "When will the war be over?" The home-going desire was once so dominant that I believe our soldiers over here would have voted—if the question had been put—to go home immediately, even if it meant peace on terms of something less than unconditional surrender by the enemy.

That isn't true now. Sure, they all still want to go home. So do I. But there is something deeper than that, which didn't exist six months ago. I can't quite put it into words —it isn't any theatrical proclamation that the enemy must be destroyed in the name of freedom; it's just a vague but growing individual acceptance of the bitter fact that we must win the war or else, and that it can't be won by running excursion boats back and forth across the Atlantic carrying homesick vacationers.

A year is a long time to be away from home, especially if a person has never been away before, as was true of the bulk of our troops. At first homesickness can almost kill a man. But time takes care of that. It isn't normal to moon in the past forever. Home gradually grows less vivid; the separation from it less agonizing. There finally comes a day—not suddenly but gradually, as a sunset-touched cloud changes its color—when a man is living almost wholly wherever he is. His life has caught up with his body, and his days become full war days, instead of American days simply transplanted to Africa.

That's the stage our soldiers are in now—the ones who have been over since the beginning, I mean. It seems to take about that long. It's only in the last few weeks that I've begun to hear frequent remarks, said enthusiastically and sincerely, about the thrill it will be to see Paris and to march down the streets of Berlin. The immediate goal used to be the Statue of Liberty; more and more it is becoming Unter den Linden. When all of our army has bridged that gap we shall be in the home stretch.

Our men can't make this change from normal civilians into warriors and remain the same people. Even if they were away from you this long under normal circumstances, the mere process of maturing would change them, and they would not come home just as you knew them. Add to that the abnormal world they have been plunged into, the new philosophies they have had to assume or perish inwardly, the horrors and delights and strange wonderful things they have experienced, and they are bound to be different people from those you sent away.

They are rougher than when you knew them. Killing is a rough business. Their basic language has changed from mere profanity to obscenity. More than anything else, they miss women. Their expressed longings, their conversation, their whole conduct show their need for female companionship, and the gentling effect of femininity upon man is conspicuous here where it has been so long absent.

Our men have less regard for property than you raised them to have. Money value means nothing to them, either personally or in the aggregate; they are fundamentally generous, with strangers and with each other. They give or throw away their own money, and it is natural that they are even less thoughtful of bulk property than of their own hard-earned possessions. It is often necessary to abandon equipment they can't take with them; the urgency of war prohibits normal caution in the handling of vehicles and supplies. One of the most striking things to me about war is the appalling waste that is necessary. At the front there just isn't time to be economical. Also, in war areas where things are scarce and red tape still rears its delaying head, a man learns to get what he needs simply by "requisitioning." It isn't stealing, it's the only way to acquire certain things. The stress of war puts old virtues in a changed light. We shall have to relearn a simple fundamental or two when things get back to normal. But what's wrong with a small case of "requisitioning" when murder is the classic goal?

Our men, still thinking of home, are impatient with the strange peoples and customs of the countries they now inhabit. They say that if they ever get home they never want to see another foreign country. But I know how it will be. The day will come when they'll look back and brag about how they learned a little Arabic, and how swell the girls were in England, and how pretty the hills of Germany were. Every day their scope is broadening despite themselves, and once they all get back with their global yarns and their foreign-tinged views, I cannot conceive of our nation ever being isolationist again. The men don't feel very international right now, but the influences are at work and the time will come.

I couldn't say truthfully that they are very much interested in foreign affairs right now, outside of battle affairs. Awhile back a friend of mine in Washington wrote me an enthusiastic letter, telling of the Ball Resolution in the Senate calling for the formation of a United Nations organization to co-ordinate the prosecution of the war, administer reoccupied countries, feed and economically re-establish liberated nations, and to assemble a United Nations military force to suppress any future military aggression.

My friend told of the enthusiasm the bill had created at home, hailed it as the first definite step in winning the peace as well as the war, and asked me almost pleadingly to send back a report on what the men at the front thought of the bill.

I didn't send any report, because the men at the front thought very little about it one way or the other. I doubt that one out of ten of them remembered the thing two days, even though they may have read about it in *Stars and Stripes*. There wasn't anything specific to get their teeth into and argue about. It sounded too much like another Atlantic Charter or committee meeting.

Of course, by digging, a person could find plenty of politically and internationally minded men in our army—all the way from generals to privates—who do spend considerable time thinking of what is to come after the victory, and how we are to handle it. But what I'm trying to get over is that the bulk of our army in Africa, the run-of-the-mine mass of soldiers, didn't think twice about this bill if they heard of it at all. Their thoughts on the peace can be summed up, I believe, in a general statement that after this war is won they want it fixed so it can't happen again and they want a hand in fixing it, but our average guy has no more conception of how it should be done than to say he supposes some kind of world police force is the answer. There is a great deal more talk along the line of, "Those bluenoses back home better not try to put prohibition over on us while we're away this time," than you hear about bills and resolutions looking toward the postwar world.

Your men have been well cared for in this war. I suppose no soldiers in any other war in history have had such excellent attention as our men overseas. The food is good. Of course we're always yapping about how wonderful a steak would taste on Broadway, but when a soldier is pinned right down he'll admit ungrudgingly that it's Broadway he's thinking about more than the steak, and that he really can't kick on the food. Furthermore, cooking is good in this war. Last time good food was spoiled by lousy cooking, but that is the exception this time. Of course, there were times in battle when the men lived for days on nothing but those deadly cold C rations out of tin cans, and even went without food for a day or two, but those were the crises, the exceptions. On the whole, we figure by the letters from home that we're probably eating better than you are.

A good diet and excellent medical care have made our army a healthy one. Statistics show the men in the mass healthier today than they were in civil life back home.

Our men are well provided with clothing, transportation, mail, and army newspapers. Back of the lines they had Post Exchanges where they could buy cigarettes, candy, toilet articles, and all such things. If they were in the combat zone, all those things were issued to them free.

Our fighting equipment was the only thing that didn't stand head and shoulders above everything issued to soldiers of any other country, and that was only because we weren't ready for war at first, and for two years we have been learning what was good and what was bad. Already many of our weapons are unmatched by any other country. Give us another year and surely it can be said that our men are furnished better weapons, along with better food, health and clothing, than any other army.

Here it is June of 1943 and it seems a long time since we landed at Oran in November of 1942. Of course there were thousands of us even in those first days in Africa, and yet it seemed like a little family then. And specially so when we went on to Tunisia—in those bitter January days we were so small that I knew almost every officer on the staff of every unit, in addition to hundreds of the soldiers. Nothing was very official in our lives then; there was almost no red tape; we correspondents at the front were few and were considered by the army rather like partners in the firm. We made deep friendships that have endured.

During the winter I dropped in frequently at Corps Headquarters, buried deep in a gulch beyond Tebessa. They put up a little tent for me, and I tried to work and sleep in it, but was never very successful at either because of being constantly, paralyzingly cold throughout the twenty-four hours of the day. We ate in a tent with a crushed-stone floor and an iron-bellied stove in the center. It was the only warm place I knew, and so informal was the war in those first days that often I sat around the stove after supper and just gabbed country-storelike with Lieutenant General Lloyd Fredendall, then commander of our armies in Tunisia. I was very fond of General Fredendall, and I admired and respected him. For some unknown reason I always thought of him to myself as "Papa" Fredendall, although I don't think anybody else ever did. I still wear the Armored Corps combat jacket he gave me.

The first pioneering days of anything are always the best days. Everything is new and animating, and acquaintanceships are easy and everyone is knit closely together. In the latter part of the Tunisian war things were just as good for us correspondents—we had better facilities and the fighting army continued to be grand to us—and yet toward the end it became so big that I felt like a spectator instead of a participant. Which is, of course, all that a correspondent is or ever should be. But the old intimacy was gone.

And then finally the Tunisian campaign was over, spectacularly collapsed after the bitterest fighting we had known in our theater. It was only in those last days that I came to know what war really is. I don't know how any of the men who went through the thick of that hill-by-hill butchery could ever be the same again. The end of the Tunisian war brought an exhilaration, then a letdown, and later a restlessness from anticlimax that I can see multiplied a thousand times when the last surrender comes. That transition back to normal days will be as difficult for many as was the change into war, and some will never be able to accomplish it.

Now we are in a lull and many of us are having a short rest period. I tried the city and couldn't stand it. Two days drove me back to the country, where everything seemed cleaner and more decent. I am in my tent, sitting on a newly acquired cot, writing on a German folding table we picked up the day of the big surrender. The days here are so peaceful and perfect they almost give us a sense of infidelity to those we left behind beneath the Tunisian crosses, those whose final awareness was a bedlam of fire and noise and uproar.

Here the Mediterranean surf caresses the sandy beach not a hundred yards away, and it is a lullaby for sleeping. The water is incredibly blue, just as we always heard it was. The sky is a cloudless blue infinity, and the only sounds are the birds singing in the scrub bushes that grow out of the sand and lean precisely away from the sea. Little land terrapins waddle around, and I snared one by the hind leg with a piece of string and tied it in Photographer Chuck Corte's tent while he was out, just for a joke. Then I found myself peeking in every few minutes to see how the captive was getting along, and he was straining so hard to get away that I got to feeling sorry for the poor little devil, so I turned him loose and ruined my joke.

An occasional black beetle strolls innocently across the sandy floor. For two hours I've been watching one of them struggling with a cigarette butt on the ground, trying to move it. Yesterday a sand snake crawled by just outside my tent door, and for the first time in my life I looked upon a snake not with a creeping phobia but with a sudden and surprising feeling of compassion. Somehow I pitied him, because he was a snake instead of a man. And I don't know why I felt that way, for I feel pity for all men too, because they are men.

It may be that the war has changed me, along with the rest. It is hard for anyone to analyze himself. I know that I find more and more that I wish to be alone, and yet contradictorily I believe I have a new patience with humanity that I've never had before. When you've lived with the unnatural mass cruelty that mankind is capable of inflicting upon itself, you find yourself dispossessed of the faculty for blaming one poor man for the triviality of his faults. I don't see how any survivor of war can ever be cruel to anything, ever again.

Yes, I want the war to be over, just as keenly as any soldier in North Africa wants it. This little interlude of passive contentment here on the Mediterranean shore is a mean temptation. It is a beckoning into somnolence. This is the kind of day I think I want my life to be composed of, endlessly. But pretty soon we shall strike our tents and traipse again after the clanking tanks, sleep again to the incessant lullaby of the big rolling guns. It has to be that way, and wishing doesn't change it.

It may be I have unconsciously made war seem more awful than it really is. It would be wrong to say that war is all grim; if it were, the human spirit could not survive two and three and four years of it. There is a good deal of gaiety in wartime. Some of us, even over here, are having the time of our lives. Humor and exuberance still exist. As some soldier once said, the army is good for one ridiculous laugh per minute. Our soldiers are still just as roughly good-humored as they always were, and they laugh easily, although there isn't as much to laugh about as there used to be.

And I don't attempt to deny that war is vastly exhilarating. The whole tempo of life steps up, both at home and on the front. There is an intoxication about battle, and ordinary men can sometimes soar clear out of themselves on the wine of danger-emotion. And yet it is false. When we leave here to go on into the next battleground, I know that I for one shall go with the greatest reluctance.

On the day of final peace, the last stroke of what we call the "Big Picture" will be drawn. I haven't written anything about the "Big Picture," because I don't know anything about it. I only know what we see from our worm's-eye view, and our segment of the picture consists only of tired and dirty soldiers who are alive and don't want to die; of long darkened convoys in the middle of the night; of shocked silent men wandering back down the hill from battle; of chow lines and atabrine tablets and foxholes and burning tanks and Arabs holding up eggs and the rustle of high-flown shells; of jeeps and petrol dumps and smelly bedding rolls and C rations and cactus patches and blown bridges and dead mules and hospital tents and shirt collars greasy-black from months of wearing; and of laughter too, and anger and wine and lovely flowers and constant cussing. All these it is composed of; and of graves and graves and graves.

That is our war, and we will carry it with us as we go on from one battleground to another until it is all over, leaving some of us behind on every beach, in every field. We are just beginning with the ones who lie back of us here in Tunisia. I don't know whether it was their good fortune or their misfortune to get out of it so early in the game. I guess it doesn't make any difference, once a man has gone. Medals and speeches and victories are nothing to them any more. They died and others lived and nobody knows why it is so. They died and thereby the rest of us can go on and on. When we leave here for the next shore, there is nothing we can do for the ones beneath the wooden crosses, except perhaps to pause and murmur, "Thanks, pal.